PEARSON EDUCATION

AP* TEST PREP SERIES

AP Government and Politics: United States

to accompany

O'CONNOR | SABATO | YANUS

AMERICAN GOVERNMENT: ROOTS AND REFORM

2011 EDITION, AP* EDITION, 11E

PREPARED BY:

DAVID PRICE

Santa Fe College

Longman

Boston   Columbus   Indianapolis   New York   San Francisco   Upper Saddle River

Amsterdam   Cape Town   Dubai   London   Madrid   Milan   Munich   Paris   Montreal   Toronto

Delhi   Mexico City   São Paulo   Sydney   Hong Kong   Seoul   Singapore   Taipei   Tokyo

AP Government and Politics: United States Test Prep to accompany *American Government: Roots and Reform, AP* Edition 11e* by Karen O'Connor, Larry J. Sabato, and Alixandra B. Yanus

2 3 4 5 6 7 8 9 10—EB—14 13 12

*Advanced Placement, Advanced Placement Program, AP, and Pre–AP are registered trademarks of the College Board, which was not involved in the production of, and does not endorse, these products.

Longman
is an imprint of

PearsonSchool.com/Advanced

ISBN-13: 978-0-13-258247-6

ISBN-10: 0-13-258247-3

CONTENTS

CHAPTER 3:

Federalism   46

About Your Pearson AP* Test Prep Workbook

Pearson Education is the leading publisher of textbooks worldwide. With operations on every continent, we make it our business to understand the changing needs of students at every level, from kindergarten to college. We think that makes us especially qualified to offer this series of AP* test prep books linked to our best-selling programs.

Our reasoning is that as you study for your course, you are preparing along the way for the AP exam. If you can tie the material in the book directly to the exam it makes the material that much more relevant and enables you to focus your time most efficiently. And that's a good thing!

The AP Government and Politics: United States exam is an important milestone in your education. A high score means you're in a better position for college acceptance, and it possibly puts you a step ahead with college credits. Our goal is to provide you with the tools you need to succeed on the exam.

Good luck!

Part I

Introduction to the AP Government and Politics: United States Examination

This section provides an overview of the advanced placement program, introduces the types of questions you will encounter on the exam, offers helpful test-taking strategies, and explains the grading procedure used by the College Board. In addition, a correlation chart is provided that shows where key information commonly tested on the exam is covered within *American Government: Roots and Reform, AP* Edition*. Review this section carefully before trying the sample items in the following parts.

The Advanced Placement Program

This book will help prepare you to take the Advanced Placement (AP) Government and Politics: United States Exam at the end of the year. To succeed on the exam, you need to follow a plan of curriculum review and practice. This book offers both of these. First, you will review each content area of government and politics that appears on the AP Government and Politics: United States Exam. Then, for each section, you will complete some practice drills that replicate actual AP exam questions. You will not only receive extra, guided study for your coursework, but you will also have the opportunity to apply what you have learned in class to a testing situation. You will become familiar with the types of questions on the AP Government and Politics: United States Exam and how to approach them. Go through each review section thoroughly and complete all of the accompanying drills. If you have difficulty with particular sections, that is your cue to refer to your textbook for a more detailed review.

For even more practice, this book includes two full-length AP Government and Politics: United States Exams. These will help you practice taking the exam under real-life testing conditions. The more familiar you are with the AP Government and Politics: United States Exam ahead of time, the more comfortable you will be on testing day. The more comfortable you are, the better your chances of achieving a high score.

The AP Program is sponsored by the College Board, a nonprofit organization that oversees college admissions tests. The AP Program offers high school students the opportunity to take advanced college-level courses. According to the College Board, AP courses are intended to offer a curriculum equivalent to that of an introductory college class. If you receive a score of 3 or higher (5 is the highest possible grade), you may be eligible for college credit. Thousands of colleges and universities grant credit to students who score well on AP exams. If you are taking several AP courses and score well on multiple AP exams, you may even be eligible to enter college as a sophomore. Some institutions grant sophomore status to incoming first-year students who have demonstrated mastery of many AP subjects. In addition, the College Board confers a number of AP Scholar Awards on students who score 3 or higher on three or more AP exams. Additional awards are available to students who receive very high grades on four or five AP exams.

The curriculum for each of the 34 AP courses is designed by a development committee, consisting of college professors and high school teachers. Every AP course is different, and your textbook, *American Government: Roots and Reform* AP* Edition, 11e is widely and successfully used in AP classes across the nation. The committee develops guidelines for a test that represents equally and accurately the skill levels of over 100,000 AP Government and Politics: United States students across the country. Your score on the AP Government and Politics: United States Exam reflects your abilities in comparison to other high school students enrolled in the course. Colleges use this information not only to award credit for introductory college classes but also to choose the most suitable applicants.

.

Why Take an AP Course?

You may be taking one or more AP courses simply because you are thirsty for knowledge. Of course, the fact that selective colleges look favorably on applicants who have AP courses on their transcripts is another powerful incentive. Because AP classes should involve rigorous lessons, they signal to college admissions officers that AP students are willing to challenge themselves to get the most from their educations. Because AP course work is more difficult than average high school work, many admissions officers evaluate AP grades on a kind of curve—if you receive a *B* in an AP class, for example, it might carry the same weight as an *A* in a regular high school class. Furthermore, the score you achieve on the AP exam places you in the context of your peers across the nation and across years.

Your AP Government and Politics: United States course teaches you many of the skills you will need in college. For example, your teacher will make writing assignments and encourage you to use resources beyond your textbook. Some of these resources may be primary sources that permit you to analyze events, issues, and data as a political scientist does. The AP Government and Politics: United States course will challenge you to gather and consider information in new—and sometimes unfamiliar—ways. Your ability to use these methods and skills will give you an advantage as you enter college.

Taking an AP Examination

You should challenge yourself further by taking the AP Government and Politics: United States Exam at the end of your high school course. A wealth of information—which colleges grant credit for AP exam scores and for what score, the exam schedule, when you need to sign up, the cost, the availability of fee reductions—is available either from your AP teacher or school guidance counselor at www.collegeboard.com. Some information on the College Board's website is only available to those who have registered an account, but registration is free. You can use the website as a primary source of information, but you should also communicate with your AP teacher or school guidance counselor. There are many state and local programs that help you defray the costs of taking the exam.

When you register for the AP exam, you can arrange to have your score sent automatically to a number of colleges for free. In fact, your score can be received at colleges and universities only if it has been sent there directly by the College Board. If you would like your score to be sent to other schools, you must pay an additional fee. You can also cancel your score (you must do so before you find out your score), but either of these requests must be made directly to the College Board. Your exam grade will be sent to you by mail in early to mid-July. If you simply cannot wait to find out your score, Educational Testing Service (the organization that develops and scores tests for the College Board) will release your score to you over the phone around July 1 for an additional fee.

AP Government and Politics: United States: Course Goals

The goal of the AP Government and Politics: United States course is to provide students with an understanding of the operation of American national government. Specifically, you will develop

- an understanding of the principal themes in U.S. government and politics

- the ability to analyze evidence—historical, quantitative, and presented graphically

- skills to express your knowledge in writing

AP Government and Politics: United States courses vary somewhat from teacher to teacher and from school to school. Yet the focus of your course should reflect these goals, and the instruction you receive will grow out of these basic principles. The Government and Politics: United States Development Committee has created a list of major topics and has divided them into the six groups below. These topics are the focus of your AP course, and will be revisited in questions on the AP Government and Politics: United States Exam.

Constitutional Underpinnings of United States Government

- Historical development and adoption of the Constitution

- Separation of powers

- Checks and balances

- Federalism

- Theories of modern government

Civil Rights and Civil Liberties

- The Bill of Rights and how it evolved

- The incorporation of the Fourteenth Amendment

- Judicial review and key Supreme Court cases

- The fight for minority rights

Political Beliefs and Behaviors

- Theories of modern government, including elitist, pluralist, and hyperpluralist

- Views that people have about government and their elected officials

- Characteristics and impact of public opinion

- Voting patterns of citizens

- Characteristics of political beliefs and the differences between liberals and conservatives

Political Parties, Interest Groups, and Mass Media

- Characteristics, organization, and history of political parties

- Impact of key elections

- Voting patterns and the effect on the political process

- Laws that affect elections

- Interest groups and political action committees

- Legislation affecting the political process

- The mass media and its effect on politics

Institutions of National Government

- Characteristics and power of each institution

- Relationships among each institution

- Linkage between these institutions and the political process, political parties, interest groups, the media, and public opinion

- How public policy is formulated and implemented

Public Policy

- The nature of public policy

- The creation of public policy

- The impact of the three branches of government on public policy

- The impact of the bureaucracy on public policy

- The relationship between public policy and linkage institutions

Using class lectures, assignments, and activities, you can immerse yourself in all six themes of AP Government and Politics: United States. Extensive classroom preparation and your own regular practice and study will be the foundation for your success on the AP Government and Politics: United States Exam.

Understanding the AP Government and Politics: United States Examination

The AP Government and Politics: United States Exam incorporates graphical, cartographic, and quantitative materials. This cross-disciplinary approach reflects the methods used today in colleges and universities to present subject matter.

The AP Government and Politics: United States Exam takes two hours and 25 minutes. It consists of a multiple-choice section and a free-response section. You can expect to see graphs, charts, and quotations in both sections of the test. You are expected to know the foundations of U.S. government and how and why it has evolved, but this is not an exam on history. The AP Government and Politics: United States course is a course in political science.

Section I: Multiple-Choice Questions

You will have 45 minutes to complete the 60 questions in the multiple-choice section of the test. This section accounts for 50 percent of your overall score. Each question has five answer choices, and only one choice is correct. Most of the questions in this section will be fairly straightforward. Some may require interpretation, such as determining cause and effect or drawing a comparison. Others will ask you to analyze data in charts or graphs or to evaluate a political cartoon or other illustration. The questions vary in degree of difficulty.

Not all multiple-choice questions are the same. The AP Government and Politics: United States Exam will contain the following types of questions:

Definition or Identification Questions

These questions ask you to recognize something and know what it is. Here is an example.

1. Class action suits
    (A) permit a small number of people to sue on behalf of all other people similarly situated.
    (B) are filed by students seeking to force a school district to offer additional sections of perpetually overenrolled courses.
    (C) have to do with constitutional issues, thus broadening the standing to sue.
    (D) are routinely filed by teachers' groups to prepare the way or strikes.
    (E) may be filed only if all of those with standing to sue agree to participate.

The correct answer is *A*. A small group of people who believe, for example, that they have been harmed by a product can sue the manufacturer on behalf of all the people who believe they were harmed. This is the definition of class action.

Cause-and-Effect Questions

This type of question asks which event caused another, or what is the result of something. Here is an example:

2. The increasing speed of technological advance
   (A)   has significantly reduced the scope of American government.
   (B)   helps reduce and accelerate government policymaking.
   (C)   has helped reduce the cost of health care in the United States.
   (D)   has dramatically affected health policy, but has had no effect on environmental and energy policy.
   (E)   has created many new practical and moral problems for the political system.

The answer is *E*. You can use the process of elimination. The scope of government has not gotten smaller; policymaking has not become faster; health care costs have risen; if technology has affected health policy, it is unlikely that it has not also affected environmental and energy policies. Answers *A, B, C, and D* are obviously wrong, leaving *E*.

"Roman Numeral" Questions

Here you are given a question, then several statements, phrases, or words relating to the question. You must decide which of the statements, phrases, or words are correct. It may be one or more than one.

3. Registered voters directly elect which of the following?
   I.   the president and vice president
   II.   Supreme Court justices
   III. senators
   IV.   the Electoral College
   (A)   I only
   (B)   IV only
   (C)   I and II only
   (D)   III and IV only
   (E)   II, III, and IV only

The answer is *D*. Registered voters vote for electors who then vote for the president and vice president. This is not *direct* election. So any choice that includes *I* is wrong (*A, C*). Justices of the Supreme Court are appointed by the president and approved by the Senate, so you can also eliminate choice *E*. Voters vote directly for both senators and, as noted above, the Electoral College.

EXCEPT/NOT Questions

In this type of question, four of the answer choices are correct, and you must find the answer that is *wrong.* Be sure to read the question carefully. Here is an example of this type of question.

4. Which of the following is NOT specifically mentioned in the Constitution, including its amendments?
   (A)   protection against double jeopardy
   (B)   right to bear arms
   (C)   freedom of speech
   (D)   right to privacy
   (E)   right to trial by jury

The answer is *D.* Double jeopardy is addressed in the Fifth Amendment. The right to bear arms is mentioned in the Second Amendment. Freedom of speech is protected by the First Amendment. Article III provides for trial by jury. Only the right to privacy is not specifically mentioned in the Constitution.

Supreme Court Decisions

You will be asked to identify, interpret, or compare one or more well-known Supreme Court decisions. Here is an example:

5. *New York Times* v. *Sullivan* addressed
   (A)   equal opportunity in the workplace.
   (B)   libel.
   (C)   prior restraint.
   (D)   business monopolies.
   (E)   obscenity.

The answer is *B.* The Court held that statements about public figures are libelous only if made with "reckless disregard for the truth." There is no way to guess here. All the choices are topics the Supreme Court has ruled on, and all might involve a newspaper. You need to remember significant cases and the issues they address.

Graphic Questions

You can expect to see questions based on graphs, tables, and maps.

DISTRIBUTION OF INCOME AMONG FAMILIES

(percentage share by economic level)

	1970	1980	1990	2000
Lowest fifth	5.5	5.1	4.6	3.6
Second fifth	12.0	11.6	10.8	8.9
Third fifth	17.4	17.5	16.6	14.9
Fourth fifth	23.5	24.3	23.8	23.0
Highest fifth	41.6	41.6	44.3	49.6

6. Which of the following conclusions about income distribution is supported by the table?
   (A) The share of income received by the lowest fifth increased, and the share received by the fourth fifth decreased.
   (B) The share of income received by the second fifth increased, and the share received by the fourth fifth decreased.
   (C) The share of income received by the highest fifth increased, and the share received by the lowest fifth decreased.
   (D) The number of people earning high incomes increased.
   (E) The middle class disappeared.

The numbers clearly show that *C* is the answer. Choice *D* might be attractive, but note that the table gives percents. Although the *percent* of families in the highest fifth increased, you know nothing about the actual number of people. Always read the questions and answer choices carefully.

Section II: Free-Response Questions

The second portion of the AP Government and Politics: United States Exam is an hour-and-40-minute free-response section consisting of four questions (i.e., 25 minutes per question). You must answer all four—none of them are optional. You may, however, have some choice within a question. All four questions count equally, and together they account for 50 percent of your overall score.

Because the free-response questions are open-ended, this is your opportunity to demonstrate your understanding of U.S. government and politics. You will see directives like *define, identify, describe,* and *explain.* Knowing facts or terms may earn you points if the task is to *define* or to *identify*, but to *describe* or to *explain* requires using your knowledge to construct an argument. You should use your knowledge to construct a thorough and intelligent response.

1. Scan all four questions quickly to form initial impressions of the topics about which you are being asked to write. You do not have to answer the questions in the order in which they are presented. Begin with the question you think you can respond to best. (If you are to run short on time, you would rather run short on a question about which you think you know the least than the one about which you know the most.)

2. Read and reread the question to be sure you understand exactly what is being asked. Underline directives such as *define, identify, describe,* and *explain.* These are the tasks that must be accomplished for you to earn credit for a response. You can jot notes in the margins of the exam booklet.

3. Take a couple of minutes to brainstorm about the topic. Write down the things that come to your mind. Then look them over to see which ideas will go well together to serve as examples for your response to the question and to determine the order in which you will present them. This, in essence, is the outline for your response. Remember, you have, on average, 25 minutes for each response. Five minutes invested in brainstorming and outlining up front can produce a much better response with less expenditure of time overall. But do keep track of time.

4. You may use any organizational approach that makes sense to you as long as you respond to the question and all of its parts. When in doubt, use the question format as your guide to your outline.

5. Now you are ready to begin writing. What you write is the only evidence that the Reader has about what you know regarding the question that has been posed. Flesh out the ideas you used to construct your outline, using examples to bolster you points. Correctly used, appropriate examples give the Reader confidence that you have an understanding of the question that merits awarding the points allocated to that part of the question. Your answer will be judged based on whether or not you have accomplished your task—to define, identify, describe, or explain—as laid out in the question. You earn points for accomplishing the assigned tasks. There is no need to venture beyond the scope of the question. You will not earn extra points, and, because each question is scored independently, you will not be able to make up for a question you feel you did not answer well enough by overcompensating on another question. Many free-response questions on the AP Government and Politics: United States Exam will ask you to address a single topic in a straightforward way. Here is an example of such a question:

    1.   The system of checks and balances ensures that no branch of government has unfettered power. Describe—using examples—how each branch has exercised this power over another branch.

In your response to this question, you need to furnish *examples* that help you *describe* how each of the three governmental branches has used the system of checks and balances to wield power.

Some free-response questions are divided into several parts, or subquestions. You might be presented with a list of items, such as specific court cases or interest groups, which you are asked to address in your response. These partitioned questions often contain directives like *identify, describe,* and *explain.* Here is an example:

2. Choose two of the following Supreme Court cases.

   - *California Board of Regents* v. *Bakke*
   - *Roe* v. *Wade*
   - *Gideon* v. *Wainwright*
   - *Rust* v. *Sullivan*
   - *Miranda* v. *Arizona*
   - *Korematsu* v. *United States*

For each case you selected, do each of the following:

   a. Describe the position of each side.

   b. Describe the Supreme Court's ruling.

   c. Explain whether the ruling increased or decreased the rights of individuals.

First, you need to recognize (at least two of) the cases and choose the two you want to use in the remainder of your response. Do not be intimidated by a list of six cases. You could know absolutely nothing about four of the cases and still earn all of the points for the question.

Second, you would need to describe the positions of the opposing sides in each of the two cases chosen (four descriptions).

Third, you must describe the court's ruling (i.e., a simple statement of the court's holding in the cases chosen).

Finally, you must take a position on whether the rights of individuals were increased or decreased in each of the chosen cases and support your position. A simple statement of your conclusion about the increase or decrease of individual rights by the court in your chosen cases would be insufficient to earn credit for the *explain* part of the question. The Reader must finish your response knowing how you think rights were expanded or contracted or why you have taken the position you have for each of the chosen cases. It is often the *explain* part of a question that separates the best-prepared students from the rest. You must answer all of the subquestions. Your personal opinions may affect how you explain something, but you will not be asked about your personal political opinions, so do not include them. You do not get extra credit for going beyond the scope of a question, and that just wastes your valuable time. This is a political science exam, not a forum for political position taking.

It cannot be overemphasized: Pay close attention to exactly what the question asks you to do, and do it—nothing more, nothing less. For example, in the question posed above, asking you to describe the positions of the parties in two cases, the Supreme Court's ruling, and to explain the cases' impact on the expansion or contraction of individual rights, you might know the full story of Clarence Gideon and how his case made it to the Supreme Court, but even a brilliant explanation of this saga would earn you no points because that is not requested in the question. To earn points, answer the question that is asked—not the one you wish had been asked.

Grading Procedures for the AP Government and Politics: United States Examination

The raw scores of the exam are converted into the following 5-point scale:

5—Extremely Well Qualified

4—Well Qualified

3—Qualified

2—Possibly Qualified

1—No Recommendation

How these scores are used in admission, credit, or placement decisions varies from college to college, with credit and placement decisions often being made at the departmental level. Some colleges give undergraduate course credit to students who achieve scores of 3 or better on AP exams. Other colleges require students to achieve scores of 4 or 5. If you are considering using your AP exam score for college credit, check with individual colleges at www.collegeboard.com to find out their specific requirements for credit. Below is a breakdown of how the grading of the AP Government and Politics: United States Exam works.

Section I: Multiple-Choice Questions

The multiple-choice section of the exam is worth 50 percent of your total grade. The raw score of Section I is determined by crediting one point for each correct answer and by deducting one-fourth of one point for each incorrect answer. No points are gained or lost for unanswered questions. If you have no idea what the correct answer is, do not make a wild guess—leave the answer blank. But if you can eliminate two or more of the five choices, you should make an educated guess.

Section II: Free-Response Questions

The free-response section of the exam is worth 50 percent of your total grade. It is graded by a group of AP Government and Politics: United States instructors and professors known as "faculty consultants." Each essay may be read by anywhere from one to 20 Readers. The Readers do not know whose essay they are reading, nor from which school the essay originates. Each faculty consultant generally will only read responses to one of the free-response questions during the reading and will not know what you scored on either the multiple-choice part of the exam or on the other three free-response questions. You begin with a 0 score on each free-response question, and earn points as you correctly respond to the question. The scale for scoring each free-response question is specifically adapted to the question. For example, one question may be scored using a "5-point rubric" while another is scored using a "9-point rubric." Then, your score on each free-response question is weighted so that it counts the same as each of the other three free-response questions. These weighted scores are then summed, and this total counts the same as your total multiple-choice score in your final score. The Chief Reader, the person in charge of scoring all of the exams, in consultation with statisticians from the Educational Testing Service and personnel from the College Board, then determines what total scores will be required for an AP score of 5, of 4, etc. Great care goes into assuring that your score accurately reflects where you stand in relation to the other students who took the exam you did and in relation to the students who took the exam in prior years. Colleges want to know that your score of 5 means the same as the 5 presented last year from a school across the country from where you are.

Test-Taking Strategies for the AP Government and Politics: United States Examination

To become comfortable with both the content and the format of the AP Government and Politics: United States Exam, begin preparing for the test in advance. You want to have plenty of time to devote to each of the six main subject areas on the test while practicing your free response skills at the same time. The more relaxed study time you allow yourself, the more prepared you will be and the better you will do on the exam.

Aim to finish the review sections about a week and a half before the exam. Then take the first practice exam at the back of this book. Treat the practice test exactly like the real exam. Find a quiet place where you can work without interruption and give yourself only two hours and 25 minutes. This allows you to become familiar with the actual testing conditions so that you will be less nervous on testing day.

After you have scored your practice test, take a day just to review your answers. Look at the types of questions you got wrong. Do they fall under the same content area or areas? If so, you should focus further study on those particular areas for the next two days or so. Count the number of questions you skipped. Did they fall near the end of the section? This could mean that you were running out of time. Did you feel rushed? It might be wise, then, to plan ahead of time which kinds of questions you should skip over. For example, if you got every data question right and a lot of questions about Supreme Court cases wrong, plan to skip a few of those case questions so that you can answer all of the data questions in the section. You need to make sure that you answer the questions you are more likely to know and that you skip the ones that might slow you down.

Now that you know what adjustments to make to your test-taking strategy, give yourself a few days of extra practice with your problem areas and then take the second practice test at least three days before the real exam. (Do not overwhelm yourself before the real thing!) Again, analyze your performance. Did your adjustments pay off? Is there anything you should do differently? Use your last few days to do any fine-tuning and to relax before the exam.

Below is a brief list of basic tips and strategies to think about *before* you arrive at the exam site.

- Try to plan your schedule so that you get *two* very good nights of sleep before exam day. On the day of the exam, make sure that you eat good, nutritious meals. These tips may sound corny or obvious, but your body must be in peak form for your brain to perform well.

- Arrive at the exam site 30 minutes before the start time. This saves you additional worry about arriving late.

- It is a good idea to have a photo I.D. with you when you arrive at the exam site. (It is essential if you are taking the exam at a school other than your own.) Carrying a driver's license or a student I.D. card will allow you to prove your identity if anyone needs such proof.

- Bring at least two pencils for the multiple-choice section, as well as two black pens for the free-response section of the exam. Make sure that your pencils are labeled #2 and that they have good erasers. The machine that scores Section I of the exam cannot recognize marks made by other types of pencils. Also, it cannot read a correct answer if a previous answer has not been erased completely.

- It is helpful to have a watch with you at the exam. Most testing rooms will have clocks, and most test administrators will give you periodic reminders of how much time you have remaining. Still, having your own watch makes it easy to keep close track of your own pace. The watch cannot have a calculator or an alarm, however, as these are not permitted in the exam room.

- Do not bring books of any kind, laptop computers, wireless instant-messaging devices, cameras, or portable radios. If you must bring a cellular phone with you, turn it off and give it to the test proctor until you are finished with your exam.

The test administrators are very clear and very serious about what is *not* allowed during the examination. Below is a list of actions to avoid at all costs, since each is grounds for your immediate dismissal from the exam room.

- Do not consult any outside materials during the exam period. Remember, the break is technically part of the exam—you are not free to review any materials at that time either.

- Do not speak during the exam, unless you have a question for the test proctor. Raise your hand to get the proctor's attention.

- When you are told to stop working on a section of the exam, you must stop *immediately.*

- Do not open your exam booklet before the test begins.

- Never tear a page out of your test booklet or try to remove the exam from the test room.

- Do not behave disruptively—even if you are distressed about a difficult test question or because you have run out of time. Stay calm and make no unnecessary noise. Remember, too, the worst-case scenario: If you are displeased with your performance on test day, you can cancel your exam scores.

Section I: Strategies for Multiple-Choice Questions

Having a firm grasp of U.S. government and politics is, of course, the key to your doing well on the AP Government and Politics: United States Examination. In addition, being well informed about the exam itself increases your chances of achieving a high score. Below is a list of strategies that you can use to increase your comfort, your confidence, and your chances of excelling on the multiple-choice section of the exam.

- Pace yourself and keep track of the remaining time as you complete the multiple-choice section. Remember, you have 45 minutes to answer all 60 questions. It is important that you do not get stuck on one question for too long.

- Make a mark in your test booklet next to any questions you cannot answer. Return to them after you reach the end of Section I. Sometimes questions that appear later in the test will refresh your memory of a particular topic, and you will be able to answer one of those earlier questions.

- Always read the entire question carefully and underline and define key words or ideas. You might want to circle words such as *NOT* or *EXCEPT* in that type of multiple-choice question.

- Read *every* answer choice carefully before you make your final selection.

- Use the process of elimination to help you choose the correct answer. Even if you are sure of an answer, cross out the letters of incorrect choices in your test booklet as you eliminate them. This cuts down on distraction and allows you to narrow the remaining choices even further.

- If you are able to eliminate two or three answer choices, it is better to make an educated guess at the correct answer than to leave the answer blank.

- Make yourself completely familiar with the instructions for the multiple-choice questions *before* you take the exam. You will find the instructions in this book. By knowing the instructions cold, you will save yourself the time of reading them carefully on the day of the test.

Section II: Strategies for Free-Response Questions

Here is a list of strategies that you can use to increase your chances of excelling on the free-response section of the exam.

- You have one hour and 40 minutes to outline and write four essays. This is plenty of time to accomplish your task, but not so much that you have any to waste. You must manage your time carefully.

- Be careful not to stray from the focus of the question asked. As you read a question, underline any key words and directives that indicate how you should address the material in your response. Some frequently used directives are listed below, along with descriptions of what you need to do in writing your answer.

- *compare:* address similarities and differences between two or more things

- *describe:* give a detailed account

- *identify:* give a brief definition or listing

- *explain:* communicate how or why

- As you formulate your answer, always consider whether or not it answers the question directly.

AP Correlation to *American Government: Roots and Reform, AP* Edition*

The following table is intended for your use as a study device. The left column shows one way to break down into historical eras the time period covered in AP Government and Politics: United States courses. The two columns to the right include detailed breakdowns of chapters in your textbook where you can learn more about those topics. You may want to use this table throughout the year to review what you've learned. It is also an excellent place to begin your pre-exam review of subjects.

SAMPLE AP COURSE UNITS	CORRELATIONS TO: *AMERICAN GOVERNMENT: ROOTS AND REFORM, AP* Edition*

Constitutional Underpinnings of United States Government

The Constitution

Chapter 2: The Constitution
- Roots of a New Nation
- The First Attempt at Government: The Articles of Confederation
- The Miracle at Philadelphia: Writing the U.S. Constitution
- The U.S. Constitution
- The Drive for Ratification of the U.S. Constitution
- Toward Reform: Methods of Amending the U.S. Constitution

Chapter 5: Civil Liberties
- Roots of Civil Liberties: The Bill of Rights
- First Amendment Guarantees: Freedom of Religion
- First Amendment Guarantees: Freedoms of Speech, Press, Assembly, and Petition
- The Second Amendment: The Right to Keep and Bear Arms

Federalism

Chapter 3: Federalism
- Roots of the Federal System and the Constitutional Allocation of Governmental Powers
- Federalism and the Marshall Court
- Dual Federalism: The Taney Court, Slavery, and the Civil War
- Cooperative Federalism: The New Deal and the Growth of National Government
- New Federalism: Returning Power to the States
- Toward Reform: A New Judicial Federalism?

Separation of Powers

Chapter 2: The Constitution
- The U.S. Constitution

Chapter 7: Congress
- Toward Reform: Congressional Checks on the Executive and Judicial Branches

Chapter 8: The Presidency
- The Constitutional Powers of the President

Theories of Democratic Government	**Chapter 1: The Political Landscape** • Roots of American Government: What Are They and Why Are They Important • The Philosophical Origins of American Government • American Political Culture and the Basic Tenets of American Democracy • Political Ideology: Its Role in the World and in American Politics • Changing Characteristics of the American People • Toward Reform: Population Changes and Americans' Attitudes Toward Government

Civil Rights and Civil Liberties

Civil Liberties and Judicial Interpretation	**Chapter 5: Civil Liberties** • The Rights of Criminal Defendants • The Right to Privacy • Toward Reform: Civil Liberties and Combating Terrorism
Civil Rights and the Fourteenth Amendment	**Chapter 6: Civil Rights** • Roots of Suffrage: 1800-1890 • The Push for Equality: 1890-1954 • The Civil Rights Movement • The Women's Rights Movement • Other Groups Mobilize for Rights • Toward Reform: Civil Rights, Affirmative Action, and Pay Equality

Political Beliefs and Behaviors

Citizens' Political Beliefs	**Chapter 11: Political Socialization and Public Opinion** • Public Opinion and Polling
Processes of Learning About Politics	**Chapter 11: Political Socialization and Public Opinion** • Roots of Political Values: Political Socialization • Why We Form and Express Political Opinions
Voting and Participation in Politics	**Chapter 11: Political Socialization and Public Opinion** • Toward Reform: The Effects of Public Opinion on Government and Politics **Chapter 13: Voting and Elections** • Roots of Voting Behavior

Political Parties, Interest Groups, and Mass Media

The Mass Media

Chapter 15: The Mass Media
- Roots of News Media in the United States
- Current Media Trends
- Rules Governing the Media
- How the Media Cover Politics
- Toward Reform: Media Influence, Media Bias, and Public Confidence

Political Parties

Chapter 12: Political Parties
- Roots of the American Party System
- The Functions of the American Party System
- The Party Organization
- The Party in Government
- The Party in the Electorate
- Toward Reform: Dealignment and the Strength of Political Parties

Campaigning and Elections

Chapter 13: Voting and Elections
- Elections in the United States
- Presidential Elections
- Congressional Elections
- The 2008 Congressional Elections
- Toward Reform: Strengthening the Electoral Process

Chapter 14: The Campaign Process
- Roots of Modern Political Campaigns
- The Key Players: The Candidate and the Campaign Staff
- Coverage of the Game: The Media's Role in Defining the Playing Field
- The Rules of the Game: Campaign Finance
- The Main Event: The 2008 Presidential Campaign
- Toward Reform: Campaign Finance and the 527 Loophole

Interest Groups

Chapter 16: Interest Groups
- Roots of the American Interest Group System
- The Development of American Interest Groups
- What Do Interest Groups Do?
- What Makes an Interest Group Successful?
- Toward Reform: Regulating Interest Groups and Lobbyists

Institutions of National Government

Congress

Chapter 7: Congress
- Roots of the Legislative Branch of Government
- How Congress Is Organized
- The Members of Congress
- How Members Make Decisions
- The Lawmaking Function of Congress
- Congress and the Judiciary

The Presidency

Chapter 8: The Presidency
- Roots of the Office of President of the United States
- The Constitutional Powers of the President
- The Development and Expansion of Presidential Power
- The Presidential Establishment
- Presidential Leadership and the Importance of Public Opinion
- Toward Reform: The President and Policymaker

The Federal Courts

Chapter 10: The Judiciary
- Roots of the Federal Judiciary
- The American Legal System
- The Federal Court System
- How Federal Court Judges Are Selected
- The Supreme Court Today
- Judicial Philosophy and Decision Making
- Toward Reform: Power, Policymaking, and the Court

The Bureaucracy

Chapter 9: The Executive Branch and the Federal Bureaucracy
- Roots of the Federal Bureaucracy
- The Modern Bureaucracy
- How the Bureaucracy Works
- Toward Reform: Making Agencies Accountable

Balance of Power

Chapter 2: The Constitution
- The U.S. Constitution

Chapter 7: Congress
- Toward Reform: Congressional Checks on the Executive and Judicial Branches

Chapter 8: The Presidency
- The Constitutional Powers of the President

Public Policy

Policymaking in a Federal System

Chapter 8: The Presidency
- Toward Reform: The President as Policymaker

Chapter 9: The Executive Branch and the Federal Bureaucracy
- How the Bureaucracy Works

Chapter 10: The Judiciary
- Toward Reform: Power, Policymaking, and the Court

Chapter 19: Foreign and Defense Policy
- Roots of U.S. Foreign and Defense Policy

Formation of Policy Agendas

Chapter 17: Domestic Policy
- Roots of Public Policy: The Policymaking Process

Economic Policy

Chapter 18: Economic Policy
- Roots of Government Involvement in the Economy
- Stabilizing the Economy
- Balancing Military and Domestic Expenditures: Funding the War in Iraq
- Toward Reform: The Subprime Mortgage Crisis and Regulation

Social Policy

Chapter 17: Domestic Policy
- The Evolution of Income Security and Health Care Policies
- Income Security and Health Care Policies Today
- Toward Reform: Energy and Environmental Policy

Foreign Policy

Chapter 19: Foreign and Defense Policy
- The United States as a World Power
- Foreign and Defense Policy Decision Making
- Twenty-First-Century Challenges
- Toward Reform: Choosing Between Unilateralism and Multilateralism

Part II

Topical Review with Sample Questions and Answers and Explanations

This section is keyed to the chapters in *American Government: Roots and Reform, AP* Edition, 11e*. Part II overviews important information in bullet form, provides sample questions for every question type, and includes additional review items on core concepts. Use these practice questions to arm yourself thoroughly for all kinds of test items you will encounter on the AP examination. Answers and explanations are provided for each question for your further review.

CHAPTER 1

The Political Landscape

American government is richly grounded in the ideas and beliefs of a wide range of philosophers who came before the founding of the new nation. These ideals, combined with the values and the beliefs of the framers, have led to a uniquely American political culture. These characteristics, as well as the ideology and characteristics of the American public, shape the demands that Americans place on their government.

Roots of American Government: What Are They and Why Are They Important?

- A **government** is the formal vehicle through which policies are made and affairs of state are conducted.

The Theoretical Foundations of American Government

- During the Enlightenment, people began to question the divine right of kings.

- Thomas Hobbes and John Locke crafted the **social contract theory**, which required that all people give their consent to be governed.

- **Social contract:** An agreement between the people and their government signifying their consent to be governed.

- **Mayflower Compact:** Document written by the Pilgrims while still at sea, enumerating the scope of their government and its expectations of citizens.

- **Thomas Hobbes** was one of the two primary social contract theorists. He suggests that without government, life would be "solitary, poor, nasty, brutish, and short"—a constant struggle to survive against the evil of others. For these reasons, governments had to intrude on people's rights and liberties to better control society and to provide the necessary safeguards for property. Hobbes argued strongly for a single ruler, no matter how evil, to guarantee the rights of the weak against the strong

- **John Locke** believed that having a chief executive to administer laws was important, but that he should necessarily be limited by law or by the social contract with the governed. Locke's writings influenced many American colonists, especially Thomas Jefferson, who based the Declaration of Independence on Locke's arguments.

- When it came time to craft a government in the colonies, the framers believed that a **direct democracy**—a system of government in which members of the polity meet to discuss all policy decisions and then agree to abide by majority rule—would be unworkable. They chose to create an **indirect democracy**, in which citizens voted for representatives who governed on their behalf.

- Citizens did not like the term "democracy" because it conjured up images of mob rule. They preferred the term **republic**.

- There are a number of different types of governments:

  - A **monarchy** places power in hereditary kings.

  - If a leader rules in his or her own self-interest, without regard for individual rights and liberties, the government is called **totalitarian**.

  - Governments where participating is conditioned on wealth or some other defining characteristic are known as **oligarchies.**

  - **Democracies** give power to the people, directly or through elected representatives.

American Political Culture and the Basic Tenets of American Democracy

- **Political culture** is the commonly shared attitudes, beliefs, and values about how government should operate.

- **Personal liberty** includes freedom to act without government intervention.

- **Political equality** means that all citizens have the same voice in the political process.

- **Popular consent** means that governments draw their powers from the consent of the governed.

- **Majority rule** is the central premise of direct democracy in which only policies that collectively garner the support of a majority of voters will be made into law.

- **Popular sovereignty** is the notion that the ultimate authority in society lies with the people. It has its basis in **natural law**, a doctrine that holds that society should be governed by certain ethical principles that are a part of nature and, as such, can be understood by reason.

- **Civil society** is the society created when citizens organize and express their views publicly in a debate about public policy.

- The emphasis is on individualism, or on citizens and not groups.

- **Religious faith and Religious Freedom:** America was settled by many religious groups, some seeking to escape oppression from the official established churches in Europe. Some of these groups, however, did not wish to extend toleration to other faiths within their new communities. This resulted in religious persecution at various places and various times during the colonial period. These clashes led the Framers to universally agree that the new nation had to be founded on notions of religious freedom

The Changing American Public

- Population change has been a constant in American society.

  - Population has grown tremendously since the founding.

  - The Unite States is a nation of immigrants.

  - Hispanic population is growing rapidly; white population is shrinking.

  - America is aging, average age is rising.

  - Family size is shrinking and the number of two-parent households is declining.

Political Ideology: Its Role in the World and in American Politics

- **Political ideology** is the coherent set of values and beliefs people hold about the scope and purpose of government.

- There are a number of prevailing political ideologies in the United States.

  - **Libertarians** oppose government interference in personal liberties.

  - **Conservatives** believe that government is best when it governs least, particularly with regard to the economy.

  - **Social conservatives** believe the government should regulate morality.

  - **Liberals** favor an activist government, especially in the provision of social services.

  - **Moderate: A** person who takes a relatively centrist or middle-of-the-road view on most political issues.

  - **Libertarian:** One who believes in limited government and no governmental interference in personal liberties.

- Political labels can be problematic because many Americans have mixed political beliefs.

Toward Reform: People and Politics

Politics: The study of who gets what, when, and how—or how policy decisions are made.

- **American dream**: An American ideal of a happy, successful life, which often includes wealth, a house, a better life for one's children, and for some, the ability to grow up to be president.

- Americans have high expectations of their government. As the nation and its economy grew in size and complexity, the federal government took on more responsibilities. Each generation expected the government to take on more responsibilities.

- Today, many Americans lack faith in the country's institutions. These concerns make it even easier for citizens to blame the government for all kinds of woes—personal as well as societal—or to fail to credit governments for the things they do well. Many Americans, for example, enjoy a remarkably high standard of living, and much of it is due to governmental programs and protections.

- These high expectations can make it hard to appreciate the good things that government does.

- Government is pervasive in our lives and provides a wide array of goods and services.

- Politics are always changing.

- This frustration is leading to calls for Americans to redefine their ideas about and expectations of government and how it can be reformed. This process is likely to define politics well into the future, although the expectations of people are difficult to alter to fit the lack of faith many seem to have in the institutions of government. Many Americans say they want less government, but as they get older, they don't want less Social Security. They want lower taxes and better roads, but they don't want to pay road tolls. They want better education for their children, but lower expenditures on schools. Some clearly want less for others but not themselves, a demand that puts politicians in the position of nearly always disappointing voters.

For Additional Review

Make a list of changes that have occurred in the American population in recent years. Consider how each of these changes affects the demands placed on government.

Multiple-Choice Questions

1. Personal liberty refers to
(A) demands for freedom to engage in a variety of practices without governmental interference or discrimination.
(B) a system of government that gives power to the people, whether directly or through elected representatives.
(C) the principle that governments must draw their powers from the consent of the governed.
(D) the notion that the ultimate authority in society rests with the people.
(E) the principle that all citizens are the same in the eyes of the law.

2. All of the following are characteristic beliefs associated with American political culture EXCEPT
(A) liberty.
(B) equality of opportunity.
(C) individualism.
(D) government regulation of the economy.
(E) political equality.

3. Which of the following did NOT lead to American settlement in the 17th century?
(A) questioning the divine right of kings
(B) the split from the Church of England
(C) belief in self-government
(D) belief in intelligent design
(E) Hobbes's and Locke's social contract theories

4. Which of the following is/are among the policies favored by social conservatives?
(A) efforts to make abortion illegal
(B) cuts in defense spending
(C) increasing the separation between church and state
(D) decreasing government regulation of personal behavior
(E) greater government regulation of the economy

5. At its core, democracy is based on
(A) the doctrine that society should be governed by certain ethical principles that are part of nature and, as such, can be understood by reason.
(B) freedom of religion.
(C) majority rule.
(D) a bicameral Congress.
(E) a republican form of government.

6. Basic functions common to all national governments include all of the following EXCEPT
(A) collecting taxes.
(B) maintaining a national defense.
(C) providing universal health care.
(D) preserving order.
(E) socializing young citizens.

7. In general, the U.S. population is
I. quite young.
II. getting older.
III. becoming less diverse.
IV. less affected by immigration than in other years.
(A) II
(B) II and III
(C) III and IV
(D) I, II, and III
(E) II and IV

8. A society in which in which power resides in a leader who rules according to self-interest and without regard for individual rights and liberties is called
(A) collectivism.
(B) communism.
(C) totalitarianism.
(D) socialism.
(E) oligarchy.

9. The creation of the Department of Homeland Security is an example of the national government attempting to
(A) establish justice.
(B) secure the blessings of liberty.
(C) provide for the common defense.
(D) promote the general welfare.
(E) ensure domestic tranquility.

10. Government has grown to be big and active because
I. the public expects government to solve problems.
II. it is hard to cut programs such as Social Security and national defense.
III. Democrats, the party of big government, have been in power in recent years.
IV. the government is committed to reducing income inequality.
(A) I and II
(B) II and III
(C) III and IV
(D) I, II, and III
(E) II and IV

Free-Response Questions

1. At the end of the Constitutional Convention, Benjamin Franklin said that the framers had created "a republic, if you can keep it."

   a. Define a republican form of government. Explain how a republican form of government fits with the principles of a democracy.

   b. Identify one change in the institutional arrangements of American government and explain how that change has moved us away from the framers' concept of a republican form of government.

   c. Identify a second change in the institutional arrangements of American government and explain how that change has moved us away from the framers' concept of a republican form of government.

2. In the preamble of the Constitution, the framers set out several key functions of government. List, discuss, and provide examples of three of these five functions.

ANSWERS AND EXPLANATIONS

Multiple-Choice Questions

- **1. (A) is correct.** Personal liberty, a key characteristic of U.S. democracy, refers to both freedom from governmental interference, and demands for freedom to engage in a variety of practices without governmental interference or discrimination. The other choices refer to other key characteristics of American democracy such as political equality, popular sovereignty, popular consent, and natural law.

- **2. (D) is correct.** Americans generally believe that a largely unregulated economy, similar to a laissez faire system, would be in the national interest. To the extent that government regulates the economy, Americans often believe that economic health is jeopardized.

- **3. (D) is correct.** Intelligent design is a modern development in the creationism-evolution debate. The rest of the options led to American settlement in the 17th century.

- **4. (A) is correct.** Social conservatives are also known as the "religious right." They favor greater government efforts to legislate morality, including policies that restrict the right to an abortion and prohibit gay marriage.

- **5. (C) is correct.** A democracy is founded on the needs and wants of the people. All people might not have the same needs, but the closest representation of the whole populace is the majority. Therefore, in a theoretical democracy, decisions are made by majority rule.

- **6. (C) is correct.** While universal medical care might be desirable, and while all governments provide some social services, not all governments can afford universal coverage. The other four answers all characterize basic functions of a national government.

- **7. (A) is correct.** The U.S. population is rapidly aging. This is the only accurate statement in the list, as the nation is becoming more diverse and struggles with the same sorts of immigration problems it has addressed throughout history.

- **8. (C) is correct.** This is a simple definitional question. Totalitarianism is a form of government in which power resides in a leader who rules according to self-interest and without regard for individual rights and liberties.

- **9. (E) is correct.** All of these are set out in the preamble as goals of government. The Department of Homeland Security, which deals with issues of domestic security and peacekeeping, best exemplifies the goal of "insuring domestic tranquility."

- **10. (A) is correct.** Government is big and active because people expect government to take action, and once programs are enacted it is hard to scale them back. The other choices are simply factually incorrect.

Free-Response Questions

This rubric provides examples of many, but not all, of the possible correct responses to the free-response questions.

1.

a. A republican form of government is one in which the people are represented by elected representatives. In the United States government, that means that instead of people speaking for themselves in government decision making, the people elect representatives who represent them. In a representative government, the members of Congress should attempt to represent the will of their constituents.

b. The framers originally set up the election of senators so that it was done indirectly by legislatures in the states. The Seventeenth Amendment changed this, and now U.S. senators are directly elected by the people in the states. This moved the United States away from the original intent of the framers, who did not want the government to be directly controlled by the people.

c. During the Progressive movement, many states adopted direct democracy procedures—the initiative, referendum, and recall—that put lawmaking in the hands of citizens instead of only lawmakers.

2. The preamble dictates that the government should "establish justice." This means that governments should create a uniform set of laws that citizens abide by. The Constitution created a federal judiciary to assure that citizens comply with federal criminal and civil statutes.

The preamble also states that the government should "provide for the common defense." This means that governments should protect citizens from threats within and outside their boundaries. One of the ways the U.S. achieves this goal is by giving Congress the power to raise an army and the president the power to act as commander in chief of the armed forces.

The preamble also states that the government should "promote the general welfare." The exact meaning of this clause has expanded dramatically over time, but it encompasses a wide range of tasks that allow the government to ensure that citizens are generally enjoying the best standard of living possible. Today, programs like Social Security and Medicare and Medicaid fall under this clause.

CHAPTER 2

The Constitution

The United States' break with Great Britain played a major role in shaping the first American governing document, the Articles of Confederation. This document, however, fashioned a system of government that proved unworkable in the new nation. Today, the foundation of the American political system rests on the Constitution, a document that established the United States as a federal republic composed of three branches: legislative, executive, and judicial. Over time, the Constitution has been amended to account for the growth of the nation and changes to the political system.

Roots of the New American Nation

- For 140 years, Great Britain allowed the American colonists significant ability to self-govern.

    - Colonists were able to levy taxes, while British controlled foreign relations and trade under the system of **mercantilism**.

- The French and Indian War led to significant debt for Great Britain.

    - Levied a series of increasingly oppressive taxes on the colonists to make up revenue shortfalls.

    - Included the Sugar Act, the Stamp Act, and the Quartering Act.

- Colonists mobilized in opposition to these acts.

    - Samuel Adams and Patrick Henry formed the Sons of Liberty.

    - **Stamp Act Congress** met in 1765 to detail a list of British violations of the colonists' fundamental rights.

        - Oppressive British rule increased after this meeting; the Townshend Acts were passed in 1767.

    - Samuel Adams formed the **Committees of Correspondence** to keep the colonies apprised of developments with the British.

        - Tea Act and Coercive Acts followed; these acts had the greatest impact in Massachusetts, where the Boston Tea Party and Boston Massacre took place.

- Colonists held meetings to decide how to respond to these acts.

  - **First Continental Congress** was held in 1774 to iron out differences with the king. The Declaration of Rights and Resolves was drafted at this meeting. It demanded that the Coercive Acts be repealed.

  - **Second Continental Congress was** held in 1775.

    - Fighting had already begun at Lexington and Concord, Massachusetts.

    - Original intention was still to heal wounds with Great Britain, and they extended the Olive Branch Petition.

    - Thomas Paine released *Common Sense*, galvanizing the colonists in favor of independence.

    - Eventually drafted the **Declaration of Independence**, which explained why the colonies were establishing their own sovereign country separate from Britain.

- Declaration was the official break with Great Britain.

  - Listed grievances against the king and justified revolution.

  - Borrowed heavily from the social contract theories of John Locke.

The First Attempt at Government: The Articles of Confederation

- **Articles of Confederation** created a loose league of friendship between the states with the national government drawing its powers from the states.

  - Based on the idea of a **confederation** government, in which the states retain most of the governing power.

  - The only national institution was a Congress made up of one member from each state.

  - Ratified by all states by 1781.

- A national government without any centralized power proved to be ineffectual.

  - No power to coin money.

  - No ability to make foreign agreements.

- No executive or judiciary.

- No power to tax.

- **Shays's Rebellion:** 1786 rebellion in which an army of 1,500 disgruntled and angry farmers led by Daniel Shays marched to Springfield, Massachusetts, and forcibly restrained the state court from foreclosing mortgages on their farms. The government's inability to respond quickly to this uprising of Massachusetts farmers illustrated the very real problems with the Articles.

The Miracle at Philadelphia: Writing the U.S. Constitution

- **Constitution:** A document establishing the structure, functions, and limitations of a government.

- Constitutional Convention met in Philadelphia in 1787 to revise the Articles.

- All of the delegates to the Constitutional Convention were male and well educated.

- Has been significant debate over the motives of the framers. Some scholars argue that they wrote the new Constitution to ensure their own economic well-being.

- The biggest compromise was in legislative representation of big and small states.

  - Large states favored the **Virginia Plan**. Under this plan, representation in a bicameral legislature would be determined by the population of each state.

  - Small states favored the **New Jersey Plan**. Under this plan, states' representation in a unicameral legislature would be the same regardless of size or population.

  - This debate was resolved by the **Great Compromise**. This created a bicameral legislature that borrowed elements from both plans. The Senate was made up of two representatives from each state. Representation in the House was determined by the population of each state.

- Conflict between Northern and Southern states was resolved by the **Three-Fifths Compromise**. This mandated that representation in the House would be based on the whole number of "free persons" plus three-fifths of the number of slaves living in a state.

- The executive branch was resolved by the Committee on Unfinished Portions.

  - Chose a single chief executive serving a four-year term

  - President elected by the Electoral College

  - President could be removed from office through impeachment

The U.S. Constitution

- Preamble declared that the source of the government's power was with the people.

  - The U.S. Constitution created a **federal system**, a system of government in which powers and responsibilities were divided between the state and national governments, both of which got their power from the people.

- Document was based on the ideas of **separation of powers** and **checks and balances**.

  - Separation of powers parcels out power among the three branches. Each branch is staffed separately, with equality and independence from the other branches. The functions of each branch are as follows:

    - The legislature makes the law.

    - The executive enforces the law.

    - The judiciary interprets the law.

  - Checks and balances give each branch a way to limit and counteract the powers of every other branch.

- The new **Constitution** has seven articles.

  - Article I creates the legislative branch.

    - Sets out the duties and qualifications for the office.

    - Article I, Section 8 is one of the most important parts, as it lists the powers of Congress. These are known as **enumerated powers**.

      - Concludes with the **necessary and proper clause**, which allows Congress to pass all laws necessary and proper to carry out the enumerated powers.

      - This is the basis for the **implied powers** of Congress, which are powers derived from the enumerated powers and the necessary and proper clause. These powers are not stated specifically but are considered to be reasonably implied through the exercise of delegated powers.

  - Article II creates the executive branch.

    - Sets out the duties and qualifications for office.

- Lists the powers of the president, including acting as commander in chief, making appointments, and making treaties.

  - Details how the president can be removed from office.

- Article III creates the judicial branch.

  - Creates the Supreme Court.

  - Declares that judges "shall hold their Offices during good Behavior."

- Article IV includes the **full faith and credit clause**, which mandates states to honor the laws and judicial proceedings of other states, and the provisions for admitting new states to the union.

- Article V specifies how the constitution may be amended.

- Article VI includes the **supremacy clause**, which states that national law is supreme to (that is, supersedes) all other laws passed by the states or by any other subdivision of government, and specifies that the government cannot use any religious tests.

- Article VII includes provisions for ratification.

The Drive for Ratification of the U.S. Constitution

- The approval of at least nine states was needed to ratify the constitution.

- There were two factions during the ratification period.

  - **Federalists** supported the new Constitution and a stronger central government.

    - Leading Federalists Alexander Hamilton, John Jay, and James Madison wrote *The Federalist Papers* to defend the new constitution.

  - **Anti-Federalists** believed that a strong central government would limit the power of the states and would run rampant over citizens' rights and liberties.

    - Demanded a **Bill of Rights** to protect rights and liberties from government infringement. Today, this is the first 10 amendments to the U.S. Constitution.

- Small states and states where Federalists were well organized ratified the Constitution quickly.

- Larger states, such as New York and Virginia, held out much longer, and only ratified after the publication of *The Federalist Papers* and concessions for a Bill of Rights.

Toward Reform: Methods of Amending the U.S. Constitution

- The formal amendment process has two stages.

  - Proposal may be done by a two-thirds vote in both houses of Congress or by a national constitutional convention.

  - Ratification may be done by three-fourths of state legislatures or by conventions in three-fourths of the states.

    - The traditional process is proposal with the approval of two-thirds of both houses of Congress and ratification by three-fourths of legislatures.

    - A ratifying convention has only been used once, with the Twenty-First Amendment.

- The Constitution can also change informally.

  - The judiciary can reinterpret the provisions of the Constitution.

  - Social and cultural change can also lead citizens and policymakers to reexamine the relevance and meaning of constitutional provisions.

For Additional Review

Make a chart grouping amendments to the Constitution by common themes. What topics do most amendments to the Constitution address? What amendments, if any, would you expect to be proposed or ratified in the coming years?

Multiple-Choice Questions

1. Under America's first constitution, the Articles of Confederation,
(A) the national government dominated state governments.
(B) the executive branch had more power than Congress.
(C) Congress was a unicameral body.
(D) states were represented in Congress proportionally according to population.
(E) a national standing army was established.

2. Which of the following framers was the "principal architect" of the Constitution?
(A) Edmund Randolph
(B) George Washington
(C) Thomas Jefferson
(D) Alexander Hamilton
(E) James Madison

3. The Three-Fifths Compromise at the Constitutional Convention
(A) allowed cloture to be invoked, ending a filibuster in the Senate, with the support of 60 senators.
(B) prescribed the proportion of states required to ratify a constitutional amendment.
(C) provided a formula by which slaves would be counted for apportioning the House of Representatives.
(D) established the percentage of votes necessary for electors to be chosen under the original provisions of the Electoral College system.
(E) established the percentage of members of the House required to pass a bill raising revenue.

4. A state must honor the public acts and records of any other state under the
(A) full faith and credit clause.
(B) supremacy clause.
(C) elastic clause.
(D) commerce clause.
(E) extradition clause.

5. The idea of limiting the role of government to protecting "life, liberty, and property" is generally attributed to
(A) Karl Marx.
(B) Thomas Jefferson.
(C) Thomas Hobbes.
(D) John Locke.
(E) Alexander Hamilton.

5. Which of the following is an informal way of amending the Constitution?
(A) passage of an amendment by a simple majority vote in two consecutive sessions of Congress
(B) a vote of two-thirds of the state legislatures specifically requesting Congress to call a national convention to propose amendments.
(C) passage of an amendment by a vote of two-thirds of the state legislatures without congressional approval.
(D) changes in social and cultural attitudes that lead to substantive changes in how people interpret the Constitution.
(E) passage of an amendment by a vote of two-thirds of Congress.

6. The outcome of a conflict between the Constitution and the states is determined by
(A) the Great Compromise.
(B) the supremacy clause.
(C) *Federalist No. 10.*
(D) judicial review.
(E) ex post facto laws.

7. The framers designed a system of checks and balances for the national government. Which of the following illustrate that concept?

I.   Congress overrides a president's veto.
II.   The Supreme Court declares a law unconstitutional.
III.   The president issues an executive order reducing the size of the bureaucracy.
IV.   The House and Senate cannot agree on a Conference Committee report.

(A I and II
(B) II and III
(C) III and IV
(D) II and IV
(E) I and IV

8. The Articles of Confederation failed for all of the following reasons EXCEPT
(A) The federal government lacked the power to tax.
(B) The federal government lacked the ability to regulate trade.
(C) There was no national judiciary.
(D) The central government was too weak.
(E) There was no provision to amend the Articles.

9. Which plan proposed at the Constitutional Convention called for a bicameral legislature, with one chamber having members from states calculated proportionally based upon population and the other having two members per state?
(A) Great Compromise
(B) Virginia Plan
(C) Annapolis Convention Plan
(D) Philadelphia Plan
(E) New Jersey Plan

10. Which of the following was stipulated in Article III of the Constitution?
(A) creation of the Supreme Court
(B) executive powers
(C) powers of Congress
(D) full faith and credit clause
(E) the separation of powers

Free-Response Questions

1. The Constitution has had 17 formal amendments since the adoption of the Bill of Rights, yet there are basic elements that have changed because of informal processes as well.

   a. Identify the most common means of formally amending the Constitution.

   b. Identify and explain how one informal process has changed the meaning of the Constitution even without formal amendment.

c.   Identify and explain how another informal process has changed the meaning of the Constitution even without formal amendment.

2. The framers' new Constitution tried to balance the need for "proper energy" in government with a clear limitation on governmental power.

   a.   Identify and discuss two features the framers created for keeping any branch of government from becoming too powerful.

   b.   Identify and discuss how the framers divided powers between national and state governments.

ANSWERS AND EXPLANATIONS

Multiple-Choice Questions

- **1. (C) is correct.** All but one of the answer choices misidentify a characteristic of the Articles. The only correct statement is that it provided for a unicameral legislature.

- **2. (E) is correct.** James Madison provided the intellectual impetus for the Constitution. As a result, in terms of his impact on the Constitution, Madison was in many ways the "first among equals." The others listed had an impact on the Constitution, but their roles were far more limited than Madison's, especially Jefferson's, since he was out of the country at the time of the Constitutional Convention.

- **3. (C) is correct.** Although all of the options could provide for a three-fifths ratio, only the treatment of slaves was specified in the Constitution. As a result, the others, though they may be correct (as in the case of invoking cloture), do not stem from the Constitution.

- **4. (A) is correct.** The full faith and credit clause, found in Article IV of the Constitution, guarantees that the legal records, laws, and judicial proceedings of one state will be honored by another state.

- **5. (D) is correct.** An informal method of amending the Constitution would be a practice or development that led to a change in how the Constitution was applied, even with no direct changes to it through the formal ratification process. For example, while there is no specific amendment guaranteeing women equal protection of the law, the federal courts have interpreted the Constitution to prohibit many forms of gender discrimination, thereby recognizing cultural and societal change. Formal ways of amending the Constitution include Congress, by a two-thirds vote, proposing an amendment and then three-fourths of the states ratifying that amendment. Also, Congress can be pressured to begin the amendment process by a vote of two-thirds of the state legislatures specifically requesting Congress to call a national convention to propose amendments. Amendments cannot be added by simple majority vote in two consecutive sessions of Congress or passage of an amendment by a vote of two-thirds of the state legislatures without congressional approval.

- **6. (B) is correct.** One of the major features of the new Constitution, as opposed to the Articles of Confederation, was that all states would have to adopt laws that conformed to limits of the U.S. Constitution. This was a core concept of the Constitution.

- **7. (A) is correct.** Checks and balances require the interaction between two branches of government. Hence, the overriding of a president's veto by Congress or the invalidation of a congressional law by the Supreme Court would be examples of checks and balances, while presidential orders within the executive branch or conflict within the legislative branch would not.

- **8. (E) is correct.** The Articles of Confederation could be amended with the unanimous consent of all of the states. This amendment provision, however, was less than ideal. It was difficult to get all of the states to agree on necessary changes. All of the other reasons listed are also reasons for the failure of the Articles.

- **9. (A) is correct.** The Virginia and New Jersey Plans were contradictory proposals regarding representation. Philadelphia was the city in which the convention was held while Annapolis had been the location of a failed convention in 1786. The "great compromise" that led to a Senate based upon equal state representation and a House allocated proportionally based upon population was the Great Compromise.

- **10. (A) is correct.** Article III of the Constitution established the judicial branch of the new federal government. The text was quite limited because the framers felt the court was little more than a theoretical necessity. The only court specifically established in this article was the Supreme Court.

Free-Response Questions

This rubric provides examples of many, but not all, of the possible correct responses to the free-response questions.

1.

a. Amending the Constitution is a two-step process. The most common way to amend the Constitution is, first, for a proposed amendment to be approved by a two-thirds vote in both houses of Congress. The proposed amendment is then approved by the legislatures in three-fourths of the states. This process has been used for every amendment except the Twenty-First, which repealed prohibition.

b. The Constitution can informally be changed by judicial interpretation. The courts review and interpret the Constitution and statutes to allow the meaning of the language and provisions to change over time. For example, the court's decision in *Marbury* v. *Madison* (1803) carved out the power of judicial review for the courts, although it is never explicitly stated in the Constitution.

c. The Constitution has also been informally amended with social and cultural change. For example, the powers of Congress have been allowed to increase at the expense of the powers of state governments as a result of national crises, such as the Great Depression.

2.

a. In order for any branch to be kept from being too powerful, the framers designed a government that included the twin concepts of separation of powers and checks and balances. This system divides power among three branches of government—the legislative, the executive, and the judicial. Each branch has a specific grant of power and each is given "checks over the other." For example, Congress must approve presidential treaties and can override a president's veto. The president can veto a bill of Congress. And the Supreme Court can declare acts of the president or laws of Congress unconstitutional. With ambition always ready to counteract ambition, no branch can step too far without another branch stepping in and reversing its actions. Since institutions do not want to waste time or lose prestige by having their actions reversed by another branch, separation of powers and checks and balances are a very effective system.

b. In order to keep the federal government from gaining too much power, the Constitution creates a system of federalism, that is, a system that divides power between the national government and the state governments. The powers of the national government are listed in Article I of the Constitution, and the Tenth Amendment makes it clear that powers not listed in Article I are reserved for the states.

CHAPTER 3

Federalism

In a federal system, the national and state governments derive all of their power from the people. The Constitution divides powers between the two governments, although the balance of these powers has changed over time. During the earliest days of the new republic, the governments operated in a system of dual federalism, in which state and national governments had separate spheres of power, like a layer cake. Beginning with the New Deal, the government entered a time of cooperative federalism, in which the two governments became more intertwined, like a marble cake. The presidency of Ronald Reagan ushered in a new federalism and a return of power to the states. The Supreme Court has also played a major role in defining the balance of federal-state power.

Roots of the Federal System and the Constitutional Allocation of Governmental Powers

- The United States was the first country to have a **federal system**, in which the national government and the state governments derive all power from the people.

    - This is in contrast to a **confederation**, in which all governments derive power from the states.

    - Also in contrast to a unitary government, where all authority comes from the national government.

- The powers of the national government are known as **enumerated powers**. They include coining money, regulating commerce, and providing for defense.

    - Also have **implied powers** derived from the **necessary and proper clause**.

    - The **supremacy clause** also guarantees that the national government will be superior to state governments.

- The powers of the state government are known as **reserve powers**. They include regulating elections and legislating for the health, welfare, and morals of their citizens. The **Tenth Amendment** provides the basis for state claims to reserve powers by stating that any power not given to the national government in the Constitution is reserved for the states.

- Some powers, known as **concurrent powers**, are shared by national and state governments.

- Some powers are expressly denied under the Constitution. These include passing **bills of attainder**, a law declaring an act illegal without a judicial trial, and **ex post facto laws**,

laws that make an act punishable as a crime even if the action was legal at the time it was committed.

- There are a number of provisions regulating relations between the states.

    - The **full faith and credit clause** assures that judicial actions and contracts made in one state will be binding in another state.

    - The **privileges and immunities clause** guarantees that citizens of all states are afforded the same rights.

    - States are required to **extradite** criminals from one state to the other.

    - States also work together through **interstate compacts** on issues such as driver licensing and emergency management. Interstate compacts are contracts between states that carry the force of law; generally now used as a tool to address multistate policy concerns.

Federalism and the Marshall Court

- The Marshall Court carved out an important role for the judiciary in defining the federal-state relationship.

    - *McCulloch* v. *Maryland* **(1819)** was the first major decision on federalism. The court ruled that the constitution denied states the ability to tax the federal government. The court's broad interpretation of the necessary and proper clause paved the way for later rulings upholding expansive federal powers.

    - The court also upheld the federal government's ability to regulate commerce in *Gibbons* v. *Ogden* **(1824)**. The court's broad interpretation of the Constitution's commerce clause paved the way for later rulings upholding expansive federal powers.

    - *Barron* v. *Baltimore* **(1833):** The Supreme Court ruled that the due process clause of the Fifth Amendment did not apply to the actions of states. This decision limited the Bill of Rights to the actions of Congress alone.

Dual Federalism: The Taney Court, Slavery, and the Civil War

- **Dual federalism** was an era of federalism when the national and state governments had separate spheres of power, like a layer cake.

    - Philosophy articulated by the Supreme Court in decisions such as *Dred Scott* v. *Sandford* (1857), which declared the Missouri Compromise unconstitutional and upheld the system of slavery.

- Civil War signaled the beginning of the end for dual federalism, as the responsibilities of the federal government began to grow.

- The **Sixteenth Amendment** and the **Seventeenth Amendment** took powers away from the state governments by allowing a federal income tax (Sixteenth) and removing election of senators from the hands of state legislatures (Seventeenth).

Cooperative Federalism: The Growth of National Government

- The Great Depression and the federal government's response in the form of the New Deal gave birth to a new era known as **cooperative federalism**. Under this system, the responsibilities of state and national governments became intertwined like a marble cake.

- This system grew during the Great Society of the 1960s. During this time, the use of **categorical grants** from the federal to state government increased. A categorical grant is one that allocates federal funds to states for a specific purpose.

New Trends in Federalism

- Ronald Reagan advocated for a **new federalism** and a return of power to the states.

    - Reagan pushed for the use of less restrictive **block grants**, grants given to a state by the federal government with only general spending guidelines.

- Movement continued through the 1990s and the Republican Congress's "devolution revolution."

    - One of the cornerstones of this movement was an attempt to end **unfunded mandates**, or federal requirements given to states with no money to aid in compliance.

- Bush administration pledged to continue this trend while on the campaign trail, but post–9/11 the reality of governing did not allow for as much devolution as Bush had planned.

- Also saw a growth in **preemption**, or the national government overriding state actions. No Child Left Behind is an example of this trend.

- From the New Deal until the 1980s, the Supreme Court's impact on the federal system generally was to expand the national government's authority at the expense of the states.

- Starting in the 1980s, the Rehnquist Court took a special interest in federalism issues. At first its decisions exhibited a strict states' rights perspective consistent with the ideas of new federalism, but later decisions were more mixed.

- Decisions by the Roberts Court on federalism issues have been mixed; it remains too early to determine the trajectory of the current court.

Toward Reform: Attempts to Balance National and State Powers

- The Problem:

Government makes two types of policies, redistributive and developmental. **Redistributive policies** are ones where the government collects money (usually through taxation) from one group of citizens to finance a service, such as health care or welfare, for another group of citizens. **Developmental policies** are those that are designed to strengthen a government's economic standing, such as building roads and other infrastructure. The national government's greater financial resources and ability to assure a uniform standard, makes it better suited to handle redistributive programs. In contrast, developmental programs would be best left to state governments, which are closer to the people and better able to assess and address regional needs. Historically, the division of labor has not followed this pattern. The national government, and particularly members of Congress, have had reelection incentives to create and fund developmental programs (often in the form of "pork") that have a direct impact on constituents. As a result, administration of redistributive policies was often left to the states.

- **Progressive federalism**: Movement that gives state officials significant leeway in acting on issues normally considered national in scope, such as the environment and consumer protection.

For Additional Review

To understand federal grants more completely, brainstorm a list of some services that your state provides. Then conduct Internet research to see how those programs are funded.

Multiple-Choice Questions

1. Which of the following allows the states the broadest financial discretion?
(A) categorical grants
(B) block grants
(C) mandates
(D) foreign assistance
(E) U. S. military funding

2. The Constitution grants Congress the power to establish post offices and post roads. This is an example of
(A) enumerated powers.
(B) implied powers.
(C) reserved powers.
(D) concurrent powers.
(E) exclusive powers.

3. In a confederation,
(A) power is divided between a central government and regional governments.
(B) the sovereignty within a nation is held entirely by the central government.
(C) sovereignty is shared at the national, state, and local levels.
(D) power is held at the regional level.
(E) regional governments hold sovereignty regarding domestic policy while the national government holds sovereignty in national security policy.

4. The fiscal relationship between the national and state governments involves complex relationships. Which would *least* likely be favored by state governments?
(A) unfunded mandates
(B) categorical grants
(C) block grants
(D) revenue sharing
(E) formula grants

5. Enumerated powers are those given to
(A) the Supreme Court.
(B) the federal bureaucracy.
(C) state governments.
(D) the military.
(E) the national government.

6. The Supreme Court of which era put in place the idea that the national government should not exceed its constitutionally enumerated powers, and also greatly solidified the idea of dual federalism, as stated in the Tenth Amendment?
(A) Marshall Court.
(B) New Deal.
(C) Taney Court.
(D) Rehnquist Court.
(E) Roberts Court.

7. The case of *McCulloch* v. *Maryland* (1809) ruled that
I. the federal government could exercise only the enumerated powers of the Constitution.
II. the implied powers in Article I of the Constitution allowed Congress to create a nationally chartered bank.
III. the state governments could levy taxes on national government institutions.
IV. neither states nor the federal government could tax one another.
V. the state courts had sole jurisdiction over regulatory affairs within their boundaries.
(A) I, III, and V
(B) I and IV
(C) II and III
(D) II and IV
(E) IV and V

8. Dual federalism refers to the fact that
(A) the Constitution provides two layers of government in the nation—the national and the state.
(B) there are two major forms of aid from the national government to the states—categorical and block grants.
(C) both the national and state governments can levy taxes on citizens.
(D) there are two distinct eras in American history—the era before cooperative federalism and the era since the development of cooperative federalism.
(E) there is a distinct line between policies surrounding public education and private education in the states.

9. The power of the national government to regulate interstate commerce was expanded in the landmark case of
(A) *Marbury* v. *Madison*.
(B) *Plessy* v. *Ferguson*.
(C) *McCulloch* v. *Maryland*.
(D) *Miranda* v. *Arizona*.
(E) *Gibbons* v. *Ogden*.

10. The notion that when state and federal laws conflict, the national laws will prevail is specified in the
(A) necessary and proper clause.
(B) supremacy clause.
(C) extradition clause.
(D) full faith and credit clause.
(E) privileges and immunities clause.

Free-Response Questions

1. The Constitution designed a system in which various types of powers were assigned to different levels of government. Those types of powers are variously described as:

    -   enumerated powers

    -   reserved powers

    -   concurrent powers

    -   implied powers

    Select three of the types of powers listed above.

    a. Define each of the chosen types of powers.

    b. Explain how each of the chosen types of powers affects the distribution of powers between national and state governments.

2. Cooperative federalism is a term often used to describe the complex fiscal relationship between the national and state governments. Write an essay in which you do the following:

    a. Discuss the concept of categorical grants.

    b. Explain an advantage and a disadvantage of categorical grants.

    c. Discuss the concept of block grants.

    d. Explain an advantage and a disadvantage of block grants.

ANSWERS AND EXPLANATIONS

Multiple-Choice Questions

-   **1. (B) is correct.** One of the major fiscal federalism issues in recent years is the "devolution" of powers from the national government to the states in the form of block grants. Categorical grants give very limited discretion to states while mandates leave states with no discretion. Foreign and military policies are solely the province of the national government.

-   **2. (A) is correct.** The enumerated powers are listed in Article I, Section 8, and one example is the establishment of post offices and roads. Other options describe different types of power.

-   **3. (D) is correct.** Under the Articles of Confederation, the state governments held the final power while the national government had only such powers as the 13 regional (or state) governments gave it. The other definitions provided as options describe different arrangements of power.

- **4. (A) is correct.** Mandates allow the states no discretion in spending money. Of course, from the state's position, the least liked of mandates are unfunded mandates, which require states to spend money without any financial assistance from the national government. All of the other options allow the states some modicum of control over the supervision of spending and therefore would be preferred over mandates.

- **5. (E) is correct.** This is a simple definitional question. The other options are not the correct terms to describe the definition in the root of the question.

- **6. (C) is correct.** The Taney Court really emphasized the authority of the states to make laws "necessary to their well-being and prosperity," clarifying their equal position in dual federalism. The Marshall Court's actions primarily clarified the powers of the national government. The New Deal brought about an era of cooperative federalism, which was based on the intertwined relationship between the national, state, and local governments, and was eventually given sanction by the Supreme Court. The Rehnquist Court did attempt to limit federal power over states, but not so far as to revive dual federalism. The Roberts Court's record on federalism cases is mixed, and it is really too early to discern a particular direction in its decisions.

- **7. (D) is correct.** The *McCulloch* case is a landmark decision that had two major findings: (1) that state and national governments could not destroy one another by taxing and (2) that the implied powers allowed the establishment of a national bank, even though that was not explicitly mentioned in Article I, Section 8. Answers I and III contradict the correct answers, and answer V is not related to the decision in any way.

- **8. (A) is correct.** Dual federalism is used to describe the original view of the relationship between the levels of government as clearly separated, or layered. The other four responses also refer to contrasts between two things, but not to dual federalism.

- **9. (E) is correct.** *Gibbons* v. *Ogden* had to do with expanding the national government's power to regulate interstate commerce and is one of the two most important early Supreme Court federalism decisions. (The other being *McCulloch* v. *Maryland*.) The other court cases listed have to do with different issues.

- **10. (B) is correct.** The supremacy clause assures that states comply with guiding provisions of the national government. Where the Constitution is silent, states have a great deal of discretion in their decision making. But where there is a constitutional requirement, states cannot have laws that are at variance with the national requirement.

Free-Response Questions

This rubric provides examples of many, but not all, of the possible correct responses to the free-response questions.

1.

a. Reserved powers are powers retained by the states. They extend from an enumerated list in Article I of the Constitution and are codified by the Tenth Amendment. They include the power to regulate elections and ratify amendments to the constitution.

   Enumerated powers are powers specifically granted to the federal Congress under Article I, Section 8 of the Constitution. They include coining money, regulating commerce, and providing for defense

b. Taken together, these powers define the purposes of federal and state power and assure their mutual coexistence. They also can be construed as limitations on the activity of each government. The federal government, for example, cannot regulate elections, and the state governments have no power to establish post offices and post roads. These powers are often considered by the U.S. Supreme Court in adjudicating decisions on issues of federalism.

2.

a. Categorical grants are grants from the national government to the state government for specific purposes and with strings attached. Usually, categorical grants give money to states to spend with almost no discretion—if the states agree to receive categorical grants they agree to spend the money in specific ways.

b. One advantage of a categorical grant is that it allows the national government to have greater fiscal responsibility for the money that it collects. Members of Congress may feel that since they are ultimately responsible for the money they have collected from their constituents, they should exercise specific control over how that money is spent. For example, the Interstate Highway Act is a categorical grant. As a result, if states accept money under that act, then Congress knows that it will be spent for building and maintaining the interstate highways. However, a disadvantage of categorical grants is that the states can be blackmailed by the national government. The Interstate Highway Act illustrates that as well. In order to receive that money, states must comply with all of the provisions of the grant. As a result, when the national government stipulated that in order to receive this grant, states would have to raise their drinking age to 21, all 50 states complied.

c. Block grants are grants from the national government to the state government that are given for broad classifications of expenditure, such as health or welfare. States prefer block grants to categorical grants because they have greater discretion in how to spend the money.

d. One advantage of block grants is that they allow the state governments, which are closer to the people, the ability to tailor the use of that money to the specific needs of the state. Northern states might have needs that are different from Southern states, and urban states might have needs that are different than rural states. For example, if the national government wants to improve science and math education, needs might be different in Texas, where a lot of students speak Spanish, than in Minnesota, where language barriers are not as big an issue. One disadvantage of block grants is that the national government does not have as much control over the money and states might "waste" the free money that the federal government gave them. That would mean that the national government was not a good steward of its money.

CHAPTER 4

State and Local Government

States and localities have taken on more responsibilities as the roles played by government have increased. In turn, the powers of governors, legislators, and state courts have also grown tremendously.

States also have authority over the many local governments that comprise the United States. They do not, however, have significant authority over the many Indian tribes that may live within their boundaries. States and localities raise revenue from citizens through a variety of forms of taxation.

The AP exam does not cover state and local government *per se*, but subnational governments are obviously very important in the federal system. Because of the way the AP exam is structured, there are no free-response questions at the end of this chapter. You should refer back to chapter 3, "Federalism." Material covered in this chapter could enrich your responses to those questions.

Roots of State and Local Governments

- State governments' responsibilities and representativeness have increased over time.

  With the exception of governors and a handful of big-city mayors, for much of American history, officeholders were farmers, teachers, lawyers, and shop owners who did public service during their spare time. This was true for many judges and local government bureaucrats as well. As the responsibilities and challenges of government grew, more state and local jobs became full time. The need for urban services led to more full-time local governments.

- One person, one vote: Since the 1962 *Baker* v. *Carr* Supreme Court decision, state legislative districts must represent the same number of eligible voters, which is the principle of one person, one vote. This has increased the representative nature and the responsiveness of governments.

State Governments

- **State constitution:** The document that describes the basic policies, procedures, and institutions of the government of a specific state, much as the U.S. Constitution does for the federal government.

  - Originally, state constitutions emphasized limiting executive power and protecting civil liberties.

- Constitutions adopted after the Civil War were initially more permissive and inclusive, particularly in the Reconstruction South. But, when federal occupation ended, whites reasserted control and wrote very restrictive, discriminatory constitutions.

- Western states had constitutions written during the Progressive movement that were intended to limit the power of political machines.

- Since the 1960s, the trend has been to amend constitutions to increase the power of governors, legislatures, and courts.

- State constitutions are much easier to amend than federal constitutions.

- **Political machine:** An organization designed to solicit votes from certain neighborhoods or communities for a particular political party in return for services and jobs if that party wins.

- **Progressive movement:** Advocated measures to destroy political machines and instead have voters participate directly in the nomination of candidates and the establishment of public policy.

- **Governors** are the chief executives of states and the most visible elected officials.

  - Governors' most important role is identifying state policy priorities and setting an agenda and a budget.

  - Governors have significant powers to **veto** legislation. They can use the **package or general veto** to reject a bill in its entirety, or they can reject specific parts of a bill through a **line-item veto**.

  - **Policy Implementation:** The governor's responsibility as head of the executive branch and all of the bureaucratic agencies therein provides him or her with an additional opportunity to affect public policies after laws have been passed. The speed and care with which implementation occurs are often under the influence of the governor. Likewise, governors can affect the many details and interpretations that must be decided. Governors can influence these kinds of decisions primarily through appointing the heads of state administrative agencies. The appointment powers of governors vary greatly by state.

  - Governors have several powers with respect to convicted criminals.

  - **Pardon:** The authority of a governor to cancel someone's conviction of a crime by a court and to eliminate all sanctions and punishments resulting from the conviction.

  - **Commute:** The action of a governor to cancel all or part of the sentence of someone convicted of a crime, while keeping the conviction on the record.

- **Parole:** The authority of a governor to release a prisoner before his or her full sentence has been completed and to specify conditions that must be met as part of the release.

- **Extradite:** To send a person who has been accused of a crime to another state to face criminal charges.

- **Legislatures** were originally designed to be the most powerful institutions in state government. While they are still primarily citizen bodies, they have become increasingly professionalized in recent years.

  - **Term limits:** Rules that exist in some states limiting how long an individual may serve in a state or local elected office. Currently, 15 states have term limits, down from a high point of 20 in the 1990s.

- **State courts** handle most of the disputes in the American political system.

  - Most states have a variety of general and specific trial courts, appellate courts, and courts of last resort.

    - **Municipal and specialized courts:** These have jurisdiction over a broad array of issues established by municipal or city ordinances, and specific issues such as family disputes, traffic, small claims (less than $500 or $1,000), or probate (wills).

    - **Circuit or county courts:** Circuit courts, which in most states follow county boundaries, can hear appeals from municipal or specialized courts. They are the first courts to hear cases in rural areas where towns and villages are too small to warrant a court. Like municipal courts, circuit courts hear the full range of civil and criminal cases.

    - **Appellate courts:** In appellate cases, attorneys present written and oral arguments about why a decision should be modified or reversed, but plaintiffs, defendants, and witnesses do not appear before the judges. Appeals are based primarily on whether laws were applied correctly and whether the right procedures were followed.

    - **State supreme courts**: State supreme courts offer litigants who are not satisfied with the decision of an appeals court the possibility of a reversal or amendment. As in appellate courts, state supreme courts base decisions on the arguments of attorneys rather than the testimony of witnesses. In general, supreme courts can pick and choose which cases to take.

  - Under a process called **inclusion**, state courts are required to defer to federal law if the two are in conflict.

  - **Judicial selection**: Most state judges are elected and serve for fixed terms. A few states allow governors or the legislature to appoint judges. The remaining states use a process called the **Missouri (or merit) Plan**, a method of selecting judges in which a governor must appoint someone from a list provided by an independent panel. Judges are then kept in office if they get a majority of "yes" votes in general elections.

Local Governments

- **Dillon's rule:** A court ruling that local governments do not have any inherent sovereignty but instead must be authorized by state government. Localities derive all of their power from state governments.

- **Municipalities** are the most local community governments. They are governments with general responsibilities, such as a city, town, or village, which is created in response to the emergence of a relatively dense population.

- **County**: Geographic district created within a state, with a government that has general responsibilities for land, welfare, environment, and, where appropriate, rural service policies.

- **Town**: Small communities governed by a mayor and town council instead of an open town meeting.

- **Cities**: Relatively densely populated areas that have jurisdiction over a wide variety of issues. Some of the most intense struggles among governments occur in cities.

- **Special district**: A local government that is responsible for a particular function, such as schools, water, sewerage, or parks.

- **Charter:** A document that, like a constitution, specifies the basic policies, procedures, and institutions of a municipality.

- **Special charters**: Historically, as urban areas emerged, each community desiring to be recognized as a town or city wrote and sought approval for its own unique, individual charter. To avoid inconsistencies, most state constitutions now prohibit the granting of special charters.

- **General charters**: Some states use a standard charter, written by the state legislature, for all jurisdictions, regardless of size or circumstance.

- **Classified charters**: The legislatures in several states have established a classification for cities according to population and then specified a standard charter for each classification.

- **Optional charters**: A more recent development is for the state to provide several acceptable model charters and let voters in a community choose from among them.

- **Home-rule charters**: The state legislature authorizes a community to legislate on any issue that does not conflict with existing state or federal laws.

- **Municipal Governance**

- **Town meetings**: Form of local government in which all eligible voters are invited to attend a meeting and vote on policy and management issues.

- **Mayor-council:** An elected chief executive, the **mayor,** governs the municipality along with the **city council**, which serves as the legislature of the municipality.

- **Council-manager**: A model of government in which an appointed, professional manager implements the will of an elected city council and handles the day-to-day operations of government. School districts, with very few exceptions, follow the council manager model, as do most other special districts.

- **Public corporation (authority):** Government organization established to provide a particular service or run a particular facility that is independent of other city or state agencies and is to be operated like a business. Examples include a port authority or a mass transit system.

- **Commission:** Form of local government in which several officials are elected to top positions that have both legislative and executive responsibilities.

Political Participation

- **Nonpartisan election**: A contest in which political parties do not nominate candidates and ballots do not include any party identification of those running for office. In these cases, the media play a key role, as do powerful citizens or families in a community.

- **District-based election:** Election in which candidates run for an office that represents only the voters of a specific district within the jurisdiction.

- **At-large election:** Election in which candidates for office must compete throughout the jurisdiction as a whole.

- States also use a number of forms of direct democracy to make policy and check governmental power.

  - Initiatives can be direct or indirect. **Direct initiatives** occur when voters place propositions on the ballot for an up or down vote. **Indirect initiatives** occur when the legislature places a proposal on the ballot for an up or down vote.

  - Can also use a **direct referendum**, in which voters can veto a bill recently passed by the legislature, or an **advisory referendum**, in which voters cast nonbinding ballots on an issue the legislature is considering.

- In some states citizens can remove elected officials through **recall,** a process in which voters can petition for a vote to remove officeholders before the next scheduled election.

Relations with Indian Nations

- Treaties with Indian nations affect most states.

- Indian nations have **domestic dependent nation** status, a type of sovereignty that places them outside the authority of state governments but makes them reliant on the federal government for the interpretation and application of treaty provisions.

- **Trust relationship**: The legal obligation of the federal government to protect the interests of American Indian tribes.

- **Reservation land:** Land designated in a treaty to be controlled by American Indian tribes and is not subject to taxation or regulation by state or local governments.

- **Trust land:** American Indian tribes can acquire trust land by securing ownership of a parcel and then petitioning to have it placed in trust status by the secretary of the Department of the Interior. Like reservation land, it is not subject to taxation or regulation by state or local governments. The acquisition of trust land has the potential for disruption of a community's development plans or tax base and is an obvious challenge to cordial, working relationships between tribes, the federal government, and state or local governments

- **Compacts:** State governments have limited authority to negotiate formal, legal agreements, called compacts, with tribes who wish to have casino gambling on reservation or trust land.

Toward Reform: State and Local Finances

- States differ widely in their sources of funding. Most of their revenues are from sales and income taxes. Ten states have no income taxes and five states have no sales tax.

- Local governments rely primarily on property taxes. These are particularly important for funding schools.

- **User fees:** Local and state governments levy user fees, such as admission to parks, licenses for hunting and fishing, tuition for public universities, and charges based on water use. User fees are typically placed in segregated funds.

- **Segregated funds:** Money that comes in from a certain tax or fee and then is restricted to a specific use, such as a gasoline tax that is used for road maintenance.

- **Balanced budget:** A financial plan in which the revenue from taxes and fees equals the amount of money spent.

- **Progressive tax**: The tax level increases with the wealth or ability of an individual or business to pay.

- **Regressive tax:** The tax level increases as the wealth or ability of an individual or business to pay decreases. This places a greater burden on poorer citizens.

For Additional Review

Draw a diagram of the major federal, state, and local governmental institutions. Draw arrows to show where authority is directed and briefly describe the responsibilities of each institution you have included.

Multiple-Choice Questions

1. Which of the following is a true statement about state constitutions?
(A) They have been changed over time to increase the power of governors.
(B) They must be recertified by popular vote every 10 years.
(C) They must be recertified by state legislatures every 10 years.
(D) Most states have no method for amending their constitutions.
(E) They have been changed over time to decrease the power of governors.

2. Which of the following are procedures for direct democracy?
I. a recall
II. an initiative
III. a line-item veto
IV. a referendum

(A) IV only
(B) I and II only
(C) I, II, and IV only
(D) II, III, and IV only
(E) All of the above

3. Which best describes the trend in state legislatures?
(A) State legislatures have increased their power as the power of governors to veto legislation has declined.
(B) There has been a consistent rise in the number of states that have enacted term limits for their legislators.
(C) State legislative sessions have grown shorter with the increase in federal government responsibility.
(D) They are increasingly elected in nonpartisan elections.
(E) State legislative sessions are longer.

4. In most states, the governor has line-item veto powers that allow him or her to
(A) veto state supreme court decisions.
(B) veto referenda.
(C) veto laws previously signed into law.
(D) veto unfunded federal mandates.
(E) veto specific parts of a bill.

5. Which of the following is a trend in state governments in recent decades?
(A) enactment of reforms designed to enhance the capacity of governors, legislatures, and courts to address problems
(B) a growing tendency of legislative elections being won by upper-income white-collar professionals
(C) the increasing imposition of dress codes on legislators and legislative staff
(D) state legislatures assuming primary governing responsibility in policy areas like education, crime, and social welfare
(E) increasing number of states enacting term limits

6. Most state judges are selected using
(A) elections.
(B) gubernatorial appointment.
(C) legislative appointment.
(D) the Missouri Plan.
(E) merit nominating commissions.

7. Which of the following methods of organizing policymaking in local government most embodies the concept of direct democracy?
(A) town meetings
(B) mayor-council
(C) council-manager
(D) public corporation
(E) commission

8. Which of the following is the largest source of revenue for state governments?
(A) state lotteries
(B) public utilities
(C) sales and income taxes
(D) federal grants
(E) transfers from local governments

9. Dillon's Rule is the idea that
(A) state governments should maintain balanced budgets in order to govern most efficiently.
(B) counties and municipalities should be empowered to determine local tax rates.
(C) laws passed by the legislature can be invalidated by a majority vote of the council of governments.
(D) the use of the patronage system in state governments is beneficial for public morale.
(E) local governments have only those powers that are explicitly given to them by the states.

10. All of the following are true statements about special districts EXCEPT:
(A) They often use the council-manager method governance.
(B) They usually exist to provide only a single service.
(C) They tend to be highly flexible units of government.
(D) They do not have independent sources of funds.
(E) They help local governments carry out their responsibilities more efficiently.

ANSWERS AND EXPLANATIONS

Multiple-Choice Questions

- **1. (A) is correct.** From the 1960s onward, state constitutions have been amended in order to enhance the ability of governors, legislatures, and courts to address problems. Amending state constitutions is easier than the U.S. Constitution. Although the checks and balances in state constitutions vary with each state, all contain at least some checks and balances. State constitutions do not need to be periodically recertified.

- **2. (C) is correct.** Direct democracy is government controlled directly by citizens. In some states, procedures such as the initiative, recall elections, and referenda give voters a direct impact on policymaking by means of the voting booth.

- **3. (E) is correct.** State legislative sessions are getting longer. Originally, state legislatures generally met every other year for a few short weeks. As of 2010, 43 state legislatures met every year and only seven every other year. Moreover, floor sessions are now longer, and between sessions, legislators and their staff increasingly do committee work and conduct special studies. Few governors used to have veto power, now all do. Although term limits were on the increase in the 1990s, several states have repealed term limits since 2000. While nonpartisan elections are used in some local elections, state legislative elections are generally very partisan.

- **4. (E) is correct.** The line-item veto allows a governor to veto only certain parts of a bill while allowing the rest of it to pass into law. Most governors have this power.

- **5. (A) is correct.** The trend from the 1960s onward, throughout the United States, was to amend state constitutions in order to enhance the ability of governors, legislatures, and courts to address problems. Governors have increasingly taken on more, not less, responsibility in most states. Although term limits were on the increase in the 1990s, several states have repealed term limits since 2000. White-collar professionals, such as lawyers and businesspeople, have long dominated state politics and their current dominance is certainly not a recent development.

- **6. (A) is correct.** Although a variety of methods are used to elect state court judges, most states use either partisan or nonpartisan elections to choose their state court judges.

- **7. (A) is correct.** In a direct democracy, all citizens are able to vote on laws and policies. In town meetings, all eligible voters are invited to attend a meeting and vote on policy and management issues. Mayor-council, council-manager, and commission arrangements all involve voters electing representatives to set policy, the implementation of which in the case of the mayor-council and commission models is then is overseen by elected officials. In a public corporation, a government organization is established to provide a particular service or run a particular facility that is independent of other city or state agencies and is operated like a business.

- **8. (C) is correct.** State government revenues are derived from a variety of sources, but the largest share comes from income and sales taxes. Taxes make up almost 43 percent of state revenue.

- **9. (E) is correct.** Dillon's rule, named after an Iowa judge who expressed the idea in a court decision, is the principle that local governments have only those powers that are explicitly given to them by the states. This means local governments are totally subservient to the state government.

- **10. (D) is correct.** Special districts are often set up to relieve municipalities from the burden of carrying out certain functions. As such, they are generally funded by user fees, which are placed in segregated fund accounts. Generally they provide only a single service like flood control, fire protection, public transportation, or education. Special districts tend to be highly flexible units of government because their boundary lines can be drawn across county and municipal borders. They help local governments carry out their responsibilities more efficiently. School boards are the most widely known and used example of a special district. They often have an elected or appointed board, which sets policy for a professional manager to implement.

CHAPTER 5

Civil Liberties

Civil liberties are the individual freedoms guaranteed in the Bill of Rights. They are primarily concerned with protecting citizens from too much government control. These individual freedoms include the First Amendment protection of religion, speech, press, and assembly; the Second Amendment right to bear arms; and the due process rights guaranteed in the Fourth through Eighth Amendments. The judiciary has also interpreted these amendments to imply a constitutionally protected right to privacy. In recent years, civil liberties have changed dramatically in the United States.

The Roots of Civil Liberties: The Bill of Rights

- **Civil liberties** are individual guarantees and freedoms that the government cannot abridge.

- Anti-Federalists wanted a **bill of rights** before they ratified the Constitution. These included the right to free speech and press, the right to bear arms, and a number of due process rights.

  - Federalists insisted on the **Ninth** and **Tenth Amendments** to assure that the Bill of Rights was not an exclusive document. The Ninth Amendment makes it clear that while particular rights are enumerated in the Constitution and Bill of Rights, this does not mean that others do not exist. The Tenth Amendment reiterates that powers not delegated to the national government are reserved to the states or to the people.

  - The Fourteenth Amendment was added to the U.S. Constitution in 1968, suggesting that at least some of the protections guaranteed by the Bill of Rights might be interpreted to prevent state infringement of those rights.

  - The due process clause is contained in the Fifth and Fourteenth Amendments. Over the years, it has been construed to guarantee individuals a variety of rights, ranging from economic liberty to criminal protection from arbitrary governmental action.

  - The Supreme Court increased its jurisdiction over the states by holding states to a substantive due process. **Substantive due process** refers to judicial interpretation of the Fifth and Fourteenth Amendments' due process clauses, which protect citizens from arbitrary or unjust state or federal laws.

  - The interpretation of the Constitution that holds that the due process clause of the Fourteenth Amendment requires that state and local governments also guarantee those rights is called **incorporation doctrine**.

- **Selective incorporation** is a judicial doctrine whereby most of the protections found in the Bill of Rights are made applicable to the states via the Fourteenth Amendment. Among other liberties, states must respect freedoms of press, speech and assembly.

- The Supreme Court has used the process of selective incorporation to limit the rights of states by protecting against abridgement of fundamental freedoms.

- Fundamental freedoms are those rights defined by the court to be essential to order, liberty, and justice. As such, fundamental freedoms are entitled to the highest standard of review.

First Amendment Guarantees: Freedom of Religion

- The **First Amendment**'s freedom of religion clause has two parts:

  - The **establishment clause** directs the government not to involve itself in religion.

    - In *Lemon* v. *Kurtzman* (1971), the Supreme Court allowed federal funding of parochial schools, provided that the money neither advances nor inhibits religious teaching, but instead is used for administrative purposes. This case led to what we call the *Lemon* test, a three-part test created by the Supreme Court to examine the constitutionality of religious establishment issues. Under the lemon test, a policy is constitutional if it:

      - Has a legitimate secular purpose

      - Does not advance nor inhibit religion

      - Does not foster an excessive government entanglement with religion

    - Today, the court often side steps this law in allowing prayer in school and federal funding to private religious schools.

  - The **free exercise clause** prohibits the U.S. government from interfering with a citizen's right to practice religion. Nevertheless, the court has upheld that the government can regulate religious behavior when governmental interests outweigh free exercise rights.

First Amendment Guarantees: Freedoms of Speech, Press, Assembly, and Petition

- Freedom of speech and the press have a rich history in the United States. Generally, thoughts have received the greatest protection, and actions or deeds the least. Words have come somewhere in the middle, depending on their content and purpose. When the First Amendment was ratified, it was thought to protect against prior restraint of speech or expression. **Prior restraint** is the constitutional doctrine that prevents the government from prohibiting speech or publication before the fact.

- The Adams administration limited expression with the Alien and Sedition Acts, which banned any criticism of the Federalist government. Because of public outcry, the national government later refrained from regulating speech. However, through selective incorporation, the states began to prosecute those who published articles critical of governmental policies.

- In the North, the publication or dissemination of any positive information about slavery became a punishable offense.

- In the South, supporters of slavery enacted laws to prohibit the publication of anti-slavery sentiments.

- In 1925, states' authority to regulate speech was severely restricted by the Supreme Court's decision to incorporate the free press provision of the First Amendment in *Gitlow* v. *New York*.

- The Espionage Act limited expression during World War I. In *Schenck* v. *U.S.* (1919), the court carved out a test for when speech could be limited. If speech posed a "clear and present danger" it could be limited. The clear and present danger test draws the line between protected and unprotected speech; the court looks to see whether the words used could "create a clear and present danger that they will bring about substantive evils" that Congress seeks to prevent.

- With *Brandenburg* v. *Ohio* (1969), the court ruled that speech could only be limited by the government if it met the direct incitement test.

  - The **direct incitement test** holds that advocacy of illegal action is protected by the First Amendment unless imminent lawless action is intended and likely to occur.

  - Some speech and publications are protected by the government.

    - With few exceptions, the court will not tolerate **prior restraint**, or limitations on expression before that expression occurs.

    - Protection also extends to **symbolic speech** or symbols, signs, and other methods of expression.

    - **Hate speech** that arouses anger, resentment, or alarm on the basis of race, creed, color, gender, sexual orientation, or disability is also allowed under the First Amendment, as long as it does not incite violence.

    - Speech that is unpopular is also allowed under the First Amendment, as long as it does not incite violence.

- Some speech and publications are not protected by the government.

    - **Libel**, or written defamation, and **slander,** or spoken defamation.

        - More difficult for public officials to sue for these due to the court's decision in *New York Times Co.* **v.** *Sullivan* (1964).

    - **Fighting words**, words that "by their very utterance inflict injury or tend or incite an immediate breach of peace," are not subject to the restrictions of the First Amendment.

    - Obscenity, which is defined on the basis of community standards.

- Freedoms of assembly and petition are also guaranteed, as long as the words or actions taken do not cross any of the boundaries of legality.

The Second Amendment: The Right to Keep and Bear Arms

- Second Amendment was added to make sure that citizens could maintain militias to protect themselves both from outside attack and a tyrannical central government.

- Little litigation on this subject for much of the nation's history.

- Recently, in *D.C.* v. *Heller* (2008), the court broadened Second Amendment protections to include the right to own a firearm for personal use.

- Much legislation, including the Brady Bill, has been passed in state and national legislatures in recent years.

The Rights of Criminal Defendants

- The Constitution protects the accused in a number of ways.

    - Citizens are guaranteed **writs of habeas corpus**. These are court orders that require authorities to prove that a prisoner is being held lawfully and that allow the prisoner to be freed if the judge is not persuaded by the government's case.

    - Habeas corpus rights imply that prisoners have a right to know what charges are being made against them.

    - The government cannot pass **ex post facto laws**, which criminalize an action after it has occurred.

    - The government cannot pass **bills of attainder**, which inflict punishment on the accused without judicial action.

71

- The **Fourth Amendment** protects citizens from unreasonable searches and seizures.

  - Police investigators cannot search private property without a search warrant issued by a court unless there is reason to believe that the evidence will disappear or be destroyed or removed in the meantime.

  - The Supreme Court has interpreted the Fourth Amendment to allow the police to search: (1) the person arrested, (2) things in plain view of the accused person, and (3) places or things that the arrested person could touch or reach, or that are otherwise in the arrestee's immediate control.

  - Warrantless searches may occur if police suspect that someone is committing or is about to commit a crime. Warrantless searches may also be made if consent is obtained.

  - The police cannot arrest someone unless there is probable cause to believe that he or she is guilty.

- The **Fifth Amendment** provides several protections to those that have been accused of a crime. In the most serious cases, the accused are allowed to present their cases before a grand jury. A grand jury is group of citizens charged with determining whether there is enough evidence for a case to go to trial.

  - The accused cannot be forced to supply evidence against themselves.

  - The government is required to give just compensation for taking citizens' property.

  - The accused are protected from double jeopardy.

  - The double jeopardy clause provides protection for being tried twice for the same crime in the same jurisdiction.

  - All suspects must be informed of their constitutional rights, protected by the Fifth Amendment, including the right to remain silent, and the right to an attorney provided by the court if the suspect cannot afford one.

  - *Miranda* v. *Arizona* (1966) established that suspects must be informed of their constitutional rights before they are questioned by the police. Today, suspects are read their *Miranda* **rights.**

  - The **exclusionary rule** prevents prosecutors from using evidence acquired through unreasonable search and seizure. It is derived from the Fourth and Fifth Amendments.

  - The case of *Mapp* v. *Ohio* (1961) extended the exclusionary rule to state as well as federal cases.

- In recent years, the Supreme Court has made exceptions to the exclusionary rule. For example, when police are thought to have acted in "good faith," even if their actions technically violate the rule, the court has allowed use of the evidence seized.

- The **Sixth Amendment** states that the accused have the right to speedy and public trials, impartial juries, trials in the state where crime was committed, notice of the charges, the right to confront witnesses against them and obtain favorable witnesses, and the right to counsel.

- *Gideon* v. *Wainwright* (1963) was important because it extended the right to counsel to the poor and to cases tried in state courts.

- The Sixth Amendment also requires lawyers to take reasonable steps to prepare for their clients' trial and sentencing.

  - Juries have become much more representative of the general public, thanks to changes in registration for jury duty and procedures for the use of peremptory challenges.

- Cruel and unusual punishment, excessive bail, and excessive fines are prohibited by the **Eighth Amendment**.

  - In *Gregg* v. *Georgia* (1976) and *McCleskey* v. *Kemp* (1987), the Supreme Court confirmed that the death penalty does not violate the Bill of Rights—that is, it is not considered "cruel and unusual."

  - In *McCleskey* v. *Kemp* (1987), the Supreme Court made it much more difficult for death row inmates by ruling that new issues could not be raised on appeal, even if there was some state error.

  - Debate over the death penalty continues as DNA tests sometimes prove the innocence of inmates on death row.

  - Recent court decisions have also limited the application of the death penalty to some classes of citizens, such as the mentally retarded and minors.

The Right to Privacy

- The **right to privacy** is not specifically guaranteed by the Bill of Rights, but the Supreme Court has used penumbras of the First, Third, Fourth, Ninth, and Fourteenth Amendments to infer this right.

  - *Griswold* v. *Connecticut* (1965) asserted the right to privacy in a case surrounding a married couple's use of contraception.

  - The right became more controversial when the principle was applied to abortion in **Roe v. Wade** (1973).

    - *Roe* unleashed political controversy that continues to brew today. Although the decision has not been completely overturned, it has been limited.

      - In **Webster v. Reproductive Health Services** (1989), the Supreme Court upheld a Missouri law that prevented the use of state funds for abortion clinics and that prohibited state employees from performing abortions.

      - In **Planned Parenthood v. Casey** (1992), the Supreme Court ruled that states could limit abortions as long as those limitations do not pose an "undue burden" on women.

      - The constitutionality of the federal partial birth abortion law has also been upheld.

  - More recently, the right has also been applied to homosexuality. In 2003, the U.S. Supreme Court prevented the state of Texas from criminalizing private sexual behavior.

Toward Reform: Civil Liberties and Combating Terrorism

- The USA Patriot Act, the Military Commissions Act, and a number of other laws and executive orders have altered the state of civil liberties in the United States.

  - There have been limitations placed on nearly every piece of the Bill of Rights.

  - These include punishing those who spoke out against the U.S. government, conducting broad searches without warrants, and imprisoning enemy combatants without according them traditional due process rights and overriding the need to demonstrate probable cause.

  - Under the Military Commissions Act, the rules on illegal incarceration, torture, writs of habeas corpus, and trial by jury are limited.

For Additional Review

Make a three-column table. In the first column, write all of the civil liberties discussed in this chapter. In the second column, list all Supreme Court cases that have addressed each liberty, including the date, the chief justice, and a brief synopsis of the case. In the third column, list the corresponding amendment or any previous court cases on which the Supreme Court based its decisions about each civil liberty.

Multiple-Choice Questions

1. *Roe* v. *Wade* (1973) ruled that a woman's right to an abortion came from the
(A) right of symbolic speech.
(B) right of the people to "be secure in their persons, houses, papers, and effects."
(C) "right to remain silent."
(D) due process of law.
(E) right to privacy.

2. In *Engel* v. *Vitale* (1962), the Supreme Court ruled that
(A) the reciting of a state-required prayer in public school constituted an impermissible establishment of religion under the First Amendment.
(B) the Gideon Society could distribute Bibles in public schools under the free exercise clause of the First Amendment.
(C) the eminent domain clause of the Fifth Amendment prevents government from taking religious property for public purposes.
(D) public school children may wear crosses as necklaces as a permissible mode of symbolic speech under the First Amendment.
(E) the Second Amendment "right to bear arms" does not apply in religious facilities.

3. The "exclusionary rule" was created to
(A) allow the Senate to remove a member from voting membership because of a violation of ethics rules.
(B) allow the House Rules Committee to refuse to schedule a debate on a bill.
(C) ensure that bureaucracy enforces unpopular legislation.
(D) enable the president to "impound" programmatic money appropriated by Congress.
(E) prohibit police from using illegally seized evidence at trial.

4. Which of the following cases made decisions regarding the establishment of religion?
I. *Mapp* v. *Ohio* (1965)
II. *Texas* v. *Johnson* (1989)
III. *Schenck* v. *U.S.* (1963)
IV. *Lemon* v. *Kurtzman* (1919)
(A) IV only
(B) II and III
(C) IV only
(D) I and III
(E) II and IV

5. Which of the following forms of expression is protected by the First Amendment?
(A) obscenity
(B) libel
(C) fighting words
(D) symbolic speech
(E) slander

6. Which of the following rights is protected by the Fifth Amendment?
(A) the right of privacy
(B) protection against self-incrimination
(C) the right to bear arms
(D) the right to counsel
(E) the right to a speedy and public trial

7. The Bill of Rights begins with the words "Congress shall make no law . . . ," telling the reader that the Bill or Rights is intended to protect citizens only from the national government. Yet, most of the provisions of the Bill of Rights now limit the states as well. Which of the following provisions is most relevant in explaining that change?
(A) the equal protection clause of the Fourteenth Amendment
(B) the double jeopardy clause of the Fifth Amendment
(C) the rights "retained by the people" in the Ninth Amendment
(D) the grand jury indictment provision in the Fifth Amendment
(E) the due process clause of the Fourteenth Amendment

8. The right of citizens to be made aware of their constitutional guarantees against self-incrimination and to be represented by counsel was established in
(A) *Gitlow* v. *New York* (1925).
(B) *Mapp* v. *Ohio* (1965).
(C) *Miranda* v. *Arizona* (1966).
(D) *Gideon* v. *Wainwright* (1963).
(E) *Lemon* v. *Kurtzman* (1971).

9. All of the following concepts are guaranteed to a citizen accused of a crime EXCEPT
(A) a speedy and public trial by an impartial jury.
(B) security against unreasonable search and seizures.
(C) protection from capital punishment.
(D) protection from put in jeopardy of life or limb twice for the same offense.
(E) having the assistance of counsel.

10. The right of government to keep a newspaper from publishing information that would be harmful to the morale of troops deployed in a military conflict
(A) would be denied as "prior restraint."
(B) would be allowed under the "no quartering of soldiers" provision of the Third Amendment.
(C) would be denied as entailing a "clear and present danger."
(D) would be allowed as denying "seditious speech."
(E) would be allowed under the USA Patriot Act.

Free-Response Questions

1. The USA Patriot Act was passed after the terrorist attacks of September 11, 2001.

    a. Describe the USA Patriot Act.

    b. Identify and describe a provision in the Bill of Rights that the USA Patriot Act affects.

2. The Supreme Court has incorporated many of the rights included in the Bill of Rights.

    a. Define selective incorporation.

    b. Describe the application of selective incorporation to the decisions in two of the following cases:

        • *Gitlow* v. *New York* (1925)

        • *D.C.* v. *Heller* (2008)

        • *Mapp* v. *Ohio* (1961)

        • *Gideon* v. *Wainwright* (1963)

ANSWERS AND EXPLANATIONS

Multiple-Choice Questions

- **1. (E) is correct.** In *Roe* v. *Wade,* the Supreme Court extended the right to privacy to include a right to abortion. The other answers are liberties in the Bill of Rights but are not relevant to the *Roe* decision.

- **2. (A) is correct.** The *Engel* decision was based on the establishment clause of the Constitution.

- **3. (E) is correct**. The exclusionary rule prohibits police from using illegally seized evidence at trial. The other possible answers all suggest exclusions of some variety but have nothing to do with the "exclusionary rule."

- **4. (C) is correct**. The *Lemon* decision dealt with defining the boundaries of excessive entanglement between church and state. The other three decisions have nothing to do with religious liberty.

- **5. (D) is correct.** Freedom of speech is subject to almost no limits regarding symbolic acts like flag burning. Obscenity, libel, slander, and fighting words have been ruled not to be protected under the First Amendment.

- **6. (B) is correct.** The most famous provision of the Fifth Amendment is that no one is required to provide testimony against himself or herself in court. The other options are liberties protected by other amendments.

- **7. (E) is correct.** The Bill of Rights has largely been incorporated by the states through the due process clause of the Fourteenth Amendment. That amendment, adopted after the Civil War, has been ruled to make states comply with provisions of the national constitution.

- **8. (C) is correct.** *Miranda* v. *Arizona* extended the rights of the accused to those who did not know the constitution. In that case, the Supreme Court said that knowing that the rights existed was as fundamental as having the rights.

- **9. (C) is correct.** Capital punishment has never been ruled to violate the cruel and unusual provision of the Eighth Amendment. The other options are protected rights in the Bill of Rights.

- **10. (A) is correct.** Under the First Amendment, banning of prior restraint of publication is a very strong rule.

Free-Response Questions

This rubric provides examples of many, but not all, of the possible correct responses to the free-response questions.

1.

a. In the aftermath of the terrorist attacks on the World Trade Center on September 11, 2001, Congress passed a law called the USA Patriot Act that was designed to give law enforcement agencies more power to investigate and arrest terrorists. Congress thought that under the crisis circumstances that existed, it was reasonable to give those expanded investigation powers even if it meant that some of the protections of the Bill of Rights would be compromised. The significance of the Patriot Act was that civil libertarians thought that it provided a dangerous compromise for average citizens who might be investigated.

b. The Fourth Amendment requires that if people are to be investigated, it must be with a valid search warrant signed by a judge and based upon probable cause. This amendment was meant to keep people safe from investigations and is based on the idea that people are innocent until proven guilty.

2.

a. Selective incorporation is the gradual process of binding state governments to the provisions contained in the Bill of Rights. It is done through judicial interpretation. Today, most clauses of the Bill of Rights have been incorporated by the courts. Only portions of the Third, Fifth, and Seventh Amendments remain unincorporated.

b. In the case of *D.C.* v. *Heller*, the court implicitly incorporated one of the last remaining unincorporated clauses of the Bill of Rights. The 2008 case ruled that the District of Columbia's gun ban was an unconstitutional infringement on citizens' rights and liberties. States, as well as the federal government, do not have the authority to limit citizens' right to bear arms.

In *Gideon* v. *Wainwright* (1963), the court incorporated the right to counsel. This decision was a landmark not only because it bound states to a portion of the Sixth Amendment but also because it dramatically expanded defendants' right to have the assistance of counsel.

79

CHAPTER 6

Civil Rights

Civil rights guarantee that people are not discriminated against by the government on account of race, religion, gender, national origin, or sexual orientation. African Americans were the first group to organize for civil rights. Their efforts provided inspiration for the efforts of a number of other groups, including women, Latino/as, American Indians, Asian Americans, gays and lesbians, and Americans with disabilities. These and other groups continue to face civil rights issues today.

• The Fourteenth Amendment introduced the notion of equality into the Constitution by specifying that a state could not deny "any person within its jurisdiction equal protection of the laws."

• This legislation has generated more litigation to determine and specify its meaning than any other provision of the Constitution.

• After ratification, women—and later African Americans and other minorities and disadvantaged groups—took to the courts to seek expanded civil rights in all walks of life.

Roots of Suffrage: 1800-1890

- Slavery was an issue from the moment the nation was founded.

    - The slave trade was banned in 1808.

    - The Missouri Compromise was passed in 1820, solidifying proslavery and pro-abolition groups.

- The antislavery movement was solidified by the formation of the American Anti-Slavery Association in 1833.

    - This group was the foundation for the women's movement. Women were active participants in many states but could not participate at the World Anti-Slavery Society Meeting.

        - Inspired Elizabeth Cady Stanton and Lucretia Mott to hold the Seneca Falls Convention.

- By the 1850s, tension had escalated with the publication of *Uncle Tom's Cabin* and the *Dred Scott* decision.

- In *Dred Scott* v. *Sanford* (1857), the Supreme Court ruled that the Missouri Compromise, which prohibited slavery north of a set geographical boundary, was unconstitutional. Furthermore, the court went on to add that slaves were not U.S. citizens, and as a consequence, could not bring suits in federal court.

- After the Civil War, great steps were taken to end slavery and reduce discrimination.

    - **Thirteenth Amendment** bans slavery in the United States.

    - **Fourteenth Amendment** guarantees equal protection and due process of the law to all citizens.

    - **Fifteenth Amendment** specifically enfranchised newly freed slaves.

    - Civil Rights Act of 1875 granted equal accommodation in public places and gave Congress and the federal courts the power to intervene when states attempted to restrict the citizenship rights of male African Americans in matters such as voting.

- Compliance with these laws was limited.

    - Southern states were quick to pass **Black Codes** to prohibit blacks from full involvement in society. These Black Codes prohibited African Americans from voting, sitting on juries, and even appearing in public places.

    - The Civil Rights Cases (1883) were five separate cases involving the convictions of private individuals found to have violated the Civil Rights Act by refusing to extend accommodations to African Americans in theaters, a hotel, and a railroad.

    - The judiciary upheld **Jim Crow laws**, which permitted segregation in public places.

    - Blacks were disenfranchised through the use of **poll taxes** (small taxes on the right to vote that often were due when poor African American sharecroppers had the least amount of money on hand), literacy tests, and grandfather clauses. (Grandfather clauses were voter qualification provisions that permitted people to vote even if they could not pay the tax or read, as long as their grandfathers had voted before Reconstruction. This ensured that white Southerners could vote.)

The Push for Equality, 1890-1954

- In *Plessy* v. *Ferguson* (1896) the court ruled that separate-but-equal accommodations for blacks and whites did not violate the Fourteenth Amendment.

    - This was a rallying point for activists, who were inspired to form the NAACP in 1909.

- At the same time, women's groups were beginning to mobilize for greater rights.

  - The National and American Women's Suffrage Associations merged to form a stronger movement to get women the right to vote. The drive for voting rights for women was known as the **suffrage movement**.

    - In 1920, they succeeded in winning the right to vote in the **Nineteenth Amendment**.

  - Other groups, such as the National Consumer's League, were interested in protecting women workers with maximum hour and minimum wage laws.

- The NAACP turned to the court to try to litigate for greater equality.

  - The organization mapped out a long-range test case litigation strategy to lead to greater equality.

  - Started by winning integration in law schools, then graduate schools, and eventually in primary and secondary education.

  - In *Brown* v. *Board of Education* (1954), the court ruled that segregation was inherently unconstitutional because it violated the **equal protection clause** of the Fourteenth Amendment.

The Civil Rights Movement

- Following the Supreme Court's decision in *Brown*, many states were slow to desegregate. Subsequent court decisions, like *Brown* v. *Board of Education II,* and decisive executive branch action, such as using federal troops to enforce desegregation, were needed to integrate many Southern states.

- The civil rights movement began to pick up momentum in the South.

    - Rosa Parks challenged the constitutionality of the segregated bus system, which led to the Montgomery Bus Boycott.

        - In 1956, a federal court ruled that the segregated bus system violated the equal protection clause of the Fourteenth Amendment.

    - Formation of new groups, such as the Southern Christian Leadership Conference (SCLC) and the Student Nonviolent Coordinating Committee (SNCC).

        - Groups led sit-ins, freedom rides, and mass nonviolent demonstrations to draw attention to their cause. These included the Birmingham march, during which police used dogs, clubs, and fire hoses on marchers; and the March on Washington for Jobs and Freedom, where Martin Luther King Jr. gave his "I Have a Dream" speech.

- Finally, the legislature could no longer put off getting involved.

    - The **Civil Rights Act of 1964** outlawed discrimination in voting and public accommodations, provided for federal involvement to prevent discrimination in the South, and prohibited discrimination on the basis of race, creed, color, religion, national origin, or sex. It also created the **Equal Employment Opportunity Commission,** to monitor and enforce the bans on employment discrimination.

        - It allowed the Justice Department to sue school districts that did not comply with the act.

            - Bussing was initially a solution to integration, but today the court has ruled that while the government has an interest in ending **de jure discrimination**, it can do little about **de facto discrimination.**

            - **De jure discrimination** is racial segregation that is a direct result of law or official policy.

            - **De facto discrimination** is racial discrimination that results from practice (such as housing patterns or other social or institutional, nongovernmental factors) rather than the law.

- It prohibited discrimination in employment, unless there is a "business necessity" for such discrimination.

The Women's Rights Movement

- Women faced a great deal of discrimination into the 1960s.

- The formation of the President's Commission on the Status of Women, the publication of *The Feminine Mystique*, and the passage of the Civil Rights Act brought women together.

  - The National Organization for Women (NOW) was formed in 1966 after the Equal Employment Opportunity Commission failed to enforce the law as it applied to sex discrimination. Groups began to work for an equal rights amendment for women, which passed Congress in 1972.

- Groups began to work for an equal rights amendment for women.

  - A number of states ratified this amendment quickly, but soon it hit roadblocks in more conservative states.

  - The development of a dedicated opposition ensured that the amendment never passed.

  - It continues to be reintroduced in every session of Congress as the **Women's Equality Amendment**.

- Other women's rights groups such as the American Civil Liberties Union's Women's Rights Project began to work to elevate the level of constitutional review applied to gender cases.

  - There are three standards of constitutional review today.

    - The **minimum rationality test** involves the lowest level of scrutiny. It means that governments must allege a rational foundation for any distinctions they make.

    - **Suspect classification** is the category or class, such as race, that triggers the highest standard of scrutiny from the Supreme Court.

    - **Strict scrutiny** is a heightened standard of review used by the Supreme Court to determine the constitutional validity of a challenged practice. When fundamental freedoms such as those guaranteed by the First Amendment or suspect classifications are involved, the court employs this level of scrutiny.

    - Gender was at the minimum rationality test until the court's decision in *Craig* v. *Boren* (1976), which elevated it to the intermediate standard.

- This standard has been applied in a wide range of cases.

- There are also statutory remedies for sex discrimination.

    - **The Equal Pay Act of 1963** requires employers to pay men and women equal pay for equal work.

    - **Title VII** of the Civil Rights Act of 1964 protects against sex discrimination and sexual harassment.

    - **Title IX** of the Educational Amendments of 1972 bars educational institutions receiving federal funds from discriminating against female students

Other Groups Mobilize for Rights

- Latino/as are the fastest growing minority group in the United States.

    - A push for greater rights began in the 1960s as Latino/a populations began to grow and leaders like Cesar Chavez brought attention to the rights of migrant workers.

    - Groups like MALDEF, LULAC, and the Puerto Rican Legal Defense and Educational Fund have also used the courts to secure legal change in representation, school funding, and immigration.

- American Indians are the oldest minority group in the United States.

    - Congress has had varied policies toward Indian populations, first promoting separation and later assimilation. Either way, U.S. policies have reduced Indian lands from about 140 million acres to about 47 million.

    - Today, tribes are small and often isolated. This has led to poverty for many tribes and has prevented, in part, a protest movement by this population.

    - Tribes have been successful in land rights cases, but unsuccessful with religious freedom.

- Asian Americans have also confronted significant discrimination.

    - One of the biggest difficulties for these groups is finding a Pan-Asian identity.

    - The Supreme Court has slowed Asians' progress in the United States, limiting their employment and citizenship and even allowing for internment of Japanese Americans during World War II.

    - Today, Asians have made great gains in representation.

- Gays and lesbians have struggled for much of history, but are beginning to make gains due to their above-average incomes and education.

  - Don't Ask, Don't Tell policy in the military has been widely panned.

  - In the 1996 decision in *Romer* v. *Evans*, the court ruled that an amendment to Colorado's constitution that denied homosexuals the right to seek protection from discrimination was unconstitutional under the equal protection clause of the Fourteenth Amendment.

  - Several states have recently allowed gays to marry and granted greater rights in employment. These laws are likely to be litigated for a long time to come.

- Americans with disabilities have also gained great power as a lobby.

  - The 1990 Americans with Disabilities Act (ADA) has generated much litigation and activism. The statute extends the protections of the Civil Rights Act of 1964 to all of those with physical or mental disabilities. It also guarantees access to public facilities and employment, as well as communication services, and requires employers to acquire or modify work equipment, adjust work schedules, and make existing facilities accessible to those with disabilities.

  - In 1999, the U.S. Supreme Court issued a series of decisions redefining and limiting the scope of the ADA, which dramatically reduced the number of people who can claim coverage under the act.

  - These groups often collaborate with more radical groups, such as Not Dead Yet.

Toward Reform: Civil Rights, Affirmative Action, and Pay Equity

- **Affirmative action** is a policy designed to give special attention or compensation to members of a previously disadvantaged group.

  - Issue first gained attention in the wake of *Regents of the University of California* v. *Bakke* (1978), which allowed schools to take race into account when considering college admissions.

  - This issue has been heavily litigated over the last 20 years. Most recently, in *Grutter* v. *Bollinger* and *Gratz* v. *Bollinger* (2003), in which the court affirmed the idea that race could be considered, but it could not be the defining characteristic of an applicant.

- Pay equity has also received a lot of attention recently.

  - Women continue to make significantly less than their male counterparts and are not promoted as quickly.

- This is also a concern for Latino/as, who often face language barriers and barriers posed by the immigration process.

For Additional Review

Debate continues over the policy of affirmative action. Make a chart listing arguments on each side of the issue.

Multiple-Choice Questions

1. By providing special attention to members of a previously disadvantaged group, affirmative action laws are designed to remedy which kind of discrimination?
   (A) de facto
   (B) ex post facto
   (C) de solis
   (D) habeas corpus
   (E) de jure

2. The landmark case of *Brown* v. *Board of Education* ruled that segregated schools were not acceptable because of the
   (A) constitutional provision against bills of attainder.
   (B) due process of law clause of the Fifth Amendment.
   (C) involuntary servitude clause of the Thirteenth Amendment.
   (D) equal protection clause of the Fourteenth Amendment.
   (E) command not to "deny or disparage" rights "retained by the people" under the Ninth Amendment.

3. The Thirteenth Amendment effectively invalidated which Supreme Court decision?
   (A) *Dred Scott* v. *Sandford*
   (B) *Plessy* v. *Ferguson*
   (C) *Korematsu* v. *U.S.*
   (D) *Smith* v. *Allwright*
   (E) *Guinn* v. *U.S.*

4. Which of the following are incorrectly paired?
   I. Thirteenth Amendment—right of women to vote
   II. Fifteenth Amendment—right of African American males to vote
   III. Twenty-First Amendment—banning of poll tax
   IV. Twenty-Sixth Amendment—right of 18-year-olds to vote
   (A) I and II
   (B) II and III
   (C) III and IV
   (D) I and III
   (E) II and IV

5. In the case of *Regents of the University of California* v. *Bakke,* the Supreme Court ruled that
(A) Japanese Americans could be placed in camps during World War II.
(B) migrant workers were entitled to compensation in case of injury through unemployment insurance.
(C) rejection from medical school because of strict quotas was illegal.
(D) women were entitled to equal pay for equal work.
(E) poll taxes were unconstitutional.

6. Racial discrimination in public accommodations such as restaurants and hotels was banned
(A) in the Civil Rights Act of 1964.
(B) in the Open Housing Act of 1968.
(C) in the Twenty-Fourth Amendment.
(D) in the Equal Rights Amendment.
(E) in *Reed* v. *Reed.*

7. Affirmative action refers to
(A) the U.S. Senate approving a presidential appointment to the cabinet under its "advice and consent" function.
(B) the president "faithfully executing" the appropriations of money under laws created by Congress.
(C) the Supreme Court upholding a lower court decision.
(D) interest group lobbying efforts in pursuit of the common goals of group members.
(E) a policy giving special consideration to groups that have been disadvantaged historically.

8. The Equal Rights Amendment was proposed by Congress but fell three states short of the 38 needed for ratification. If adopted, the ERA would have banned discrimination based on
(A) race.
(B) religious faith.
(C) gender.
(D) sexual orientation.
(E) physical disabilities.

9. Which of the following bars educational institutions that receive federal funds from discriminating against female students?
(A) Title IX of the Education Amendments of 1972
(B) The Equal Rights Amendment
(C) The Civil Rights Act of 1964
(D) Jim Crow Laws
(E) Black Codes

10. Which Supreme Court case upheld the relocation of Japanese American citizens to internment camps during World War II?
(A) *Craig* v. *Boren*
(B) *Smith* v. *Allwright*
(C) *Korematsu* v. *United States*
(D) *Hernandez* v. *Texas*
(E) *Yamamoto* v. *Roosevelt*

Free-Response Questions

1. One of the key issues in civil rights had to do with gaining the right to vote for groups of citizens. African Americans and women fought for and eventually earned the right to vote through Constitutional Amendments, Supreme Court decisions, and congressional laws. Among the issues related to voting rights are:
   - The poll tax
   - The grandfather clause
   - Literacy tests
   - State laws prohibiting women, African Americans, or those younger than 21 from voting
   - Discriminatory governmental practices that made it difficult to register and vote

   a. Identify and describe one law passed by Congress that made one of these practices illegal.

   b. Identify and describe one constitutional amendment that addressed one of these practices.

2. Disadvantaged groups have often turned to the judiciary to secure legal change. Choose two of the following groups and detail how they have litigated for equal rights.

   - African Americans
   - Women
   - Latino/as
   - Gays and lesbians

ANSWERS AND EXPLANATIONS

Multiple-Choice Questions

- **1. (A) is correct.** The idea of affirmative action is that preventing discrimination by law (de jure) can accomplish only so much. In order to remedy patterns of discrimination that have developed over time in fact (de facto), affirmative action is needed.

- **2. (D) is correct.** *Brown* v. *Board of Education* decided that the equal protection clause required desegregation of schools because "separate educational facilities are inherently unequal."

- **3. (A) is correct.** The Supreme Court, in the *Dred Scott* case, ruled that African American slaves were the property of their owners. The Thirteenth Amendment banned slavery, thus effectively overturning the *Dred Scott* decision.

- **4. (D) is correct.** The Thirteenth Amendment was one of the three Civil War amendments, and banned slavery. Women received the right to vote in the Nineteenth Amendment. The poll tax was banned in the Twenty-Fourth Amendment. The Twenty-First Amendment repealed prohibition.

- **5. (C) is correct.** In the case of *Regents of the University of California* v. *Bakke,* the Supreme Court found the university's quotas for enrolling minorities unconstitutional. Allan Bakke was denied enrollment in favor of a minority applicant to fulfill the university's quota, an unconstitutional "reverse discrimination."

- **6. (A) is correct**. The 1964 Civil Rights Act was a broad, sweeping law that had many characteristics. Among its provisions was one banning discrimination in public accommodations.

- **7. (E) is correct.** The purpose of affirmative action is to correct past discrimination. The other answers deal with positive, or "affirmative" things, but not with the concept of affirmative action.

- **8. (C) is correct.** All of the options have to do with different aspects of "equality," but the rights of women were only addressed in the ERA.

- **9. (B) is correct.** Title IX is the only legislation that specifically barred educational institutions receiving federal funds from discriminating against female students.

- **10. (C) is correct.** The Japanese internment camps were upheld in the *Korematsu* decision.

Free-Response Questions

This rubric provides examples of many, but not all, of the possible correct responses to the free-response questions.

1. A basic right of American citizens is the right to vote. In civil rights, the first step toward making progress regarding equality is the right to participate in the elections of members of congress and other representatives. Until all groups attain the right to vote, they can never truly be equal with other groups. To attain the right to vote, a number of barriers had to be overcome, including the poll tax, the grandfather clause, and the literacy test. Both constitutional guarantees and laws addressing governmental practices had to be written. In short, it took concerted action of all areas of government to attain the right to vote.

   a. One law passed to help African Americans vote was the Voting Rights Act of 1965. It specified that states could not use literacy tests to make it difficult for African Americans to vote. It also allowed the federal government to use voter registrars to register more African Americans to vote.

b. There were several amendments to the Constitution that expanded voting rights. The Nineteenth Amendment gave women the right to vote, the Twenty-Third gave the right to Washington D.C. to have electoral votes, and the Twenty-Fourth banned the poll tax.

2. African Americans were the first group to use litigation to secure equal rights. The NAACP Legal Defense Fund (LDF) was the pioneer of this strategy. Beginning in the 1930s, the organization began to craft a gradual test-case litigation strategy to integrate public places. One of its biggest priorities was integration in education. The LDF decided to craft an incremental strategy beginning with law schools, then graduate schools, and finally elementary and secondary schools. This strategy ultimately culminated in the court's decision in *Brown* v. *Board of Education* (1954), which overturned the court's earlier decision in *Plessy* v. *Ferguson* (1896) and ruled that separate but equal was not acceptable. This provided a gateway to the civil rights movement and other civil rights legislation passed during the 1960s.

Women followed the template of the NAACP LDF. The most visible example of this trend was the work of the American Civil Liberties Union's Women's Rights Project (WRP) to elevate gender to a higher level of constitutional scrutiny. Although the series of cases argued by Ruth Bader Ginsburg never succeeded in elevating gender to strict scrutiny, the WRP's litigation work did encourage the court to carve out a heightened level of intermediate scrutiny for gender equality cases. This standard has been applied in a wide range of cases in education, civil and criminal law, and citizenship cases.

CHAPTER 7

Congress

The legislative branch is composed of two houses, the House of Representatives and the Senate. The requirements for serving in each of these branches are laid out in the U.S. Constitution. Today, Congress is organized and its leaders are selected largely on the basis of party. Members of Congress have the difficult task of pleasing multiple constituencies but are given guidance from a variety of sources. The primary task of Congress is making laws. It also plays an important role in the checks and balances system devised by the framers.

Roots of the Legislative Branch of Government

- Great Compromise resulted in a bicameral legislature.

  - Senate has two members from each state, regardless of population.

  - House apportioned on the basis of population; 435 total members.

- Constitutional requirements for membership:

  - Members of the House must be 25 years old; senators, 30.

  - Must be residents of the state from which they are elected.

  - Senators serve six-year terms, members of the House serve two-year terms.

  - Apportionment: Every 10 years (following the census), House districts are **reapportioned** among the states and state legislatures redraw district lines in a process called **redistricting**.

- Most important task of Congress is to make law. The first step in this process is the introduction of a **bill**, which is a proposed law.

  - All revenue bills must originate in the House.

- **Impeachment**: The power delegated to Congress to remove the president, vice president, or other "civil officers," including federal judges, who commit "Treason, Bribery, or other high Crimes and Misdemeanors." This is the first step in the constitutional process of removing such government officials from office. The House of Representatives brings charges of impeachment and the Senate votes whether to remove the impeached official from office.

- Powers of the Senate without the House

- In the **advice and consent** power, the Senate has the sole authority to approve major presidential appointments, including federal judges, ambassadors, and cabinet and subcabinet positions.

- **Treaties**: The Senate must approve all presidential treaties by a two-thirds vote.

The Members of Congress

- Members must appease constituents at home and colleagues in Washington, D.C.

- Congress as a group is better educated, more white, and more male than the rest of the population.

- **Incumbency advantage**: The relative advantage an incumbent officeholder has over his or her challengers in seeking reelection.

- **Redistricting**: The process of redrawing congressional districts to reflect increases or decreases in seats allotted to the states, as well as population shifts within a state.

- **Gerrymandering**: The legislative process through which the majority party in each statehouse tries to ensure that the maximum number of representatives from its political party can be elected to Congress through redistricting.

- **Rules for Redistricting**

- Congressional and state legislative districts must be apportioned on the basis of population.

- District lines must be contiguous; you must be able to draw the boundaries of the district with one unbroken line.

- Purposeful gerrymandering of a congressional district to dilute minority strength is illegal under the Voting Rights Act of 1965.

- Redrawing of districts for obvious racial purposes to enhance minority representation is constitutional if race is not the "predominate" factor over all other factors that are part of traditional redistricting, including compactness.

How Congress Is Organized

- Political parties play a major role in organizing Congress.

  - **Majority party** is the party with the most members.

  - **Minority party** is the party with the second most members.

- Parties organize the committees, set the agenda, and choose institutional leaders. Committee membership usually reflects the partisan composition of the chamber.

- Parties are stronger in the House than in the Senate.

  - **Speaker of the House** is the leader of House business and is selected by the whole House on what is usually a party-line vote. Also, the Speaker is the only officer of the House specifically mentioned in the Constitution. It is the chamber's most powerful position and is traditionally a member of the majority party.

  - **Party caucuses or conferences** are formal gatherings of all party members in one of the Houses of Congress. They choose leaders other than the Speaker of the House.

  - **Majority leader**: The head of the party controlling the most seats in the House of Representatives or the Senate; is second in authority to the Speaker of the House, and is regarded as the Senate's most powerful member.

  - **Minority leader**: The head of the party with the second greatest number of elected representatives in the House of Representatives or the Senate.

  - **Whip**: Key member who keeps close contact with all members of his or her party and takes vote counts on key legislation, prepares summaries of bills, and in general acts as a communications link within a party.

- Senate also has party leadership.

  - The vice president of the United States is technically the head of the Senate.

  - Official chair is the **president pro tempore**, who is the longest-serving senator of the majority party. This is largely a ceremonial position.

  - Also have leaders and whips as in the House, although they may have more difficulty enforcing party unity.

- Most of the work in Congress is done in committees.

  - **Standing committees** continue from one Congress to the next and are where bills go for consideration.

  - Have considerable power to set the agenda by deciding which bills to consider.

  - **Joint committees** are committees from both houses that conduct investigations.

  - **Conference committees** reconcile differences between bills passed by the House and Senate.

- **Select (or special) committees** are temporary committees appointed for particular purposes.

- **Discharge petition**: Petition that gives a majority of the House of Representatives the authority to bring an issue to the floor in the face of committee inaction.

- Committee assignments are very valuable commodities for members.

  - Members want to be on committees that deal with issues of importance to their constituents.

  - Appropriations and budget committees are sought after because their control over the funding to implement laws passed by Congress gives them prestige and influence within Congress.

- Committee chairs are very powerful.

  - They set the agenda.

  - They are no longer selected solely on the basis of **seniority**.

Powers of Congress

- How laws are made

  - House and Senate have parallel lawmaking procedures, and a bill can be introduced in either house first, except bills dealing with revenue, which must come from the House.

  - Bill is referred to the full committee.

  - Bill is referred to the subcommittee.

  - **Markup:** A full committee session in which committee members offer changes to a bill before it goes to the floor. They then vote on the bill, and if it passes, it goes to the full House. If this occurs in the House, it goes to the Rules Committee.

  - Full House considers legislation.

  - **Methods of obstructing consideration of bills**

  - **Hold:** A tactic by which a senator asks to be informed before a particular bill or nomination is brought to the floor. This request signals leadership that a member may have objections to the bill and should be consulted before further action is taken.

- **Filibuster**: A formal way of halting Senate action on a bill by means of long speeches or unlimited debate. Filibusters can be ended by **cloture**, the procedure to end debate in the Senate. This means that an effective majority in the Senate is really 60, not 51.

- If legislation passes, it goes to the other house of the legislature, where the same process must be repeated.

- If both houses pass the bill, a conference committee is held to iron out the differences in the bill because both houses must pass identical legislation.

- Bill is sent to the president, who either signs it or vetoes it. **Veto**: Formal constitutional authority of the president to reject bills passed by both houses of the legislative body, thus preventing the bill from becoming law without further congressional activity.

- **Pocket veto**: If Congress adjourns during the 10 days the president is allowed to consider a bill passed by both houses of Congress, the bill is considered vetoed without the president's signature.

The Budgetary Function

- **Congressional Budget Act of 1974**: Act that established the congressional budget process we use today, laying out a plan for congressional action on the annual budget resolution, appropriations, reconciliation, and any other revenue bills.

- **Reconciliation**: A procedure that allows consideration of controversial issues affecting the budget by limiting debate to 20 hours, thereby ending threat of a filibuster.

- **Pork**: Legislation that allows representatives to bring money and jobs to their districts in the form of public works programs, military bases, or other programs.

- **Earmark**: Funds that an appropriations bill designates for specific projects within a state or congressional district.

The Oversight Function

- **War Powers Act**: Passed by Congress in 1973; the president is limited in the deployment of troops overseas to a 60-day period in peacetime (which can be extended for an extra 30 days to permit withdrawal) unless Congress explicitly gives its approval for a longer period.

- **Congressional review**: A process whereby Congress can nullify agency regulations by a joint resolution of legislative disapproval.

- **Senatorial courtesy**: A custom in which presidents, when selecting district court judges, defer to the senators in whose state the vacancy occurs.

How Members Make Decisions

- **Trustee**: Role played by an elected representative who listens to constituents' opinions and then uses his or her best judgment to make a final decision.

- **Delegate**: Role played by an elected representative who votes the way constituents would want, regardless of his or her own opinion.

- **Politico**: Role played by an elected representative who acts as a trustee or as a delegate, depending on the issue.

  - Party is a leading indicator of voting behavior, and its influence has grown in recent years.

  - **Divided government**: The political condition in which different political parties control the presidency and Congress. Party can be particularly important in times of divided government.

  - **Unified government**: The political condition in which the same political party controls the presidency and Congress.

  - Members are always mindful of their constituents' preferences.

  - Colleagues can provide useful advice.

  - **Logrolling**: Vote trading; voting to support a colleague's bill in return for a promise of future support. Logrolling is more likely to occur on issues that are of little interest to the member.

  - Interest groups and lobbyists provide information and research.

  - Staff and support agencies guide members' votes and provide services to constituents.

  - **Congressional Research Service (CRS)**: CRS responds to more than a quarter of a million congressional requests for information each year. Its staff conducts nonpartisan studies of public issues and conducts major research projects for committees at the request of members. CRS also prepares summaries and tracks the progress of all bills introduced.

  - **Government Accountability Office (GAO)**: The GAO performs four additional functions: (1) It sets government standards for accounting, (2) provides a variety of legal opinions, (3) settles claims against the government, and (4) conducts studies, upon congressional request.

- **Congressional Budget Office (CBO)**: The CBO was created in 1974 to evaluate the economic effect of different spending programs and to provide information on the cost of proposed policies. It is responsible for analyzing the president's budget and economic projections. The CBO provides Congress and individual members with a valuable second opinion to use in budget debates.

Toward Reform: Congressional Checks on the Executive and Judicial Branches

- Balance of power between Congress and the president has changed over time.

- From 1960s to 2000, Congress increased its oversight of the president, holding hearings and conducting investigations into bureaucratic activity.

- Congress also has the power of congressional review—the ability to disapprove of newly approved bureaucratic regulations.

- Oversight is less diligent in times of unified party control.

- Congress has also tried to assert its power in foreign relations through the War Powers Act, which limits the president's ability to deploy troops without congressional approval.

- Congress also has the ability to approve or reject presidential appointments.

- Congress can impeach the president.

Congress and the Judiciary

- Congress and the Court also have a balance of power.

  - Congress must be mindful of judicial review.

  - Congress can establish the number and jurisdiction of federal courts.

  - Senate influences judicial nominees through **senatorial courtesy.**

For Additional Review

As you read your textbook, keep a list of all the committees you come across. Jot down what kind of committee each is and what its role or policy specialty is.

Multiple-Choice Questions

1. Which demographic group is the most underrepresented in Congress?
(A) African Americans
(B) Latinos
(C) Asians
(D) women
(E) upper income

2. Which is most likely to determine candidates' chances of getting elected to Congress?
(A) their personal wealth
(B) their connections to the media
(C) their incumbency status
(D) their campaign style
(E) promises they make to the people

3. The trustee view of representation refers to
A. an elected representative who listens to their constituents' opinions on some issues and then uses her or his best judgment to make other decisions.
B. an elected representative who serves in a leadership position for her or his party in Congress.
C. an elected representative who uses her or his best judgment to make decisions.
D. a career politician.
E. an elected representative who tries to represent the views of her or his constituents' opinions even if they disagree with them.

4. Which of the following would be an attractive committee for a member of Congress who wanted to increase her or his power and influence within the chamber?
(A) Ways and Means
(B) Rules
(C) Education
(D) Government Reform
(E) Appropriations

Approval of Congress and Own Representative

Questions:

Do you approve or disapprove of the way Congress is handling its job?

Do you approve or disapprove of the way the representative from your district is handling his or her job?

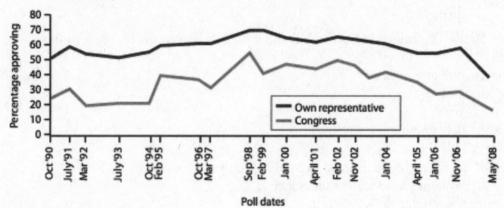

Source: Lexis-Nexis RPOLL.

5. Which of the following conclusions may be drawn based on the data in the figure above?
(A) There is no correlation between citizens' ratings of Congress and their own representative.
(B) Citizens are more likely to approve of Congress than of their own representative.
(C) Representatives' approval ratings are at an all-time high.
(D) Trust in Congress has fallen precipitously in recent years.
(E) On average, about half of the American public approves of the job their member of Congress is doing.

6. A senator can effectively prevent the Senate from voting by
(A) conducting oversight.
(B) filibustering.
(C) introducing another bill.
(D) holding hearings.
(E) no known process, because the rules are very structured.

7. Which of the following ends debate in the Senate?
(A) cloture
(B) vote by the Rules Committee
(C) conference committee
(D) markup
(E) rider

8. Most of the time, members of Congress vote with
(A) the president.
(B) their states.
(C) celebrities.
(D) their party.
(E) the lobbyists.

9. After a House committee reviews a bill and writes its report, the bill goes to the
(A) Senate.
(B) appropriate subcommittee.
(C) president.
(D) floor for debate.
(E) House Rules Committee.

10. Which of the following is the best example of legislative oversight?
(A) The vice president presides over the Senate.
(B) The Rules Committee amends a bill.
(C) Debate is limited.
(D) A hearing is held to investigate misuse of funds within a federal agency.
(E) Pork barrel legislation is not allowed.

Free-Response Questions

1. Occasionally, one party will have control of Congress and the presidency. This will give the majority party advantages in Congress, yet passing legislation is still difficult.

    a. Describe the legislative advantages of the majority party in Congress with respect to both committee structure and leadership.

    b. Explain why, even with unified party control, passing legislation is difficult. Use two examples to support your explanation.

2. Congress has several nonlegislative functions. Describe the relevance of each of the following and provide an example:

    a. oversight of the bureaucracy

    b. confirmation of political appointees

    c. impeachment

ANSWERS AND EXPLANATIONS

Multiple-Choice Questions

- **1. (D) is correct.** Women make up a small percentage of both the House and the Senate and do not come close to the percentage in the general population.

- **2. (C) is correct.** Incumbency is the most important determinant in a candidate's chance of getting elected.

- **3. (C) Is correct.** The trustee view of representation says that representatives make decisions by using their best judgment, even if that judgment leads them to decisions that their constituents would oppose. The delegate view of representation is that elected representatives need to represent the views of their constituents' opinions even if they disagree with them.

- **4. (E) is correct.** Appropriations and budget committees are sought after because their control over the funding to implement laws passed by Congress gives them prestige and influence within Congress.

- **5. (E) is correct.** On average, about 50 percent of citizens approve of the job their representative is doing. The other statements are either false or cannot be determined from this figure.

- **6. (B) is correct.** The filibuster stalls the debate process and therefore prevents the Senate from voting.

- **7. (A) is correct.** A cloture (60 votes) ends a filibuster.

- **8. (D) is correct.** While party discipline is not required, on most legislative issues members of Congress will vote with their party.

- **9. (E) is correct.** After being discussed and marked up in committee, a bill goes to the Rules Committee, which will schedule it for debate on the floor of the House.

- **10. (D) is correct.** Oversight committees routinely investigate claims of misuse of funds by holding hearings and asking questions of members of an agency.

1.

a. The majority party in Congress has numerous advantages in the legislative process. All committee chairs come from the majority party and there are more members of the majority party on committees. The chair of the committee can decide to hold a vote on moving a piece of legislation to the next stage, and is usually successful since there more members from his or her party in the committee. The Speaker of the House comes from the majority party. The majority party also makes up a disproportionate share of the Rules Committee, which schedules legislation, oversees the rules for the legislation, and oversees the debate on the legislation.

b. Even when one party controls both the White House and Congress, passing legislation is still difficult. There are many things that can stop legislation from passing. First, there is no guarantee of party discipline. One defecting member of a political party has the potential to slow the legislation. Oftentimes members within a party will disagree significantly during the markup process. One committee chair can also essentially hold a piece of legislation hostage in committee. Finally, in the Senate there are maneuvers that give the minority party power, such as filibustering. All a minority party senator has to do is declare his or her intent to filibuster, and then only cloture (60 votes) can cut off the filibuster. If the majority party does not have 60 members in the Senate, passing any legislation will be difficult.

2.

a. One nonlegislative function of Congress is oversight of the federal bureaucracy. This occurs when a committee investigates how a federal department or agency is doing its job. Normally, Congress does this by holding hearings and asking questions of federal employees. This information-gathering process results in reports, recommendations, and new legislation. This is done publicly, and video clips of these hearings are often shown on television. One example is the 9/11 Commission. This commission was created to try to figure out how our intelligence systems could perform better and avoid another 9/11 catastrophe. Hearings were held and a major report was published, which resulted in the reorganization of U.S. intelligence services.

b. Another nonlegislative function of Congress is confirming presidential appointees. This is done most often by the Senate Judiciary Committee. The committee holds a hearing and interviews the potential nominee. Former employers and those who know the nominee may also testify. The committee makes a recommendation about whether or not to approve the nominee and then the full Senate must vote by a simple majority in order for the nominee to be confirmed. One recent example of this process is Michael Mukasey's nomination as U.S. attorney general.

c. Finally, impeachment is a nonlegislative function. If the president has committed a "high crime or misdemeanor" then the House may conduct an investigation of wrongdoing. The House then votes by simple majority and the Senate can conduct a trial to see if the allegations warrant removal of the president from office. The Senate is required to vote by a two-thirds majority in order to remove the president.

CHAPTER 8

The Presidency

The president of the United States is the most powerful individual in all of American politics. The presidency as a government institution has changed dramatically since the writing of the Constitution. The essential powers of the presidency are listed in the Constitution, but over the course of history, presidents have claimed a range of inherent powers to aid them in making policy. They are also helped by a large presidential establishment that provides advice and policy expertise. Leadership and approval ratings, too, help presidents as they try to work with Congress and the bureaucracy.

Roots of the Office of President of the United States

- Framers distrusted a powerful chief executive.

- Presidential Qualifications and Terms of Office laid out in Article II.

    - Must be a natural born citizen.

    - Must be at least 35 years of age.

    - Serves four-year terms.

    - **Twenty-Second Amendment** limits presidents to two terms.

- Little attention is paid to the duties of the vice president.

- The Constitution sets forth the process of **impeachment** of a president who has abused his powers or committed a "high crime or misdemeanor" worthy of removal from office.

    - The House may vote for the impeachment of the president by a simple majority.

    - The Senate conducts the impeachment trial and the chief justice of the Supreme Court presides over the trial.

    - It takes a two-thirds vote in the Senate to remove the president from office.

- **Executive privilege** allows the president to refuse to disclose confidential information.

    - *U.S.* v. *Nixon* rules that there is no overriding executive privilege that extends to court orders.

- **Presidential Succession Act** (1947): Lists, in order, those in line (after the vice president).

- **Twenty-Fifth Amendment:** Deals with aspects of presidential succession. It directs the president to appoint a new vice president, subject to the approval (by a simple majority) of both houses of Congress and some other body determined by Congress) to deem a president unable to fulfill his duties and it sets up a procedure to allow the vice president to become acting president if the president is incapacitated. Under this procedure the vice president and a majority of the cabinet can deem a president unable to fulfill his duties.

The Constitutional Powers of the President

- The Constitution grants the president limited, specific powers.

    - Nominate **cabinet**-level government officials, Supreme Court justices, and all other federal judges.

    - **The cabinet** is the formal body of presidential advisers who head the 15 executive departments. Presidents often add others to this body of formal advisers.

    - Convene Congress.

    - Make treaties and **executive agreements,** both of which are formal international agreements entered into by the president. **Treaties** require approval by two-thirds of the Senate. **Executive Agreements** do not require the advice and consent of the U.S. Senate.

    - Legislation: Presidents cannot introduce legislation to Congress. They must rely on their party's leadership to do that for them.

    - **Veto:** The formal, constitutional authority of the president to reject bills passed by both houses of Congress, thus preventing them from becoming law without further congressional action.

    - President does not have the **line-item veto**.

    - Act as commander in chief of the armed forces.

    - **War Powers Act** attempts to limit the amount of time troops can be deployed without the permission of Congress.

    - **Pardons**: An executive grant providing restoration of all rights and privileges of citizenship to a specific individual charged or convicted of a crime.

The Development and Expansion of Presidential Power

- George Washington set a number of precedents for later presidents.

    - Established the primacy of the national government

- Established the cabinet system

- Exerted the role of the executive in foreign affairs

- Claimed the **inherent powers** of the presidency, the powers that belong to the president because they can be inferred from the Constitution

- Powers expanded slowly until the Civil War, when Abraham Lincoln took a number of legally questionable actions in the name of preserving the union.

   - Argued that inherent powers allowed him to circumvent the Constitution in a time of war.

- Growing importance of presidential decision making, post-Franklin Roosevelt presidency.

   - **New Deal:** The name given to the program of "Relief, Recovery, Reform" begun by President Franklin D. Roosevelt (FDR) in 1933 to bring the United States out of the Great Depression. FDR's style personalized the presidency and the New Deal led to a growth in the bureaucracy.

The Presidential Establishment

- Vice presidents were historically chosen to balance the ticket politically.

   - Vice presidential power has grown in recent years.

- Cabinet advisors head departments that handle broad issues of national interest.

   - Fifteen cabinet departments today.

   - Presidents' reliance on their cabinet secretaries has decreased over time.

- First ladies act as informal advisors.

- The **Executive Office of the President** helps the president to oversee the executive branch bureaucracy. It includes the National Security Council, the Council of Economic Advisors, and the Office of Management and Budget.

- The White House staff includes important personal and political advisors to the president, such as the legal counsel to the president, the president's personal secretary, and the chief of staff. This office takes care of the president's political needs and manages the press. They have no independent legal authority. Their power is derived from their personal relationship to the president

Presidential Leadership and the Importance of Public Opinion

- Presidents' ability to get their policies passed depends on a number of factors.

    - Presidential leadership and the "power to persuade."

    - "Going public" to mobilize public opinion.

- President's approval ratings can help or hinder their ability to achieve policy goals.

    - High approval ratings increase a president's political capital, while low approval alienates even presidential partisans.

    - Approval tends to follow a cyclical pattern. It is highest during the president's honeymoon period and after times of national crisis.

Toward Reform: The President as Policymaker

- Modern presidents play a significant role in setting the legislative agenda.

    - Greatest power is the ability to construct legislative coalitions.

    - Getting support in Congress is particularly difficult, especially in times of divided government or when the president's approval rating is low.

- President works with the **Office of Management and Budget (OMB)** to make a budget proposal to Congress. The OMB prepares the president's annual budget proposal, reviews the budget and programs of the executive departments, supplies economic forecasts, and conducts detailed analyses of proposed bills and agency rules.

- Can make policies without Congress by using the **executive order**, a rule or regulation issued by the president that has the effect of law.

- Growth of the use of "signing statements" to declare the president's disagreement with sections of new laws.

For Additional Review

As you read about the president, keep a list of notable events or issues surrounding particular presidents to look over before the exam.

Multiple-Choice Questions

1. Congress can override a presidential veto of legislation
(A) by appealing to the U.S. Supreme Court.
(B) by negotiating a deal with the vice president.
(C) by getting approval of the bill in three-fourths of the state legislatures.
(D) with a majority vote of the House Rules Committee.
(E) with a two-thirds vote in both houses of Congress.

2. According to the Constitution, the vice president
(A) chairs all cabinet meetings.
(B) is ineligible to run for president after two terms as vice president.
(C) can act as president if the president becomes incapacitated
(D) must be of the same party as the president.
(E) is an ex officio member of the Council of Economic Advisors.

3. Which of the following presidential appointments requires Senate confirmation?
(A) press secretary
(B) chief of staff
(C) White House counsel
(D) Council of Economic Advisors
(E) secretary of state

4. All of the following are true statements about the impeachment process EXCEPT
(A) the chief justice of the United States presides over the trial.
(B) the Supreme Court decides guilt or innocence.
(C) the trial must be held in public.
(D) the Senate serves as the jury.
(E) the House of Representatives brings the formal charges against the president.

5. A president is most likely to gain public support for a public policy proposal by
(A) sending the vice president out to conduct high-profile town hall meetings.
(B) placing ads in respected newspapers with large circulations.
(C) vetoing a bill passed by Congress.
(D) appealing to the public directly via the broadcast media.
(E) including the proposal in his or her party's campaign platform.

6. The Twenty-Fifth Amendment is significant because it
(A) clarifies the terms under which the vice president may become president as a result of the president being disabled.
(B) limits the number of terms the president can serve.
(C) clarifies the formal roles, duties, and responsibilities of all parties involved in a presidential impeachment trial.
(D) defines the process to be used for creating new cabinet positions.
(E) clarifies Congress's role in the realm of U.S. foreign policy.

7. Which of the following is a power that a president could use to control high-level officials in the bureaucracy
(A) the line-item veto.
(B) congressional oversight committees.
(C) campaign finance reform.
(D) the presidential power to appoint and remove top-level administrators.
(E) the presidential power to pardon.

8. Which of the following statements about the president as commander in chief is true?
(A) The president has the authority to declare war for up to 60 days without consulting Congress.
(B) Presidents have considered the War Powers Act an unconstitutional infringement of their executive power.
(C) Presidents with no prior military experience are not allowed to make major military decisions alone.
(D) The president is required by law to consult with the Joint Chiefs of Staff before deploying the military.
(E) The president is a nonvoting member of the Senate Armed Services Committee.

9. Which of the following are powers of the president?
I.   conducting diplomatic relations
II. negotiating treaties
III. dismissing Supreme Court justices
IV. appointing cabinet officers
(A) IV only
(B) I, II, and III only
(C) I, II, and IV only
(D) I, III, and IV only
(E) II, III, and IV only

10. Which of the following is NOT in line of presidential succession?
(A) chief justice of the Supreme Court
(B) secretary of state
(C) secretary of the interior
(D) attorney general
(E) Speaker of the House

Free-Response Questions

1. The president is the single most powerful individual in government. Some of the president's most important responsibilities and powers are in the area of national security.

    a. Identify and explain two national security powers or responsibilities granted to the president in the Constitution.

b. Identify and describe two constitutional limitations on presidential national security power.

2. The president plays an important policymaking role in the federal system.

a. Identify and explain two ways the president influences policy.

b. Identify and describe two limitations on the president's policymaking power.

ANSWERS AND EXPLANATIONS

Multiple-Choice Questions

- **1. (E) is correct.** While a presidential veto usually effectively kills proposed legislation, Congress can override the veto with a two-thirds majority vote in both houses and has done so about four percent of the time. The Constitution gives the president the power to veto as a means to check Congress, and it gives Congress the power to override a veto as a means of checking the president.

- **2. (C) is correct.** The Twenty-Fifth Amendment to the Constitution establishes procedures for presidents to be declared incompetent to serve, and makes it clear that in such cases the vice president acts as president.

- **3. (E) is correct.** Because they are a member of the president's cabinet, nominees for secretary of state must be confirmed by the Senate. The National Security Council, the chief of staff, the White House counsel, and the Council of Economic Advisors are considered to be part of the president's personal staff of advisors and are not required to be approved by the Senate.

- **4. (B) is correct.** The presidential impeachment process is as follows: (1) the House votes to impeach the president; (2) the Senate carries out the impeachment trial, with the chief justice of the United States presiding; and (3) the Senate must have a two-thirds vote to convict and remove the president. The Supreme Court plays no role in this process.

- **5. (D) is correct.** Public support is one of the president's most important resources for getting policy agenda enacted. Presidents who have the backing of the public have an easier time influencing Congress. Using the mass media to directly appeal to the public is an effective tool for gaining public support.

- **6. (A) is correct.** The Twenty-Fifth Amendment, passed in 1967, is significant because it clarifies the terms under which the vice president may become president as a result of the president being disabled. It also outlines how a recuperated president can reclaim the job.

- **7. (D) is correct.** The power to appoint and remove top-level administrators gives the president significant influence over what the federal bureaucracy does or does not do.

- **8. (B) is correct.** Despite generally complying with its provisions, presidents since Richard Nixon have continued to insist that the War Powers Act is an unconstitutional infringement of their executive power. The War Powers Act gives presidents the power to commit troops for 60 days, but not to declare war.

- **9. (C) is correct.** According to the Constitution, presidents have the power to conduct diplomacy, negotiate treaties with foreign countries, and appoint members of their cabinets. Presidents nominate federal court judges, but they cannot remove them from their seats once they have been confirmed by the Senate. In fact, once they have been nominated by the president and approved by the Senate, federal judges hold their positions for life. The Constitution specifies that Supreme Court and other federal judges have no term limit. Justices and judges can be impeached, but this has happened only 13 times in the history of the federal courts.

- **10. (A) is correct.** The chief justice is not in the line of presidential succession. The Constitution authorizes the vice president to take over the office of the presidency if the president dies, resigns, is impeached, or is otherwise unable to perform his duties. After the vice president, the succession is the Speaker of the House of Representatives, the president pro tempore of the Senate, and then cabinet members, ordered according to the date their offices were established.

This rubric provides examples of many, but not all, of the possible correct responses to the free-response questions.

1.

a. National security powers or responsibilities granted to the president in the Constitution.

- **Commander in chief**. Because the framers wanted civilian control of the military, they made the president commander in chief of the armed forces. As commander in chief, the president controls where and how the military is deployed. The president also commands the vast arsenal of weapons of mass destruction. While only Congress can declare war, the president can interject U.S. troops into armed conflict on a limited basis.

- **Diplomatic powers**. The president alone extends diplomatic recognition to foreign governments. The president can also terminate relations with other countries.

- **Power to make treaties and executive agreements with other nations**. The president has the sole power to negotiate treaties with other countries, although the Constitution requires the Senate to approve treaties by a two-thirds vote.

b. Constitutional limitations on presidential national security power.

- **Congress declares war**. Although the president has the power to deploy U.S. troops, only Congress has the constitutional power to declare war.

- **The Senate must approve treaties**. Treaties that presidents negotiate with foreign countries must be approve by a two-thirds vote in the Senate.

- **Congress has the power of the purse**. A president's national security agenda requires a willingness on the part of Congress to appropriate the necessary funds to support it.

2.

a. Identify and explain two ways the president influences policy.

- **Executive orders**. The president can issue executive orders that have the effect of law. These can be powerful tools for the president to change the course of policy. For example, President Harry Truman used an executive order to desegregate the armed forces.

- **Setting the legislative agenda**. Many presidents play major roles in setting the agenda of Congress. They not only make policy proposals but also use lobbyists to steward proposals through the policymaking process.

b. Identify and describe two limitations on the president's policymaking power.

- **Congress has the power of the purse**. Although the president can make policy proposals, only Congress can appropriate funds.

- **The Supreme Court has judicial review**. The Supreme Court can review the constitutionality of executive orders or regulations promulgated by the bureaucracy.

CHAPTER 9

The Executive Branch and the Federal Bureaucracy

The federal **bureaucracy** is composed of all of the agencies, departments, offices, and bureaus in the executive branch. It has grown tremendously since the beginning of the new nation. Most bureaucrats are career civil servants; they represent a wide array of jobs and talents. The bureaucracy is primarily responsible for implementing and enforcing laws.

Roots of the Federal Bureaucracy

- Government started out small, with only three cabinet departments.

- Began to grow in the 1830s with the creation of the Post Office.

  - Jobs were filled through the **spoils system**, the firing of public office holders of a defeated political party to replace them with loyalists of the newly elected party. This is a form of **patronage,** which refers to jobs, grants, or other special favors that are given as rewards to friends and political allies for their support.

  - This system was a way to reward party loyalists.

- Backlash against the spoils system in the 1880s.

  - Passage of the **Pendleton Act** in 1883 created a **civil service system,** a merit system by which many federal bureaucrats are now selected.

  - Development of the **merit system,** which is a system of employment based on qualifications, test scores, and ability, rather than party loyalty.

- Bureaucracy grew with the creation of new agencies.

  - Formation of **independent regulatory commissions**, agencies created by Congress outside a major executive department.

  - **Federal Trade Commission (FTC)** is an independent regulatory commission that protects small businesses and the public from unfair competition, especially from big business.

  - Development of new cabinet agencies over the course of the 20th century as a response to the Progressive movement, the New Deal, World War II, and the Great Society.

The Modern Bureaucracy

- Government employees are a very diverse group of individuals.

  - About 90 percent of federal employees are civil service and paid within the General Schedule (GS).

  - The remaining 10 percent are appointed by the president to higher-level policymaking positions.

  - Most workers do not work in Washington, D.C.

- Use of private contractors has grown in recent years.

- **Formal Organization of the bureaucracy**:

  - **Cabinet departments:** Major administrative units with responsibility for a broad area of government operations. Departmental status usually indicates a permanent national interest in a particular governmental function, such as defense, commerce, or agriculture.

  - **Independent executive agencies:** Governmental units that closely resemble a cabinet department but have narrower areas of responsibility, and perform services rather than regulatory functions.

  - **Government corporations:** Businesses established by Congress to perform functions that could be provided by private businesses.

- **Government Workers and Political Involvement**

  - **Hatch Act:** The 1939 act to prohibit civil servants from taking activist roles in partisan campaigns. This act prohibited federal employees from making political contributions, working for a particular party, or campaigning for a particular candidate.

  - It was updated in 1993 by the **Federal Employees Political Activities Act**, which liberalized the Hatch Act by allowing federal employees to run for office in nonpartisan elections and to contribute money to campaigns in partisan elections.

How the Bureaucracy Works

- Max Weber's six characteristics of a model bureaucracy:

  - A chain of command in which authority flows from top to bottom

  - A division of labor whereby work is apportioned among specialized workers to increase productivity

- Clear lines of authority among workers and their superiors

- A goal orientation that determines structure, authority, and rules

- Impersonality, whereby all employees are treated fairly based on merit and all clients are served equally, without discrimination, according to established rules

- Productivity, whereby all work and actions are evaluated according to established rules

- Main goal of bureaucracy is policy **implementation**, the process by which a law or policy is put into operation.

- **Iron triangles**: The relatively stable relationships and patterns of interaction that occur among agencies, interest groups, and congressional committees or subcommittees.

- **Issue network**: The loose and informal relationships that exist among a large number of actors who work in broad policy areas.

- **Interagency councils:** Working groups created to facilitate coordination of policymaking and implementation across a host of governmental agencies.

- Bureaucrats have a lot of **administrative discretion,** the ability of bureaucrats to make choices concerning the best way to implement congressional or executive intentions.

- Policy is made in one of two ways:

  - **Rule making** is a quasi-legislative process that results in regulations that have the characteristics of a legislative act.

  - **Regulations** Rules that govern the operation of all government programs that have the force of law.

  - To make a regulation, one must follow the Administrative Procedures Act.

  - **Administrative adjudication** is a quasi-judicial process in which a bureaucratic agency settles disputes between two parties in a manner similar to the way courts resolve disputes.

Toward Reform: Making Agencies Accountable

- The bureaucracy answers ultimately to the president, who

  - appoints agency heads who will support his policies.

  - can reorganize agencies.

- issues **executive orders** to change or implement statutes.

- The bureaucracy is also influenced by Congress, which

  - performs legislative oversight through hearings.

  - ultimately determines each agency's budget.

  - can use the process of congressional review to examine and nullify bureaucratic regulations.

  - **Police patrol oversight** is proactive and allows Congress to set its own agenda for programs or agencies to review.

  - **Fire alarm oversight** is reactive and generally involves a congressional response to a complaint filed by a constituent or politically significant actor.

- The bureaucracy may also be influenced by the judiciary, which

  - can review the constitutionality of regulations.

  - can make sure that citizens have received due process by the bureaucracy.

For Additional Review

Look through your textbook and make a list of federal agencies and departments. For each one, note the policy area that it handles and any other relevant information, such as which type of bureaucratic institution it is or how its administrators are selected.

Multiple-Choice Questions

1. All of the following are important official services performed by the federal bureaucracy EXCEPT
(A) implementing laws passed by Congress.
(B) implementing the president's policy initiatives.
(C) solving disputes between the executive and legislative branches of government.
(D) distributing information about public programs and services.
(E) issuing rules and regulations.

2. The Pendleton Civil Service Act is significant because
(A) it instituted an affirmative action policy for hiring and promoting federal bureaucrats.
(B) it created the federal civil service and prescribed that the hiring of civil servants be based on merit.
(C) it gave the president more control over federal agencies.
(D) it reduced the number of federal civil servants working outside of Washington, D.C.
(E) it established clear boundaries between state and federal bureaucracies.

3. Bureaucracies are often criticized as being undemocratic because
(A) they are not directly accountable to the people.
(B) they utilize a merit system for hiring.
(C) citizens tend to have low opinions of them.
(D) the courts have no influence over their actions.
(E) they are overly influenced by campaign contributions.

4. Presidents attempt to exercise control over the bureaucracy through which of the following means?
I. appointing heads of federal agencies that are loyal to them
II. issuing executive orders
III. proposing alterations to agencies' budgets
IV. providing incentive pay to senior agency administrators

(A) I only
(B) I and III only
(C) III and IV only
(D) I, II, and III only
(E) All of the above

5. Which of the following statements represent a prevalent myth about the federal bureaucracy?
I. The bureaucracy is growing larger each year.
II. Most federal bureaucrats work in Washington, D.C.
III. Citizens are generally dissatisfied with the bureaucracy.
IV. The bureaucracy makes government inefficient and cumbersome.

(A) I only
(B) IV only
(C) I and II only
(D) II, III, and IV only
(E) All of the above

6. An important tool Congress uses to influence the bureaucracy is
(A) submitting *amicus curiae* briefs to the federal courts.
(B) issuing executive orders.
(C) hiring civil servants to head federal agencies.
(D) frequently removing administrators from office.
(E) requiring agency heads to routinely appear before congressional committees.

7. Iron triangles are made up of which of the following?
(A) congressional committees, independent executive agencies, and private corporations
(B) bureaucratic agencies, congressional committees, and interest groups
(C) regulatory commissions, the Office of Management and Budget, and interest groups
(D) the executive, the legislative, and the judicial branches of government
(E) the president's cabinet, interest groups, and private corporations

8. All of the following are independent regulatory commissions EXCEPT the
(A) Federal Reserve Board.
(B) National Labor Relations Board.
(C) Security and Exchange Commission.
(D) Office of Management and Budget.
(E) Federal Trade Commission.

9. The Hatch Act helps maintain a nonpartisan bureaucracy because it
(A) creates a federal commission on which half the members are Democrats and half are Republican.
(B) ensures that federal employees are hired based on merit.
(C) requires all federal employees to register to vote as independents.
(D) requires all federal agencies to have staffs that are balanced along party lines.
(E) prohibits government employees from active participation in partisan politics.

10. The federal bureaucracy handles all of the following activities EXCEPT
(A) issuing rules and regulations.
(B) holding hearings to obtain information about proposed policies.
(C) implementing policies passed by Congress.
(D) appropriating funds to pay for federal government programs.
(E) acting as a quasi-judicial body.

Free-Response Questions

1. Many political scientists believe that having a nonpartisan civil service increases the likelihood that government will operate in an effective and efficient manner.

   a. Define the merit principle and explain how it helps to ensure that the civil service remains nonpartisan.

   b. Define the Hatch Act and explain how it helps to ensure that the civil service remains nonpartisan.

c. Although the federal bureaucracy is nonpartisan, the president is nominally in charge of it. Identify and describe two ways a president attempts to control the bureaucracy.

2. Political scientists have considered the complex interconnections between the bureaucracy and other actors in the political system.

   a. Define an iron triangle and give an example of an iron triangle in practice.

   b. Define an issue network, explain how it differs from an iron triangle, and give an example of an issue network in practice.

ANSWERS AND EXPLANATIONS

Multiple-Choice Questions

- **1. (C) is correct.** The bureaucracy does not referee or solve disputes between the executive and legislative branches of government. Bureaucracies are essentially implementers of policy.

- **2. (B) is correct.** The Pendleton Civil Service Act of 1883 created the federal civil service system. Hiring and promotions in this system are based on the merit system. With regards to hiring, applicants must take an exam, and those individuals in the highest scoring group are hired. Most federal bureaucratic positions are filled this way, though the president does appoint some people to high-level positions.

- **3. (A) is correct.** Although they make vital decisions and perform essential services for government and the people, bureaucrats are not directly accountable to citizens the way the president and Congress are. This has led to the criticism that the bureaucracy is an undemocratic branch of government.

- **4. (D) is correct.** Presidents have no control over the compensation bureaucrats receive. There is a fairly rigid federal pay scale that is used to determine the level of pay and benefits to which federal employees are entitled.

- **5. (E) is correct.** All of these statements are false or misleading. The federal bureaucracy is not growing bigger and bigger each year. Only about 12 percent of federal bureaucrats work in Washington, D.C. California, with more than 245,000 federal employees, leads the nation in the number of federal bureaucrats. Most citizens are generally satisfied with the service they receive from the bureaucracy.

- **6. (E) is correct.** Congress uses oversight committee hearings as a means to ensure federal agencies are meeting the goals and objectives set in laws it passes and to help keep federal agencies free of fraud, waste, and abuse.

- **7. (B) is correct.** An iron triangle is the mutually dependent relationship between bureaucratic agencies, interest groups, and congressional committees. These relationships are often detrimental to the interests of taxpayers and ordinary citizens.

- **8. (D) is correct.** The Office of Management and Budget is part of the Executive Office of the President and is not an independent regulatory commission.

- **9. (E) is correct.** The Hatch Act, originally passed in 1939 and amended most recently in 1993, prohibits civil service employees from actively participating in partisan politics while on duty. The act was intended to help ensure a fair and impartial bureaucracy and to protect bureaucrats from coercion on the part of superiors or political appointees.

- **10. (D) is correct.** Only Congress can appropriate funds to be spent by the federal government. The bureaucracy engages in all of the other activities listed.

Free-Response Questions

This rubric provides examples of many, but not all, of the possible correct responses to the free-response questions.

1.

a. Define the merit principle and explain how it helps to ensure that the civil service remains nonpartisan.

- The merit principle calls for the use of entrance exams and promotion ratings to hire and reward qualified civil servants. Under this principle individuals are hired and promoted based on their qualifications, rather than patronage or partisan ties.

b. Define the Hatch Act and explain how it helps to ensure that the civil service remains nonpartisan.

- The Hatch Act is a federal law that prohibits government employees from participating in partisan political activities while on duty. The law helps to protect civil service employees from pressures from political appointees and others to behave in a partisan manner in carrying out their professional duties.

c. Ways a president attempts to control the bureaucracy.

- **Appoint the right people to head agencies**. Presidents control the appointments of federal agency heads and subheads. Appointing individuals who share their ideologies and goals is one effective way presidents influence agencies.

- **Issue executive orders.** Executive orders carry the force of law and can be used to get agencies to take or not take certain actions.

- **Alter an agency's budget**. The Office of Management and Budget (OMB) is instrumental in determining an agency's budget. Threats to cut or add to a budget usually get an agency's attention.

2.

a. Define an iron triangle, and give an example of an iron triangle in practice.

- An iron triangle is a relatively stable pattern of interactions between congressional committees, bureaucratic agencies, and interest groups.

- An example of an iron triangle is the relationship between the House Committee on Veterans' Affairs, the Department of Veterans Affairs, and the Veterans of Foreign Wars.

b. Define an issue network, explain how it differs from an iron triangle, and give an example of an issue network in practice.

- An issue network is the system of loose and informal relationships that exist among policy actors working in an issue area.

- Issue networks include more policy actors than iron triangles and may change more frequently.

- An issue network in veterans' affairs would include all of the actors detailed above plus other interest groups (such as the American Legion), lawyers, courts, think tanks, veterans' hospital administrators, etc.

CHAPTER 10

The Judiciary

The judiciary was initially viewed as little more than a theoretical necessity under the new Constitution. Its powers, however, have grown significantly over time. Today, the American courts review a wide array of criminal and civil cases within a dual federal and state court system. The federal courts are made up of three tiers: the district courts, the courts of appeals, and the Supreme Court. These courts are filled with judges appointed by the president with the advice and consent of the Senate. Nominees to the Supreme Court are particularly important because this is the highest court in the political system, and it has great discretion over the cases it chooses to hear. Judges also have significant policymaking power.

The Roots of the Federal Judiciary

- Framers thought the judiciary was little more than a theoretical necessity.

- Only court established by the constitution is the Supreme Court; all others established by Congress.

    - **Judiciary Act of 1789** establishes the basic three-tiered structure of the American court system.

- Constitution is silent on **judicial review**, which is the power of the courts to review acts of other branches of government and the states. If exercised by the Supreme Court, the power of judicial review invalidates a law, and the decision cannot be appealed. This is the court's primary method of serving as a check on the other two branches of government.

    - Court first claims this power in *Marbury* **v.** *Madison* (1803).

    - Claiming judicial review was an essential step taken by Chief Justice John Marshall to establish the court as a coequal branch.

The American Legal System

- Two types of courts:

    - **Trial courts** are the beginning of all litigation.

    - **Appellate courts** review decisions of lower courts.

- Court must have jurisdiction to hear a case.

- Courts with **original jurisdiction** are the first courts to hear a case.

    - The court assesses and decides a case based on the facts of the case.

    - Most cases do not continue after their first ruling.

- Courts with **appellate jurisdiction** hear cases that have been appealed.

    - The court interprets the case as it relates to the law; it does not review the facts.

- There are two primary types of law:

    - **Criminal law** is used to protect property and individual safety.

    - **Civil law** is used to settle disputes between private parties.

The Federal Court System

- Courts can take one of two forms:

    - **Constitutional courts** are those specifically created or authorized in the Constitution.

    - Congress establishes **legislative courts** for specialized purposes, such as the Court of Appeals for Veterans Claims.

- There are 94 federal district courts.

    - Federal trial courts of original jurisdiction.

    - Federal district courts primarily handle the following types of cases:

        - Cases involving the federal government as a party

        - Cases that present a federal question

        - Civil suits between citizens of different states

- Thirteen courts of appeals review cases appealed from the district courts.

    - All have appellate jurisdiction.

    - They do not focus on the facts of the case. Rather, they obtain information about the case from oral arguments and **briefs**: documents containing the legal written arguments in a case filed with a court by a party prior to a hearing or trial. They evaluate the treatment of the case in the district court in terms of errors of procedure or the law.

- Usually three judges hear a case.

- Their ruling sets a **precedent** for the district courts within their geographic circuit.

- **Precedent**: A prior judicial decision that serves as a rule for settling subsequent cases of a similar nature.

- *Stare decisis*: Reliance on past decisions or precedents to formulate decisions in new cases.

- The Supreme Court is the highest court in the land.

  - Consists of nine justices who rule on cases together.

  - It reviews cases from the U.S. courts of appeals and state supreme courts (as well as other courts of last resort) and acts as the final interpreter of the U.S. Constitution. The court not only decides major cases with tremendous policy significance each year, but it also ensures uniformity in the interpretation of national laws and the Constitution, resolves conflicts among the states, and maintains the supremacy of national law in the federal system

  - Has original jurisdiction in cases between two states, the federal government and a state, or a state and a foreign country.

  - Most cases fall under its discretionary appellate jurisdiction.

How Federal Court Judges Are Selected

- The president appoints all federal judges and justices.

- The Senate must confirm nominations.

  - Confirmation of district judges is determined by **senatorial courtesy,** the process by which presidents generally defer selection of district court judges to the choice of senators of their own party who represent the state where the vacancy occurs.

- Most nominees have previous judicial experience.

- Supreme Court nominees are particularly important.

  - Nomination criteria include competence, ideology, rewards, pursuit of political support, religion, and race, ethnicity, and gender.

  - The confirmation process begins with an inquiry by the Federal Bureau of Investigation.

- The American Bar Association rates nominees on their qualifications.

- Senate Judiciary Committee holds hearings.

Interest groups are frequent participants.

- Full Senate votes on the nominee.

The Supreme Court Today

- The court hears only a small fraction of the cases presented to it.

    - Chooses to hear cases by granting a **writ of certiorari**, a request for the Supreme Court to order up the records from a lower court to review the case.

    - Process controlled by the **rule of four**, which means at least four justices of the Supreme Court must vote to consider a case before it can be heard.

    - Law clerks play a significant role at all stages of the process.

    - Cases heard by the court usually involve:

        - the federal government as a party (represented by the **solicitor general**, the fourth-ranking member of the Department of Justice; responsible for handling nearly all appeals on behalf of the U.S. government to the Supreme Court).

        - conflict between the courts of appeals.

        - civil rights or liberties questions.

        - ideological or policy preferences of the justices.

        - social or political interest, often evidenced by *amicus curiae* (literally, "friend of the court") briefs. These can be filed as briefs or presented as oral arguments before the court.

- Once the court decides to hear a case, it follows a process to the final decision:

    - Oral arguments are held.

    - Justices hold a conference and vote on the case outcome.

    - Opinions are written and a decision is handed down.

    - **Majority opinion**: Reflect the views of at least five of the justices. This opinion usually sets out the legal reasoning justifying the decision, and this legal reasoning becomes a precedent for deciding future cases.

- **Concurring Opinion**: Sometimes a majority of justices agree with the outcome of the case but not with the legal rationale. In this case, justices who did not agree with the rationale of the others would write concurring opinions.

- **Dissenting Opinion**: Opinions filed by Justices who disagree with the outcome favored by the majority.

Judicial Philosophy and Decision Making

- Judges can follow a number of theoretical perspectives in making decisions.

    - **Judicial restraint** is a theory of limited judicial intervention.

    - **Judicial activism** is a philosophy of broad judicial power.

    - **Strict constructionist** judges follow the framers' intentions.

- Political scientists model judicial decision making in a number of ways.

    - Behavioral model

    - Attitudinal model

    - Strategic model.

- Justices also pay attention to public opinion.

Toward Reform: Power, Policymaking, and the Court

- All judges make policy.

    - Have overturned laws.

    - Have overturned their own decisions.

- **Judicial implementation**: How and whether judicial decisions are translated into actual public policies affecting more than the immediate parties to a lawsuit.

    - Lack an enforcement mechanism to make citizens comply with decisions.

For Additional Review

Select two Supreme Court cases that are of particular interest to you or that had a major impact on politics or society. Read the opinion or opinions associated with the cases to better understand the reasoning on which the justices made important decisions.

Multiple-Choice Questions

1. Which of the following statement is true of the judicial system in the United States?
    (A) It is a unitary court system.
    (B) Interest groups are forbidden from participating in Supreme Court litigation.
    (C) The system prescribes that criminal cases be decided by juries and civil cases be decided by judges.
    (D) The U.S. Constitution established all federal courts.
    (E) The U.S. government enjoys great success in litigation.

2. Which of the following is part of the federal court system?
    I.   U.S. Supreme Court
    II. State supreme courts
    III. Court of Military Appeals
    IV. U.S. court of appeals
    (A) I only
    (B) IV only
    (C) I and IV only
    (D) I, II, and IV only
    (E) I, III, and IV only

3. Federal district courts are the only federal courts in which
    (A) the facts are presented by both parties in the case.
    (B) *amicus curiae* briefs are registered with the court.
    (C) the solicitor general appears for oral argument.
    (D) juries are impaneled to decide cases.
    (E) three judge panels decide the outcome of cases.

4. Which of the following statements is true about Congress's influence over Supreme Court decision making?
    (A) Congress can pass laws to prohibit judicial activism.
    (B) The Senate can filibuster court decisions.
    (C) Congress has significant control over the court's appellate jurisdiction.
    (D) The Senate can decide which cases the Supreme Court will hear.
    (E) District court judges are reviewed by Congress every 10 years.

5. Senatorial courtesy is

(A) the custom of the Supreme Court sharing its docket with the Senate Judiciary Committee before it is made public.

(B) a tradition whereby nominees for federal judgeships must meet the approval of senators of the president's party from the state in which the nominee will serve.

(C) the tradition of the full Senate approving all judicial nominees who win a majority vote in the Judiciary Committee.

(D) the practice of the Senate filling judicial vacancies with judges who share the same judicial philosophy as their most immediate predecessor.

(E) the tradition of the vice president hosting a formal reception to introduce Supreme Court nominees to members of the Senate.

6. All of the following influence the selection of federal judges and Supreme Court justices EXCEPT

(A) campaign contributions.

(B) partisanship.

(C) ideology.

(D) experience.

(E) judicial philosophy.

7. Which of the following is true about the vast majority of cases decided by the Supreme Court?

(A) They are decided by unanimous decision.

(B) The decisions tend to significantly alter current policy.

(C) They always reverse the decision of the lower courts.

(D) They result in the payout of larger damage awards than decisions rendered by lower courts.

(E) They are decided based on how similar past cases have been decided.

8. One major weakness of federal courts as policymakers is that

(A) judges are term limited, which affects their ability to implement their decisions.

(B) lower courts are not required to follow the decisions of superior courts.

(C) they must rely on other institutions to implement their decisions.

(D) they are shielded from the pressures of electoral politics.

(E) courts tend to lack legitimacy in the eyes of most citizens.

9. Interest groups play a role in the federal judicial process in all of the following ways EXCEPT by

(A) frequently testifying before the courts.

(B) lobbying the Judiciary Committee about a judicial nominee.

(C) filing *amicus curiae* briefs.

(D) having their lawyers represent a plaintiff.

(E) filing a class action suit.

10. The power of courts to determine which acts of Congress, the executive branch, and state legislatures are constitutional is known as

(A) precedent.
(B) *stare decisis*.
(C) original jurisdiction.
(D) judicial implementation.
(E) judicial review.

Free-Response Questions

1. The framers of the Constitution desired a federal judiciary that was removed from the pressures and direct consequences of electoral politics.

    a. Identify and describe two provisions in the Constitution that were intended to shield the judiciary from electoral politics.

    b. The framers' intent notwithstanding, the federal judiciary is not free of the influence of electoral politics. Identify and describe two ways electoral politics affect the federal judiciary.

2. The Constitution provides each of the three branches of government with the capacity to limit and trump the powers of the other two.

    a. Describe one way the president can check and balance the powers of the federal judiciary.

    b. Describe one way Congress can check and balance the powers of the federal judiciary.

    c. Describe one way the Supreme Court can check and balance the powers of the executive branch.

    d. Describe one way the Supreme Court can check and balance the powers of the Congress.

ANSWERS AND EXPLANATIONS

Multiple-Choice Questions

- **1. (E) is correct.** The U.S. government, represented by the solicitor general, enjoys an above-average rate of victory, especially before the Supreme Court. The solicitor general is often referred to as the court's "ninth-and-a-half" member.

- **2. (D) is correct.** All of the courts listed except state supreme courts are part of the federal judiciary. No state court is part of the federal court system.

- **3. (D) is correct.** There are no juries in the courts of appeals, the Supreme Court, or any other federal court except the district courts.

- **4. (C) is correct.** In many instances, federal courts' jurisdiction derives from Congress and not the Constitution. The Constitution provides Congress with the discretion to determine which category of cases appellate courts may hear.

- **5. (B) is correct.** Senatorial courtesy is a tradition whereby nominees for federal judgeships must meet the approval of senators of the president's party from the state in which the nominee will serve. This tradition began under George Washington, and since that time the Senate has tended not to confirm nominations for district court judges when senators of the president's party from the state in which the nominee will serve oppose them.

- **6. (A) is correct.** There is no evidence that campaign contributions are a major factor in determining who presidents nominate for federal judgeships.

- **7. (E) is correct.** Most Supreme Court rulings are grounded in precedent.

- **8. (C) is correct.** Unlike legislatures and the executive branch, the courts must always rely on other units of government to implement and enforce their rulings. This is widely viewed as a weakness for the courts as policymakers.

- **9. (A) is correct.** Unless they have sponsored the case, interest groups only appear before the federal courts during oral argument in the most extraordinary of circumstances.

- **10. (D) is correct.** Judicial review is the power of the courts to determine whether acts of Congress, the executive branch, and the states are constitutional. This power was established by the Supreme Court's decision in *Marbury* v. *Madison*.

Free-Response Questions

This rubric provides examples of many, but not all, of the possible correct responses to the free-response questions.

1.

a. Provisions in the Constitution that were intended to shield the judiciary from electoral politics

   - **Federal judges are appointed, not elected.** This feature allows judges to make reasoned decisions based on the rule of law without the fear of losing their jobs because some of their decisions may be unpopular with a group of constituents or the general public.

- **Lifetime appointment for federal judges**. Once confirmed by the Senate, federal judges have lifetime tenure on the bench, so long as they do not commit impeachable offenses. This lifetime tenure allows judges to make reasoned decisions based on the rule of law without the fear of losing their jobs, since some of their decisions may be unpopular with other government officials or the general public.

- **Federal judges' salaries cannot be reduced.** The Constitution expressly prohibits the reduction of judges' salaries during their time on the bench. This constitutional provision allows judges to make decisions without fear of reprisal from the executive and legislative branches.

b. Ways electoral politics affect the federal judiciary.

- **The president, who is a political partisan, nominates federal judges.** Presidents seek to appoint judges to the bench who share their party affiliations, ideologies, judicial philosophies, and stances on specific issues. This makes federal judges products of a partisan political process.

- **The confirmation process.** The confirmation process for federal judges is sometimes highly partisan, with Democrats and Republicans seemingly using the process as a continuation of the last election or a precursor for the next.

- **Congress controls the appellate jurisdiction of federal courts.** Because of this authority, Congress has the capacity to prohibit the courts from hearing specific categories or classes of cases.

2.

a. Ways the president can check and balance the powers of the federal judiciary.

- **Appointment power.** The president nominates Supreme Court and other federal judges.

b. Ways Congress can check and balance the powers of the federal judiciary.

- **Confirmation process.** The Senate must confirm Supreme Court justices and all other federal judicial nominees.

- **Impeachment power.** Congress can impeach federal judges.

- **Jurisdiction authority over lower federal courts.** The Constitution created just one federal court, the U.S. Supreme Court. It gave Congress the authority to create any other subordinate courts that it saw fit to create. Thus, in theory, Congress could disband all federal courts except the Supreme Court. Congress also has the capacity to prohibit the courts from hearing specific categories or classes of cases.

- **Power of the purse.** Although the Constitution expressly prohibits the reduction of judges' salaries during their time on the bench, Congress determines if federal judges receive pay raises and how much any raise will be.

c. A way the Supreme Court can check and balance the powers of the executive branch.

- **Judicial review**. Courts can declare acts of the president and federal agencies to be unconstitutional or unlawful.

d. A way the Supreme Court can check and balance the powers of the Congress.

- **Judicial review**. Courts can declare laws passed by Congress to be unconstitutional.

CHAPTER 11

Political Socialization and Public Opinion

More than two centuries of immigration to the United States has created an incredibly **diverse population** of Americans. Numerous social and economic factors therefore contribute to a varied forum of **public opinion.** However, despite their differences, Americans overall share a common **political culture** based on democracy and federalism. Today, public opinion can be a powerful tool, especially during elections. Increasingly, politicians, pundits, and even voters are paying close attention to what polls tell them is the public's opinion.

Roots of Public Opinion Research

- **Polls** are the most common means of assessing public opinion.

    - Recent polls indicate that Americans have little political knowledge and little faith that the government is acting on their behalf.

    - Public opinion polls have shown a trend indicating that Americans trust government less than they used to.

    - **Public opinion** is what the public thinks about a particular issue or set of issues at any point in time.

    - **Public opinion polls** are interviews or surveys with samples of citizens that are used to estimate the feelings and beliefs of the entire population.

    - **Straw polls** are unscientific surveys used to gauge public opinion on a variety of issues and policies.

    - A **sample** is a subset of the whole population selected to be questioned for the purposes of prediction or gauging opinion.

        - A **random sample,** or group that statistically represents the whole population of the United States, is asked to fill out a questionnaire or answer some questions over the phone. A famous nonrandom sample, *The Literary Digest* poll of 1936, wrongly predicted that Republican Alf Landon would defeat Franklin Roosevelt in the election that year because it relied on telephone and vehicle ownership to draw its sample, which skewed the sample heavily toward those with higher incomes. Commonly, modern polls rely on **random digit dialing** to draw telephone samples.

- A **stratified sample** is a variation of random sampling; census data are used to divide the country into four sampling regions. Sets of counties and standard metropolitan statistical areas are then randomly selected in proportion to the total national population.

- **Push Polls** are taken for the purpose of providing information on an opponent that would lead respondents to vote against that candidate.

- **Tracking polls** are continuous surveys that enable a campaign to chart its daily rise or fall in support.

- An **exit poll** is conducted by media as voters leave the voting booth, to predict the outcomes of elections.

- Nevertheless, there are some problems that can call poll results into question.

  - The **margin of error** is the measure of the accuracy of a public opinion poll.

  - A **sampling error**: The size and quality of the sample can also affect the accuracy of a poll and thus the level of confidence in the poll. Often the opinions of the poor and homeless are underrepresented because insufficient attention is given to making certain that these groups are sampled representatively.

  - **Ambiguous phrasing:** The wording of a question is critical, and ambiguously worded questions can affect the accuracy of a poll.

  - **Limited respondent options:** Polls can be inaccurate when they limit responses. The more constrained the choices, the less reliable and useful the poll is. (For example, "Do you like or dislike this policy?")

  Difficulty measuring intensity: A respondent might answer affirmatively to any question, but it is likely that his or her feelings about issues such as abortion, the death penalty, or support for U.S. troops in Afghanistan or Iraq are much more intense than their feelings about the Electoral College or types of voting machines. Yet, polls rarely have mechanisms to differentiate degree of passion on an issue.

Forming Political Opinions

- People learn about politics and form their political beliefs through **political socialization,** the process through which individuals get their political orientations— knowledge, feeling, and evaluations regarding the political world. Socialization is a dynamic process, with learning taking place over one's entire lifetime. Socialization is part of the very important nurturing process.

- There are several different means through which people informally acquire political information:

- **The family:** Families have a significant degree of influence, especially over younger members. Most people identify with the same party as their parents.

- **Gender:** From the time that the earliest public opinion polls were taken, women have held more liberal attitudes than men about social welfare issues such as education, juvenile justice, capital punishment, and the environment. Public opinion polls have also found that women hold more negative views about war and military intervention than men.

- **Race and ethnicity:** These are exceptionally important factors in the study of public opinion. The direction and intensity of African American and Hispanic opinions on a variety of hot-button issues often are quite different from those of whites. For example, whites are much more likely to support American military action abroad than are blacks or Hispanics. Differences can be seen in other issue areas. Guaranteeing government sponsored health insurance, for example, is a hot-button issue with Hispanic voters, with 61 percent favoring it.

- **Age:** Age seems to have a decided effect on political socialization. Our view of the proper role of government, for example, often depends on the era in which we were born and the general tone of American culture at that time. Young people, for example, resist higher taxes to fund Medicare, while baby boomers and the elderly generally resist all efforts to limit Medicare or Social Security.

- **School:** Schools educate children in American values such as democracy and capitalism, both through academics and through practices such as reciting the Pledge of Allegiance. A good education also tends to produce more politically active and aware citizens. In addition to the influence of the educational system, young people are also influenced by members of their peer groups when formulating their political attitudes and beliefs.

- **Peers:** Parental influences are greatest from birth to age five, but then a child's peer group becomes increasingly important as the child gets older, especially as he or she gets into middle school or high school.

- **The mass media:** Most Americans, especially children and teenagers, watch a significant amount of **television.** Political information is often disseminated through TV. Younger people are much less likely to watch the news than are adults, however, and as a result, the political knowledge of young people today is significantly lower than that of young people a few decades ago.

- **Cues from Leaders or Opinion Makers:** Political leaders, members of the news media, and a host of other experts have regular opportunities to influence public opinion because of the lack of deep conviction with which most Americans hold their political beliefs.

- **Political Knowledge:** Although few citizens know everything about all of the candidates and issues in a particular election, they can, and often do, know enough to impose their views and values as to the general direction the nation should take.

Toward Reform: The Effects of Public Opinion on Government and Politics

- **Founder's belief:** "All government rests on public opinion" ~ *The Federalist Papers*.

- **Contemporary example of interplay between polls and policy:** George W. Bush wanted to reform on reforming Social Security. However, when poll after poll showed little support for change, the administration pulled back on its support for reform. Examples such as this show how the public's views, registered through public opinion polls, can affect policy.

For Additional Review

Brainstorm a list of topics in the news. Then write down what you think the conservative and the liberal opinion about each issue would be. If you are not sure, do some library or Internet research to find out.

Multiple-Choice Questions

1. Which of the following is a random sample?
(A) interviewing people in a nonsystematic fashion
(B) a selection mechanism that gives each person an equal chance of being selected
(C) going up to people on the street and asking for their opinions
(D) asking every student in the Introduction to Psychology course to fill out a survey
(E) putting your survey on the web and asking readers to fill it out

2. The process through which people learn their knowledge, feelings, and evaluations about politics is called
(A) political socialization.
(B) political efficacy.
(C) propaganda acquisition.
(D) political ideology.
(E) public opinion.

3. Sampling error refers to
(A) the pollster making mistakes in selecting a sample.
(B) the sample not being representative of the population.
(C) coding mistakes that mean that responses are not accurately reported.
(D) the level of confidence in the findings of a public opinion poll.
(E) using a nonrandom procedure for drawing a sample of the population.

4. The failure of the 1936 *Literary Digest* poll occurred because
(A) the sample was too small to predict the outcome of the election.
(B) the questions on the survey were not phrased to obtain accurate results.
(C) mail surveys rarely can be representative of the population.
(D) the survey oversampled voters with high incomes.
(E) computer technology of the day was inadequate to process the data accurately.

5. Which type of poll is most likely to be used by the media to predict the outcome of an election?
(A) a benchmark poll
(B) an exit poll
(C) a matchup poll
(D) a focus group poll
(E) a purposive poll

6. Which of the following is true?

I. Children tend to support the same party as their parents.
II. Americans who are not very knowledgeable about politics tend to not vote.
III. Younger Americans today are more informed about politics than those of 50 years ago.
IV. Women hold more liberal attitudes than men.

(A) I, IV
(B) I, II, III
(C) II, III, IV
(D) II, IV
(E) I, II, IV

7. An example of the "gender gap" in American politics would be that women
(A) are denied equal protection of the law in economic matters in the United States.
(B) cannot take combat roles in the military.
(C) voted Barack Obama in substantially greater numbers than John McCain.
(D) are proportionally underrepresented among members of Congress.
(E) live on average longer than men, affecting their Social Security costs.

8. Which of the following questions uses the most neutral phrasing?
(A) "Do you favor Gestapo-style tactics to prevent smoking?"
(B) "Do you favor government infringement on your freedom to smoke?"
(C) "Do you favor government efforts to force its will on law-abiding Americans who smoke?"
(D) "Do you favor turning smokers into criminals or do you support the freedoms guaranteed by our Constitution?"
(E) "Do you favor government efforts to reduce smoking?"

9. Which of the following is a major weakness of public opinion polls?
(A) Polls can only measure the opinions of political elites.
(B) It is difficult to measure the intensity of feelings about issues.
(C) Polls are so fraught with error that their results are nearly meaningless.
(D) The opinions of the poor and homeless are overrepresented.
(E) All of the above.

10. Which of the following polls is most likely to help a candidate evaluate the short-term effect of a certain campaign event?
(A) an exit poll
(B) a tracking poll
(C) a push poll
(D) a stratified sample
(E) a cross-sectional poll

Free-Response Questions

1. List the major demographic and social factors that shape a person's political opinions and how they affect them. Based on that, explain how likely it would be for an average baby boom Latina female to support a conservative candidate calling for the privatization of Social Security and an increased military effort in Afghanistan.

2. One of the most consistent ways that Americans learn about public opinion is through polling.

   a. Describe the advantage of a random sample for public opinion polling over a nonrandom sample.

   b. Describe one advantage and one disadvantage of telephone surveys compared to person-to-person interviewing.

   c. Describe what public opinion polls tell us about Americans' levels of political information.

   d. Describe what public opinion polls tell us about Americans' political attitudes.

ANSWERS AND EXPLANATIONS

Multiple-Choice Questions

- **1. (B) is correct.** A random sample is one in which each person in the population being sampled has an equal chance of being selected. Although picking people walking down the street, or taking a particular class, or visiting a specific website does have an element of randomness, it does not necessarily give everyone in the population being sampled the ability to be in the sample.

- **2. (A) is correct.** Political socialization is defined in the root of the question. Each of the other answers refers to a different concept.

- **3. (B) is correct.** In all sampling, there is a possibility that the sample drawn is not perfectly reflective of the population as a whole. In random sampling, the likelihood of such error can be estimated mathematically. The other answers all can cause error as well, but they occur in ways that cannot be estimated and are therefore not "sampling error."

- **4. (D) is correct.** The 1936 *Literary Digest* poll is perhaps the most famous example of the problem of drawing a nonrepresentative sample. By sending surveys only to those with cars and telephones during the depths of the Great Depression, the magazine unwittingly created a sample that was wildly at variance with the population as a whole. Because of this, the poll wrongly predicted that Alf Landon would win the presidency, when he actually lost in a landslide.

- **5. (B) is correct.** Exit polls are used by media on Election Days to predict the outcome of an election. Other possible answers are polls that can be used during campaigns, but for different purposes.

- **6. (A) is correct.** Children tend to support the same party as their parents, and women generally hold more liberal attitudes than men. Studies show that Americans' degree of knowledge of history, politics, and the issue positions of candidates is less than the percentage of the population that votes, showing that a number of Americans who are not very knowledgeable about politics feel they know enough to give their input on the direction the country should take. Younger Americans today are less informed about politics than those of 50 years ago.

- **7. (C) is correct.** All of the possible answers refer to real and fictional differences between men and women. However, in politics, the gender gap only refers to the fact that since 1980, women have tended to be more supportive of Democrats than have men. The 2008 election was no exception, with 56 percent of women voting for Obama and only 49 percent of men.

- **8. (E) is correct.** "Do you favor government efforts to reduce smoking" is the most neutral phrasing because it does not use wording that plays on negative or positive feelings that people might have. The other phrasings attempt to associate smoking with the deeply held beliefs of individual liberty and limited government, which are an integral part of American political culture.

- **9. (B) is correct.** While a respondent might answer affirmatively to any question, it is likely that his or her feelings about issues such as abortion, the death penalty, or support for U.S. troops in Afghanistan or Iraq are much more intense than their feelings about the Electoral College or types of voting machines. Yet, polls rarely have mechanisms to differentiate degree of passion on an issue.

- **10. (B) is correct**. Tracking polls enable a campaign to chart its daily rise or fall in support.

Free-Response Questions

This rubric provides examples of many, but not all, of the possible correct responses to the free-response questions. Occasionally, there will be weaknesses pointed out in the suggested answer, providing students with examples of what to avoid.

1. Gender has a definite noticeable impact on one's political socialization. From the time that the earliest public opinion polls were taken, women have held more liberal attitudes than men about social welfare issues such as education, juvenile justice, capital punishment, and the environment. Public opinion polls have also found that women hold more negative views about war and military intervention than men.

    Race and ethnicity are exceptionally important factors in the study of public opinion. The direction and intensity of African American and Hispanic opinions on a variety of hot-button issues often are quite different from those of whites. For example, whites are much more likely to support American military action abroad than are blacks or Hispanics. Differences can be seen in other issue areas. Guaranteeing government sponsored health insurance, for example, is a hot-button issue with Hispanic voters, with 61 percent favoring it.

    Age seems to have a decided effect on political socialization. Our view of the proper role of government, for example, often depends on the era in which we were born and the general tone of American culture at that time. Young people, for example, resist higher taxes to fund Medicare, while baby boomers and the elderly generally resist all efforts to limit Medicare or Social Security.

    As a female, our hypothetical voter would already be inclined to oppose a conservative, especially one that emphasizes increased American military operations abroad. These tendencies to oppose the hypothetical candidate would be reinforced by the candidate's stand in favor of cutting Social Security. Baby boomers generally oppose all efforts to limit Medicare or Social Security.

2.

    a. A random sample is better than a nonrandom sample because random people can answer questions better than selected people. Random people can give "real" answers, while selected people are members of the elite and don't really know what the people are thinking. As a result, a random sample gives everyone an equal chance of being selected and therefore is more likely to be representative of the population as a whole. With a nonrandom sample, we cannot estimate how likely the sample is to represent the people.

b. Telephone surveys are both great and bad. They are great because everyone with a phone can be surveyed. They are bad because people without telephones cannot be surveyed.

c. Surveys tell us that Americans don't know much about politics. They can't answer even simple questions well. For example, in his segment, "Jaywalking," Jay Leno shows that people are really dumb in answering questions about politics.   *This paragraph almost earns a point for saying that people are not well informed. But the example is not from a survey, and there is no discussion of what polls tell us about attitudes.*

CHAPTER 12

Political Parties

Political parties are the main vehicles for nominating candidates and running campaigns. Through elections, they serve as **linkage institutions** that help bring the concerns of the electorate to the political arena. Political parties also unite groups of politicians and the electorate by offering an ideological framework with which people can choose to identify themselves. The United States has for the most part always had a **two-party system. Party competition** is the battle between Democrats and Republicans for the control of public offices.

The Roots of the Two-Party System

- A **political party** is an organized effort by officeholders, candidates, activists, and voters to pursue their common interests by gaining and exercising power through the electoral process.

- Most democratic nations have multiparty systems that allow many interests to be represented. The United States, however, has mainly had a two-party system. Historians and political scientists consider America to have had three separate two-party systems.

- **The First Party System: Federalists and Democratic Republicans 1796–1824**

  - Alexander Hamilton's short-lived **Federalist** Party was the first political party.

  - Thomas Jefferson's **Democratic-Republicans** won all presidential elections from 1800 to 1824.

- **The Second Party System: Democrats and Whigs 1828–1856**

  - **Democrats:** Andrew Jackson appealed to the masses rather than to the elite, and he formed a new coalition and, ultimately, the Democratic Party.

  - **The Whig Party** was the opposition party, although it had little political success.

- **The Third Party System: Democrats and Republicans 1860–present**

  - A **political machine** is a party organization that recruits voter loyalty with tangible incentives and is characterized by a high degree of control over member activity. It dominated in the "Golden Age" of parties from the Civil War to the 1920s.

  - The modern era seems very different from the Golden Age of parties. Many social, political, technological, and governmental changes have contributed to changes in the nature of the national parties since the 1920s.

    - The government assumed important functions previously performed by the parties, such as printing ballots and conducting elections.

    - The government started social welfare services. Beginning in the 1930s with Franklin Roosevelt's New Deal, social services began to be seen as a right of citizenship rather than as a privilege extended in exchange for a person's support of a party.

  - **Candidate-centered politics:** Politics that focuses directly on the candidates, their particular issues, and character, rather than on party affiliation.

  - **Party realignment:** A shifting of party coalition groupings in the electorate that remains in place for several elections.

  - **Critical election:** An election that signals a party realignment through voter polarization around new issues.

  - **Secular realignment:** The gradual rearrangement of party coalitions, based more on demographic shifts than on shocks to the political system.

The Organization of the American Party System

- **National committees:** Each of the two major parties maintains not only a national committee, but also a House party committee and a Senate party committee. The national committee focuses primarily on aiding presidential campaigns and conducting general party-building activities, while the House and Senate campaign committees work primarily to maximize the number of seats held by their respective parties in Congress.

- **National committee chair:** The key national party official is the chairperson of the national committee. Although the chair is formally elected by the national committee, he or she is usually selected by the sitting president or newly nominated presidential candidate, who is accorded the right to name the individual for at least the duration of the campaign. Only the post-campaign, out-of-power party committee actually has the authority to appoint a chairperson independently.

- **National convention:** A party meeting held in the presidential election year for the purposes of nominating a presidential and vice-presidential ticket and adopting a platform.

- **Superdelegate:** Delegate slot to the Democratic Party's national convention that is reserved for an elected party official, whose vote at the convention is not pledged to individual candidates.

- **State parties:** Parties are structurally based in the states and localities. Except for the campaign finance arena, virtually all government regulation of political parties is left to the states. The state governing body supervising this collection of local party organizations is usually called the state central (or executive) committee. Its members come from all major geographic units, as determined by and selected under state law.

- **Think tank:** Institutional collection of policy-oriented researchers and academics who are sources of policy ideas.

- **Soft money:** The virtually unregulated money funneled through political parties for party-building purposes, such as get-out-the-vote efforts and issue ads. Banned after 2002.

Activities of American Political Parties

- **Raising money:** Political parties, particularly during midterm and presidential election years, spend a great deal of time raising and disseminating money for candidates. The parties are able to raise huge sums of money because they have developed networks of donors who are reached by a variety of methods. Both parties have sizable mailing, emailing, and phone lists of several million people who are proven donors.

- **Mobilizing support:** Parties help candidates recruit voters and build support for ideas.

- **National party platform:** A statement of the general and specific philosophy and policy goals of a political party, usually promulgated at the national convention.

- **The congressional party:** Parties organize and operate Congress.

- **The presidential party:** The party of the president that captures the public imagination and shapes the electorate's opinion of the two parties.

- **The parties and the judiciary:** Judges are creatures of the political process, and their posts are considered patronage plums. Judges appointed by presidents or governors are chosen for their abilities, but also increasingly as representatives of some particular philosophy or approach to government.

- **The parties and state government:** The party's relationship to the legislature, the executive, and the judiciary apply to those branches at the state level, and is similar to that of the national level, with one important difference. Governors in many states have greater influence over their party's organizations and legislators than the president does.

- **Providing linkage:** Parties provide linkage between branches and levels of government and between voters and candidates.

- **Accountability:** Candidates on the campaign trail and elected party leaders in office are required from time to time to account for their performance at party-sponsored forums, nominating primaries, and conventions.

- **Party identification:** A citizen's personal affinity for a political party, usually expressed by a tendency to vote for the candidates of that party.

    o **Family:** Parents are the single greatest influence in establishing a person's first party identification. Parents who are politically active and share the same party identification raise children who will be strong party identifiers, whereas parents without party affiliations or with mixed affiliations produce offspring more likely to be independents.

    o Geographic region: Regions in which one immigrant group dominates generally embrace the political attitudes of the political leaders of that group. One of the most long-standing and dramatic regional differences in the United States is that between the South and the North. The South has continued to lag behind the rest of the nation in support for civil rights, while continuing to favor return of power to the states at the expense of the national government. The interior West, too, appears different from other sections of the nation. Many who have sought refuge there are staunchly against governmental action.

    o Gender: Women, and particularly unmarried women, are more likely to be Democrats, while white men are increasingly becoming the core of the Republican Party. Women have held more liberal attitudes about social welfare issues such as education, juvenile justice, capital punishment, and the environment. This phenomenon has been called the gender gap. Over the last two decades, and especially in the aftermath of the 9/11 attacks, the noticeable gap between the overall male and female attitudes toward use of the military has dropped, yet the others differences still remain.

    o Race and ethnicity: Members of minority groups tend to be more liberal on average. Differences in political socialization between ethnic groups appear at a very early age. Young African American children, for example, generally show very positive feelings about American society and political processes, but this attachment lessens considerably over time, falling in line with the more-critical-than-average view adult African Americans have for government. Also, there appears to be a degree of homogeneity among members of an ethnic group about the political issues that directly affect that group. For example, Hispanics tend to favor bilingual education more than whites or African Americans.

- o Age and age cohort: One's attitudes about the proper role of government are often reflective of the era in which an individual was born. Older people continue to be affected by having lived through the Great Depression and World War II. One political scientist predicts that as baby boomers age, the age gap in political beliefs about political issues, especially governmental programs, will increase. Young people, for example, resist higher taxes to fund Medicare, while the elderly resist all efforts to limit Medicare or Social Security.

- o Social and economic factors: Occupation, income, and education are closely related, so many of the same partisan patterns appear in all three classifications. Democrats lead substantially among trial lawyers, educators, blue-collar workers, and other groups. Labor union members are also Democrats by nearly two to one. The GOP remains predominant among executives, professionals, and white-collar workers, and women who do not work outside the home tend to be conservative and favor the Republicans.

- o Religious groups and associations: These groups also influence political attitudes. For example, during the last decade, fundamentalist Christians have played an ever-increasing role in the politics of the United States.

Minor Parties in the American Two-Party System

- **Third parties** occasionally arise to challenge the two major parties, but they rarely gain enough support to put a candidate in office.

  - Some parties form around a specific cause, such as the Greens, with their emphasis on environmental issues.

  - Some become the vehicle of economic protest, like the Populists of the 1890s.

  - Some are ideologically based, like the Socialists or Libertarians.

  - Some form around a specific individual, like Theodore Roosevelt's Bull Moose Party.

  - Some have a regional basis, like the states' rights Dixiecrat Party in the 1940s.

- Though they rarely win, third-party candidates do force particular issues onto the political agenda and allow Americans to express their discontent with the two major parties.

- They may also shift the votes of the electorate. Ross Perot is often credited with costing George Bush a second term in 1992, by appealing to a large number of conservative voters who might otherwise have voted for Bush. Some cite Ralph Nader as the primary reason for Al Gore's defeat in 2000, because he pulled much of his support from liberal voters.

- Third parties achieve their greatest successes when they incorporate new ideas or alienated groups, or nominate attractive candidates as their standard-bearers. Third parties do best when declining trust in the two major political parties plagues the electorate. Usually, though, third parties' ideas are eventually co-opted by one of the two major parties, each of them eager to take the politically popular issue that gave rise to the third party and make it their own, in order to secure the allegiance of the third party's supporters.

- **Proportional representation:** A voting system that apportions legislative seats according to the percentage of the vote won by a particular political party.

- **Winner-take-all system:** An electoral system in which the party that receives at least one more vote than any other party wins the election.

Toward Reform: Two Parties Endure

- **Dealignment** is a general decline in party identification and loyalty in the electorate.

- **Strengths of the current party system:**

  - Both major parties exhibit flexibility and pragmatism, which help ensure their survival.

  - They have almost always provided strong competition for each other and the voters at the national level. Of the 30 presidential elections from 1884 to 2008, for instance, the Republicans won 17 and the Democrats 15.

  - The sharp rise in party unity scores in Congress discussed earlier suggests that the party in government is alive and well.

  - The unprecedented fundraising of the party organizations suggests, moreover, that political parties are here to stay.

For Additional Review

Look at the list of United States presidents in the appendix at the back of your book. When did the presidency change hands between parties? What significant social and economic factors might have played a role in that transition? Note also the occurrences of third-party nominees. Select a third party that is unfamiliar to you and learn more about it in an encyclopedia or other reference book.

Multiple-Choice Questions

1. All of the following are activities of political parties EXCEPT
(A)   dictating policies.
(B)   recruiting candidates and campaign workers.
(C)   providing continuity in the wake of changing issues and personalities.
(D)   giving cues to voters.
(E)   coordinating policymaking between branches and levels of government.

2. The U.S. has a "single member, plurality" system, often referred to as
(A)   direct representation.
(B)   proportional representation.
(C)   winner-take-all.
(D)   winner-take-most.
(E)   winner-take-some.

3. Political machines recruited party members by
(A)   providing tremendous leeway in how party members serve the party.
(B)   offering them tangible incentives, such as jobs.
(C)   threatening physical violence.
(D)   relying on the merit principle when hiring employees.
(E)   working through unions and targeting groups, such as machinists and other factory workers.

4. Which of the following groups is likely to be Democratic?
I. white-collar workers
II. blue-collar workers
III. trial lawyers
IV. women who do not work outside the home

(A)   I and IV
(B)   II and III
(C)   I, II, and III.
(D)   I and III
(E)   I, II, III, and IV

5. Which of the following is the best definition of a realignment?
(A)   the abandonment of citizens from the two major parties to be independent
(B)   the requirement that members of a party vote together
(C)   the party that controls the White House loses control in Congress
(D)   a shifting of party coalition groupings in the electorate that remains in place for several elections
(E)   the emergence of many third parties

6. A citizen's personal affinity for a political party, which results in the citizen voting for candidates of that political party, is known as party
(A) identification.
(B) registration.
(C) alignment.
(D) coalition.
(E) representation.

7. Which of the following statements about political parties is accurate?
(A) The U.S. has never had a third party.
(B) The Democratic and Republican parties have been on the presidential ballot for every election since the presidency of George Washington.
(C) Third parties are prohibited by the Constitution.
(D) Third parties have frequently captured the White House.
(E)   While the Democrats and Republicans have dominated American politics, they have also seen competition from a wide variety of third parties.

8. Many Americans do not associate with either major political party and instead claim to "vote for the ___ and not the ___."
(A) party; person
(B) person; party
(C) challenger; incumbent
(D) free-rider; policy entrepreneur
(E) underdog; front-runner

9. A superdelegate is
(A) a spokesperson and arbitrator for the party during the four years between elections.
(B) a delegate to the Democratic Party's national convention that is reserved for an elected party official, whose vote at the convention is not pledged to individual candidates.
(C) someone elected in a winner-take-all system.
(D) someone selected by a proportional representation election.
(E) someone who won a seat by both proportional representation and winner-take-all district voting.

10. The events in which the parties formally nominate their candidates for the presidency are
(A) critical elections.
(B) national conventions.
(C) open primaries.
(D) closed primaries.
(E) national committees.

Free-Response Questions

1. The power of the political party has declined over the past 50 years. Defend this thesis by defining and describing each of the terms below.

    a. dealignment

    b. political machine

    c. national party conventions

2. The Democratic and Republican parties have gone through several realignments.

    a. Define realignment.

    b. Identify one realignment for the Democratic Party and one for the Republican Party.

    c. Explain the significance of realignments for American politics.

ANSWERS AND EXPLANATIONS

Multiple-Choice Questions

- **1. (A) is correct.** American political parties may articulate policy preferences, but they are unable to dictate policy. They do however recruit candidates and campaign workers, provide continuity, give cues to voters, and coordinate policymaking.

- **2. (C) is correct.** At national level elections in the U.S. use a system in which the party that receives at least one more vote than any other party wins the seat in question.

- **3. (B) is correct.** The party machines relied on providing jobs and favors to recruit and retain the loyalty of voters.

- **4. (B) is correct.** White-collar workers and women who do not work outside the home tend to favor Republicans, while blue-collar workers and trial lawyers favor Democrats.

- **5. (D) is correct.** Realignments are major changes of the groups that make up the coalition that supports each party. The change must remain in place for several elections.

- **6. (A) is correct.** A citizen's personal affinity for a political party, usually expressed by a tendency to vote for the candidates of that party, is called the citizen's party identification.

- **7. (E) is correct.** Although third-party candidates rarely win elections, several have appeared on the ballot over the years and have had some affect on the political debate, and possibly the outcome of elections.

- **8. (B) is correct.** With the decline in party identification, the plurality of voters considered themselves **Independent** rather than Democratic or Republican, and many Americans insist that they vote for "the person, not the party."

- **9. (A) is correct.** A superdelegate is a delegate to the Democratic Party's national convention that is reserved for an elected party official, whose vote at the convention is not pledged to individual candidates.

- **10. (B) is correct.** Candidates for the presidency are formally selected at a national convention.

Free-Response Questions

This rubric provides examples of many, but not all, of the possible correct responses to the free-response questions.

1.

a. The power of the parties has declined over the past 100 years. This is due to a dealignment movement. Dealignment refers to the abandonment of citizen's affiliations with the two major political parties to become "independent" voters. Such independent or "swing voters" have hurt the power of the party because members of each party must now battle for the ideological center in order to win an election. The party can no longer depend on a large number of citizens to vote a straight ticket, and thus the election results become less predictable. Also, presidents are less likely to staff government with party loyalists, and are more likely to turn to independents.

b. The decline of the party machine has also hurt the power of the party. The party machine can be described as a party organization with lots of power in large cities. Such a machine once guaranteed social services and jobs to new immigrants, ran conventions, and staffed city government. This created a group of party loyalists that lasted for generations. Some of these activities became illegal, causing the party to lose strength as the generations of party loyalists diminished.

c. Finally, the national party convention was once a source of party strength, but this strength has diminished greatly. The national party used to determine who the nominee would be for the presidency, with no voter involvement at all. The progressive reforms stripped this power from the party at the state level and eventually all states began holding primaries and caucuses to determine the nominee, taking the power away from the party.

2. A realignment usually occurs after a critical election. A realignment marks a major change in the nature of the political party. The change occurs in both the demographic groups that once supported the party as well as the agenda of the party. In a realignment, the party that was once the majority usually becomes the minority. The change is national as well as local, and the change is not simply marked by one election but has some permanence.

Most political scientists argue that there have been four major realigning periods. Perhaps the most remembered realignment for the Republican Party took place after the election of 1860—sometimes referred to as the "birth of the Republican Party." The new president, Abraham Lincoln, had captured a new group of voters and his party dominated politics (the party realigned several times after that). Perhaps the most remembered realignment for the Democratic Party came after the election of 1932. Franklin D. Roosevelt began a "New Deal" coalition, which would unify the Democratic Party for years to come.

Realignments are significant to American politics because they mark major changes in the nature of the party, and the party emerges as a completely different organization. Understanding realignments helps to explain how parties have changed. For example, it is surprising to some that Thomas Jefferson was a Democrat because he was a states' rights advocate, and the Democratic Party today has advocated federal power in most domestic policy areas. The explanation for this is that the Democratic Party has realigned since Thomas Jefferson was a member of the party.

CHAPTER 13

Voting and Elections

This chapter focuses on patterns of voting over time, the purposes served by elections, and the various kinds of elections held in the United States. Presidential and congressional elections are given special attention, as their rich histories tell us a great deal about the American people and their changing hopes and needs. We conclude by returning to contemporary presidential elections and addressing key aspects of electoral reform.

Roots of American Elections

- **Electorate:** The citizens eligible to vote.

- **Mandate:** A command, indicated by an electorate's votes, for the elected officials to carry out a party platform or policy agenda.

Elections in the United States

- **Authoritarian system:** A system of government that bases its rule on force rather than consent of the governed.

- **Electorate:** The citizens eligible to vote.

- **Mandate:** A command, indicated by an electorate's votes, for the elected officials to carry out their platforms.

- **Primary election:** Election in which voters decide which of the candidates within a party will represent the party in the general election.

- **Closed primary:** A primary election in which only a party's registered voters are eligible to vote.

- **Open primary:** A primary in which party members, independents, and sometimes members of the other party are allowed to vote.

- **Crossover voting:** Participation in the primary of a party with which the voter is not affiliated.

- **Raiding:** An organized attempt by voters of one party to influence the primary results of the other party.

- **Runoff primary:** A second primary election between the two candidates receiving the greatest number of votes in the first primary.

- **General election:** Election in which voters decide which candidates will actually fill elective public offices.

- **Ballot measure:** An election option such as the initiative or referendum that enables voters to enact public policy.

- **Initiative:** An election that allows citizens to propose legislation and submit it to the state electorate for popular vote.

- **Referendum:** An election whereby the state legislature submits proposed legislation to the state's voters for approval.

- **Recall:** An election in which voters can remove an incumbent from office by popular vote.

Presidential Elections

- **Methods of selecting the nominee:**

    - **Winner-take-all primary:** The candidate who wins the most votes in a state secures all of that state's delegates.

    - **Proportional representation primary:** Candidates who secure a threshold percentage of votes are awarded delegates in proportion to the number of popular votes won.

    - **Caucus:** Under this system, party members meet in small groups throughout a state to discuss and select the party's delegates to the national convention.

- **Frontloading:** The tendency of states to choose an early date on the primary calendar. A frontloaded primary schedule generally benefits the front-runner, since opponents have little time to turn the contest around once they fall behind. It also benefits the candidate who wins the "invisible primary," that is, the one who can raise the bulk of the money *before* the nomination season begins.

- **Party conventions:** Election year gatherings that formally draft the party's platform and nominate the party's candidate for president.

    - **Unit rule:** A traditional party practice under which the majority of a state delegation can force the minority to vote for its candidate, a practice now abolished by the Democratic Party.

    - **Superdelegate:** Delegate slot to the Democratic Party's national convention that is reserved for an elected party official.

- **Electoral College:** Representatives of each state who cast the final ballots that actually elect a president. Each state has as many electors as it has senators and representatives in Congress. Almost all states are **winner-take-all:** The candidate who receives the highest popular vote in the state gets all of that state's electoral votes.

- **Elector:** Member of the Electoral College chosen by methods determined in each state.

- **The Twelfth Amendment:** The constitutional foundation for presidential elections today, it provides for separate elections for president and vice president. Previously, in the event of a tie, or if no candidate received a majority of the total number of electors, the election still went to the House of Representatives. Now, however, each state delegation would have one vote to cast for one of the three candidates who had received the greatest number of electoral votes.

- **Reapportionment:** The reallocation of the number of seats in the House of Representatives after each decennial census. (Remember, the number of electoral votes for each state changes with the number of its House seats.)

- **Popular vote loser, Electoral College winner**
  - 1876: Hayes over Tilden

  - 1888: Harrison over incumbent president Cleveland

  - 2000: Bush over Gore

  - Coincidentally, all cases involved Republicans winning the Electoral College and Democrats winning the popular vote.

Congressional Elections

- **Incumbency:** The current system enhances the advantages of **incumbency** (that is, already being in office). Those in office tend to remain in office.

- **Redistricting:** Redrawing congressional districts to reflect increases or decreases in seats allotted to the states as well as population shifts within a state, generally done in conjunction with reapportionment.

- **Gerrymandering:** The legislative process through which the majority party in each statehouse tries to assure that the maximum number of representatives from its political party can be elected to Congress through the redrawing of legislative districts.

- **Midterm election:** An election that takes place in the middle of a presidential term.

Patterns in Vote Choice

- **Conventional political participation:** Political participation that attempts to influence the political process through well-accepted forms of persuasion, such as voting or letter writing.

- **Unconventional political participation:** Political participation that attempts to influence the political process through unusual or extreme measures, such as protests, boycotts, and picketing.

- **Party identification** remains the most powerful predictor of vote choice. Stated simply, self-described Democrats tend to vote for Democratic candidates and self-described Republicans tend to vote for Republican candidates.

- **Ticket-splitting:** The practice of voting for candidates from different parties for various offices in the same election.

- **Ideology** represents one of the most significant divisions in contemporary American politics. Liberals, generally speaking, favor government involvement in social programs and are committed to the ideals of tolerance and social justice. Conservatives, on the other hand, are dedicated to the ideals of individualism and market-based competition, and they tend to view government as a necessary evil rather than an agent of social improvement. Moderates lie somewhere between liberals and conservatives on the ideological spectrum; they favor conservative positions on some issues and liberal positions on others. Not surprisingly, ideology is very closely related to vote choice. Liberals tend to vote for Democrats, and conservatives tend to vote for Republicans.

  - **Racial and ethnic groups** tend to vote in distinct patterns. While whites have shown an increasing tendency to vote Republican, African American voters remain overwhelmingly Democratic in their voting decisions. Hispanics also tend to identify with and vote for Democrats, although not as monolithically as do African Americans.

  - **Gender:** Women, and particularly unmarried women, are more likely to be Democrats, while white men are increasingly becoming the core of the Republican Party. Women have held more liberal attitudes about social welfare issues such as education, juvenile justice, capital punishment, and the environment. This phenomenon has been called the gender gap. Over the last two decades, and especially in the aftermath of the 9/11 attacks, the noticeable gap between the overall male and female attitudes toward use of the military has dropped, yet the others differences still remain.

  - **Religious groups and associations:** These groups also influence political attitudes. For example, during the last decade, fundamentalist Christians have played an ever-increasing role in the politics of the United States.

- **Turnout** is the proportion of the voting-age public that votes.

- **Retrospective judgment:** A voter's evaluation of the performance of the party in power.

- **Prospective judgment:** A voter's evaluation of a candidate based on what he or she pledges to do about an issue if elected.

- Various factors affect patterns in voter turnout.

  - **Education and income:** Other things being equal, college graduates are much more likely to vote than those with less education. A considerably higher percentage of citizens with annual incomes over $65,000 vote than do citizens with incomes under $35,000.

  - **Age:** A much higher percentage of citizens age 30 and older vote than do citizens younger than 30, although voter turnout decreases over the age of 70.

  - **Gender:** Recent polls suggest that today women vote at the same rate as men or at a slightly higher rate. Since women comprise slightly more than 50 percent of the U.S. population, they now account for a majority of the American electorate.

  - **Race and ethnicity:** Whites still tend to vote more regularly than do African Americans, Hispanics, and other minority groups.

  - **Group membership:** Individuals who are members of civic organizations, trade and professional organizations, and labor unions are more likely to vote and participate in politics than those who are not members of these or similar types of groups. People who more frequently attend church or other religious services, moreover, also are more likely to vote than people who rarely attend or do not belong to religious institutions.

  - **Interest in politics:** It is believed that interest serves as a gateway that leads people to gather information about candidates and to more fully participate in the political process, including voting.

Toward Reform: Problems with Voter Turnout

- The United States has one of the lowest voter participation rates of any nation in the industrialized world, fluctuating from around 50 to 60 percent. Political scientists attribute this to several factors:

  - **Time conflicts:** One-fifth of registered voters cite being too busy or having conflicting work or school schedules as a reason for not voting.

- **Difficulty of registration:** While nearly every other democratic country places the burden of registration on the government rather than on the individual, in the United States individuals must assume the responsibility of registering.

- **Difficulty of absentee voting:** Recent literature in political science links liberalized absentee voting rules and higher turnout.

- **Number of elections:** Another explanation for low voter turnout in the United States is the sheer number and frequency of elections. According to a study by the International Institute for Democracy and Electoral Assistance, the United States typically holds twice as many national elections as other Western democracies.

- **Voter apathy** negatively affects turnout.

- **Weakened influence of political parties:** Political parties today are not as effective as they once were in mobilizing voters, ensuring that they are registered, and getting them to the polls.

Ways to improve voter turnout

- Make Election Day a national holiday.

- Enable early voting.

- **Online and mail voting:** Rightly or wrongly, many Americans equate Internet voting with the ideals of instant democracy and greater citizen participation. To date, persistent security concerns have hampered widespread adoption of online voting practices. The use of mail-in ballots, whereby registered voters are mailed ballots and given several weeks to mail them back with their votes, has been found to increase participation. Currently, Oregon and Washington are the only states that vote almost entirely by mail-in ballots.

- **Election Day registration**: In the nine states that permit this, turnout has averaged about 11 percentage points higher in recent elections than in other states, supporting the long-held claim by reformers that voter turnout could be increased if registering to vote were made simpler for citizens.

- **Modernizing the ballot:** The use of electronic voting systems such as touch-screen machines and optical scan readers has increased rapidly since 2000. Critics believe that the lack of a paper trail leaves electronic machines vulnerable to fraud, and they worry that the machines could crash during an election. Still others believe the machines are not worth the additional cost.

- **The National Voter Registration Act of 1993 (the Motor Voter Act)** was an attempt to ease the bureaucratic hurdles associated with registering to vote by requiring states to provide the opportunity to register through drivers' license agencies, public assistance agencies, and the mail.

For Additional Review

The 2000 presidential election was an extraordinary political event for many reasons. Not only was it one of the few elections in American history in which a candidate won the popular vote but lost the electoral vote, it was also the first presidency to be determined ultimately by the Supreme Court. Read more about the controversies of this election at www.supremecourtus.gov/florida.html

Multiple-Choice Questions

1. When does a referendum occur in the United States?
   (A) once every four years, when presidential elections occur
   (B) when states give voters an opportunity to vote on legislation
   (C) when citizens sign a petition to get a third party on the ballot
   (D) when citizens request that changes be made to the state's constitution
   (E) when citizens change their party affiliations

2. All of the following are true of the Electoral College system EXCEPT:
   (A) It is possible to win the electoral vote but lose the popular vote.
   (B) A majority of electors is required to win.
   (C) Electors are awarded proportionally in most states.
   (D) Candidates have historically focused campaigns on large states.
   (E) Many candidates today focus their campaigns on swing states.

3. Which of the following is an example of conventional political participation?
   (A) writing letters to members of Congress
   (B) launching a fake anthrax scare at the Capitol
   (C) launching a real anthrax scare at the Capitol
   (D) boycotting
   (E) protesting

4. In recent years, states have chosen early dates for their presidential primaries in order to gain influence in the process. This is called
   (A) influence peddling.
   (B) gerrymandering.
   (C) frontloading.
   (D) fish mongering.
   (E) primary staging.

5. Ticket-splitting refers to
   (A) participation in the primary of a party with which the voter is not affiliated.
   (B) voting for candidates of different parties for various offices in the same election.
   (C) a second election between the two candidates receiving the greatest number of votes in the first election.
   (D) when party members, independents, and members of the other party are allowed to participate in a primary election.
   (E) voting in the primary election of one party for some offices and in the primary of the other party for other offices.

6. In 1971, the voting age was lowered to 18 by the _____ Amendment.
(A) Twenty-Seventh
(B) Twenty-Sixth
(C) Twenty-Fifth
(D) Eighteenth
(E) Seventeenth

7. Which of the following has resulted in a definitive, noticeable increase in voter participation?
(A) voting by mail
(B) online voting
(C) same-day registration
(D) modernizing the ballot
(E) having highly polarized political parties

The demographic correlates of presidential voting behavior have changed in a number of important ways since 1960. When Kennedy was elected in 1960 Protestants and Catholics voted very differently, as Kennedy's Catholicism was a major issue during the campaign. Although John Kerry was the first major party nominee since Kennedy to be of the Catholic faith, Catholics were only slightly more likely to support him than Protestants. Today, the major difference along religious lines involves how often one attends religious services, with those who attend regularly being substantially more likely to support Republican presidential candidates. The least likely group to support Republicans these days is African-Americans. As you can see in data below, Kerry clearly drew more support from African Americans than did Kennedy. Another advantage that Democrats now enjoy is with female voters, who preferred Kerry by 7 percent more than men. Interestingly, women were actually slightly less likely than men to have supported the handsome JFK in 1960. Finally, the rapidly expanding Hispanic population in the U.S. has reshaped the electoral scene with their tendency to support Democratic candidates. Hispanics numbered only about 1 percent of voters.

	KENNEDY	NIXON	KERRY	BUSH
Protestant	36	63	40	59
Catholic	83	17	47	52
Jewish	89	11	74	25
Regularly attend religious services	49	50	39	60
Often attend regligious services	36	64	49	50
Seldom attend religious services	55	44	54	45
Never attend religious services	51	49	62	36
White	48	52	41	58
African American	71	29	88	11
Hispanic	NA	NA	57	40
Male	52	48	44	55
Female	47	53	51	48
18–29	53	47	54	45
30–44	51	49	46	53
45–64	50	50	47	52
65+	39	61	47	52
No HS diploma	55	45	50	49
High school diploma	52	48	47	52
Some college	33	67	46	54
College degree	38	62	49	50

Source: 1960 National Election Study and 2004 National Voter Exit Poll.

7. Which of the following can be concluded from the preceding table?
(A) Catholic voters were more likely to vote Democrat in 1960 than they were in 2004.
(B) Jewish voters tended to choose Republican candidates in 1960 and 2004.
(C) Those who attend religious services voted Democrat in 1960 and 2004.
(D) Those with a college degree were overwhelmingly likely to vote Republican in 1960 and 2004.
(E) Female voters voted Republican in 1960 and 2004.

8. This group now represents a majority of the electorate because they are a majority of the population.
(A) white men
(B) women
(C) African Americans
(D) Hispanics
(E) senior citizens

9. When party members meet in small groups throughout the state to discuss and select the party's delegates to the national convention, this is known as
(A)   a winner-take-all primary.
(B)   proportional representation.
(C)   a caucus.
(D)   the district plan.
(E)   raiding.

10. How did the Twelfth Amendment change the Electoral College?
(A)   It mandated a direct popular election for president.
(B)   It stipulated that if there is no majority winner in the Electoral College, the Senate will select the president.
(C)   It established that the Electoral College would conduct separate elections for president and for vice president.
(D)   It mandated that electors vote for a president and a vice president from the same state.
(E)   It decreed that any disputes about the process of selecting a president will be decided by the Supreme Court. The first time this amendment was used was in *Bush* v. *Gore*.

Free-Response Questions

The demographic correlates of presidential voting behavior have changed in a number of important ways since 1960. When Kennedy was elected in 1960 Protestants and Catholics voted very differently, as Kennedy's Catholicism was a major issue during the campaign. Although John Kerry was the first major party nominee since Kennedy to be of the Catholic faith, Catholics were only slightly more likely to support him than Protestants. Today, the major difference along religious lines involves how often one attends religious services, with those who attend regularly being substantially more likely to support Republican presidential candidates. The least likely group to support Republicans these days is African-Americans. As you can see in data below, Kerry clearly drew more support from African Americans than did Kennedy. Another advantage that Democrats now enjoy is with female voters, who preferred Kerry by 7 percent more than men. Interestingly, women were actually slightly less likely than men to have supported the handsome JFK in 1960. Finally, the rapidly expanding Hispanic population in the U.S. has reshaped the electoral scene with their tendency to support Democratic candidates. Hispanics numbered only about 1 percent of voters.

	KENNEDY	NIXON	KERRY	BUSH
Protestant	36	63	40	59
Catholic	83	17	47	52
Jewish	89	11	74	25
Regularly attend religious services	49	50	39	60
Often attend regligious services	36	64	49	50
Seldom attend religious services	55	44	54	45
Never attend religious services	51	49	62	36
White	48	52	41	58
African American	71	29	88	11
Hispanic	NA	NA	57	40
Male	52	48	44	55
Female	47	53	51	48
18–29	53	47	54	45
30–44	51	49	46	53
45–64	50	50	47	52
65+	39	61	47	52
No HS diploma	55	45	50	49
High school diploma	52	48	47	52
Some college	33	67	46	54
College degree	38	62	49	50

Source: 1960 National Election Study and 2004 National Voter Exit Poll.

1.

    a. Identify two groups according to the preceding table that voted Democratic in both elections. Explain why the Democratic Party attracts these voters.

    b. Identify two groups according to the table above that voted Republican in both elections. Explain why the Republican Party attracts these voters.

THE DECLINE OF TURNOUT: 1892 to 2004

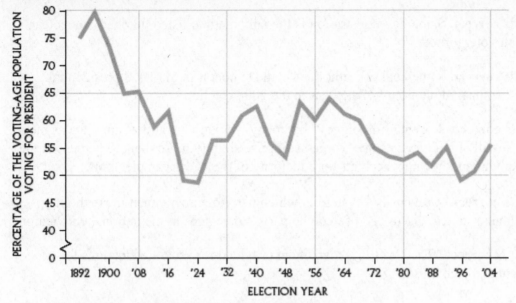

2. The chart above shows a recent trend in voting in American elections.

    a. Define voter turnout.

    b. Identify the trend in voter turnout displayed in the chart above.

    c. Identify two rules of the electoral process and explain how each impacted this trend.

    d. Describe one additional reason (not identified in *c*) to explain this trend.

ANSWERS AND EXPLANATIONS

Multiple-Choice Questions

- **1. (B) is correct.** Many states allow voters to vote on legislation. This is called a referendum.

- **2. (C) is correct.** The winner-take-all system is used in the Electoral College for all states except Maine and Nebraska.

- **3. (A) is correct.** Conventional political participation attempts to influence the political process through well-accepted, often moderate forms of persuasion, such as letter writing. The other choices are more extreme and are examples of unconventional participation.

- **4. (C) is correct.** The tendency of states to choose an early date on the primary calendar is called frontloading.

- **5. (B) is correct.** None of the other choices are amendments that deal with who is eligible to vote.

- **6. (C) is correct.** Same-day registration is the only method listed that has had a clear effect on voter turnout

- **7. (A) is correct.** 83 percent of Catholics voted Democrat in the 1960 presidential election compared with only 47 percent in the 2004 election.

- **8. (B) is correct.** Recent polls suggest that today women vote at the same rate as men or at a slightly higher rate. Since women comprise slightly more than 50 percent of the U.S. population, they now account for a majority of the American electorate.

- **9. (C) is correct.** A caucus is a system in which party members meet in small groups throughout a state to discuss and select the party's delegates to the national convention.

- **10. (C) is correct.** The Twelfth Amendment provided for separate elections for president and vice president.

Free-Response Questions

This rubric provides examples of many, but not all, of the possible correct responses to the free-response questions.

1.

a. The groups that voted Democratic in both elections were Jewish, African American, and the young. Jewish voters have typically favored religious freedoms and have sympathized with minority voters. These factors have attracted them to the Democratic Party because the Democratic Party is less likely to advocate prayer in school and supports minority rights. African American voters are attracted to the Democratic Party because the Democrats advocated legislation to improve civil rights in the 1960s and currently are more likely to support programs, such as affirmative action, that help them. The younger voters are more attracted to the Democratic Party because the Democrats are less socially conservative.

b. The groups that voted Republican in both elections include Protestant, white, and college-educated voters. Protestants are more likely to support the Republican Party because Republicans tend to support policies that religious individuals support—such as not allowing abortion or gay marriage, and advocating prayer in school. College-educated voters are more likely to have higher-paying jobs, which may lead them to support the low-tax platform of the Republican Party.

2.

a. Voter turnout can be defined as the percentage of citizens who are eligible to vote (and have completed voter registration) who vote in a given election.

b. The chart above shows that voter turnout has steadily declined over the years.

c. There are several rules of the electoral process that impacted this trend. One is the expansion in suffrage to women, African Americans, and the young (18- to 21-year-olds). Each time suffrage was expanded, the overall turnout of voters decreased. Also, there are more elections today than there once were, including primary elections that are limited to registered members of a particular party.

d. There are several reasons that also contribute to this trend, including growing mistrust of the political system, growing apathy, and dealignment. As citizens' view elected officials in a negative light, they are less likely to go to the polls to support them. Citizens are also getting more apathetic as their lives become increasingly filled with opportunities to surf the Internet or watch TV. They are less likely to make the effort to learn about the election and participate in it. Finally, fewer voters are loyal to one political party, making them less likely to care who the winner is.

CHAPTER 14

The Campaign Process

To run for a political office, a person must first receive a party's official **nomination.** Then, with the party's endorsement and assistance, the candidate must **campaign** to win the support of voters. These two processes require a great deal of money and media exposure. Presidential campaigning has become a major part of the political process in the United States. **Campaign strategy** is the plan of candidates to win the election. The nomination and campaign process is so taxing that many qualified individuals make a decision not to run.

Roots of Modern Political Campaigns

- **Nomination campaign:** Part of a political campaign aimed at winning a primary election and representing your party in the general election.

- **General election campaign:** Part of a political campaign aimed at winning a general election and assuming the office for which a candidate is running.

Assembling a Campaign Staff

- **The candidate:** The person running for office. Candidates must be willing to endure a grueling schedule and enormous amounts of stressful, hard work to win an office. Making this effort demonstrates to voters the candidate's commitment to the office. As the election grows closer and the pressure reaches its peak, candidates sometimes make mistakes and become more short-tempered.

- **The campaign staff:** Paid staff, political consultants, and dedicated volunteers who work behind the scenes to support the candidate. Collectively, they plan general strategy, conduct polls, write speeches, craft the campaign's message, and design the strategy for communicating that message in the form of television advertisements, radio spots, websites, and direct mail pieces.

- **Campaign manager:** The individual who travels with the candidate and coordinates the many different aspects of the campaign.

- **Finance chair:** A professional who coordinates the fundraising efforts for the campaign.

- **Communications director:** The person who develops the overall media strategy for the candidate, blending free press coverage with paid TV and radio spots, and mail media.

- **Press secretary:** The individual charged with interacting and communicating with journalists on a daily basis.

- **Internet team:** The campaign staff that makes use of web-based resources to communicate with voters, raise funds, organize volunteers, and plan campaign events.

- **Campaign consultant:** A private-sector professional who sells a candidate the technologies, services, and strategies required to get that candidate elected.

- **Media consultant:** A professional who produces the candidate's television, radio, and print advertisements.

- **Pollster:** A professional who takes public opinion surveys that guide political campaigns.

- **Volunteer campaign staff:** Volunteers are the lifeblood of every national, state, and local campaign. Volunteers answer phone calls; staff candidate booths at public events, such as festivals and county fairs; copy and distribute campaign literature; and serve as the public face of the campaign.

- **Voter canvass:** The process by which a campaign reaches individual voters, either by door-to-door solicitation or by telephone.

- **Get out the vote (GOTV):** A push at the end of a political campaign to encourage supporters to go to the polls.

Raising Money

- **The Federal Election Campaign Act (FECA):** In an attempt to make campaigns more fair and transparent this law enacted disclosure requirements, established the Presidential Public Funding Program, which provides partial public funding for presidential candidates who meet certain criteria, and created the Federal Election Commission (FEC).

- **Federal Election Commission (FEC):** An independent federal agency tasked with enforcing the nation's election laws.

- **Soft money:** The virtually unregulated money funneled by individuals and political committees through state and local parties.

- **Hard money:** Legally specified and limited contributions that are clearly regulated by the Federal Election Campaign Act and by the Federal Election Commission.

- **Bipartisan Campaign Reform Act (BCRA) of 2002:** Multifaceted attempt to limit the influence of donated money on campaigns. It supplanted most of the provisions of the Federal Election Campaign Act, banned soft money, and placed restrictions on several types of advertising.

- *McConnell* v. *Federal Election Commission* (2003): The Supreme Court held that the government's interest in preventing corruption overrides the free speech rights to which the parties would otherwise be entitled and, thus, found that BCRA's restrictions on soft-money donations and political advertising did not violate free speech rights.

- *Citizens United v. Federal Election Commission* (2010): The Supreme Court declared the BCRA's ban on electioneering communications made by corporations and unions unconstitutional. This decision struck a significant blow to BCRA's provisions, and many observers expect it to dramatically increase the power of interest groups and corporations in campaigns and elections in the future.

Sources of Campaign Funding

- **Individuals:** Individual contributions are donations from independent citizens. They represent the majority of money donated to campaigns. The maximum allowable contribution under federal law for congressional and presidential elections was $2,400 per election to each candidate in 2009–2010. Primary and general elections are considered separately.

- **Political Parties**: Under the current rules, national parties can give up to $5,000 per election to a House candidate and $42,600 to a Senate candidate. In competitive races, the parties may provide almost 20 percent of their candidates' total war chests.

- **Political action committee (PAC):** Federally mandated, officially registered fundraising committee that represents interest groups in the political process.

- *Buckley* v. *Valeo* (1976): Ruling that no limit could be placed on the amount of money candidates can spend from their own families' resources, since such spending is considered a First Amendment right of free speech.

- **Public funds:** Donations from the general tax revenues to the campaigns of qualifying presidential candidates.

- **Matching funds:** Donations to presidential campaigns from the federal government that are determined by the amount of private funds a qualifying candidate raises.

- **527 political committees:** Nonprofit and unregulated interest groups that focus on specific causes or policy positions and attempt to influence voters. They are prohibited from engaging in advocacy for or against a candidate, but they can advocate on behalf of political issues. Their emergence was an unintended result of the BCRA in 2004.

- **501(c)(3) committees:** Nonprofit and tax-exempt groups that can educate voters about issues and are not required to release the names of their contributors. They are prohibited from conducting political campaign activities to influence elections to public office. Like 527s, 501(c)(3)s are permitted to educate voters on political issues as long as they do not overtly advocate a specific position.

Reaching Voters

- **Traditional media:** Coverage of campaigns dominates news coverage in federal election years. The press often reports what candidates are doing, such as giving speeches or holding fundraisers. This coverage is sometimes frustrating for campaigns because they have no control over the content or spin of the coverage. News reports are often obsessed with the horserace aspect of politics—who's ahead, who's behind, who's gaining—to the detriment of the substance of the candidates' issues and ideas.

- **Strategies to Control Media Coverage:**
  1. Isolate the candidate from the press, thus reducing the chances that reporters will have negative incidents to highlight in their coverage.
  2. Sound bites: Activities designed to include brief, clever quotes, staged with appealing backdrops so that they will be covered on the television news and in the newspaper.
  3. Spin: A process in which campaigns put forward the most favorable possible interpretation of their candidate (and the most negative for their opponent) on any situation occurring in the campaign.
  4. TV talk and comedy shows: Shows like *The Tonight Show with Jay Leno*, *The Late Show with David Letterman*, and *The Daily Show with John Stewart*, give candidates an opportunity to present their views and answer questions in a less critical forum.

- **Candidate Debates:** Forum in which political candidates face each other to discuss their platforms, records, and character. Debates are important for consolidating a candidate's voter base and correcting misperceptions about the candidate's suitability for office. While candidates have complete control over what they say in debates, they do not have control over what the news media will highlight and focus on after the debates. In most cases, however, debates do not alter the results of an election, but rather, increase knowledge about the candidates and their respective personalities and issue positions, especially among voters who had not previously paid attention to the campaign.

- **New media:** New technologies, such as the Internet, that blur the line between paid and free media sources.

- **Positive ad:** Advertising on behalf of a candidate that stresses the candidate's qualifications, family, and issue positions, without reference to the opponent.

- **Negative ad:** Advertising on behalf of a candidate that attacks the opponent's platform or character.

- **Contrast ad:** Ad that compares the records and proposals of the candidates, with a bias toward the sponsor.

  Inoculation ad: Advertising that attempts to counteract an anticipated attack from the opposition before the attack is launched.

Toward Reform: The 2008 Presidential Campaign

- **The party nomination battles:** With no incumbent president or vice president running for reelection, the nomination contests in both parties drew a crowded field of candidates. The Republicans wrapped their process up first, selecting Arizona senator John McCain. He chose a political unknown, Alaska governor Sarah Palin, as his running mate. She had strong appeal with the religious right wing of the Republican Party. After a long, drawn-out contest (made longer by the Democratic policy of allocating delegates proportionally in primaries), Illinois senator Barack Obama received the Democratic nomination over New York senator Hillary Clinton. Obama, whose main appeal was youth and the theme of change, picked Senator Joe Biden, a longtime Washington insider, to assuage fears that Obama was too inexperienced to lead.

- **The Democratic convention:** The highlight of the Democratic convention was Obama's acceptance speech. He was the first African American to win the nomination of a major party for president, and the night of his speech marked the 45th anniversary of the Reverend Martin Luther King's "I Have a Dream" speech. Observers judged it a significant achievement and an important milestone in American history.

- **The Republican convention** was held with the country eyeing a massive hurricane. Recalling the negative public perception of Republican president Bush's handling of Hurricane Katrina, the first night of the convention was scaled back considerably. The night was to feature President Bush and Vice President Cheney as speakers, but both of their appearances were cancelled. Their absence may have benefited the McCain campaign, given that both men were widely unpopular. The highpoint of the Republican convention was the acceptance speech of vice-presidential nominee Sarah Palin, whose speech was rapturously received in the convention center and received high marks from media commentators and political analysts.

- **The debates and the general election campaign:** Given the high level of dissatisfaction with the incumbent Republican administration, McCain's best hope of changing the dynamics of the race rested on a strong showing in the debates, or a major misstep by Obama. However, the Democrats stayed on message, criticizing Bush's handling of the economy and tying McCain to the unpopular president and his policies. Senator McCain spent most of the campaign attempting to distance himself from President Bush and prove that he was a maverick—a more authentic agent of change than his opponent. In both cases, McCain was largely unsuccessful.

- **Election results and analysis:** Obama won a landslide in the Electoral College, 365 to 173. In the popular vote, Obama won 53 percent to McCain's 46 percent—the highest percentage of the vote won by a Democratic nominee since 1964. The Obama campaign's decision to opt out of the public financing system allowed them to raise an unprecedented sum of money to fund their ground operation and to buy extensive airtime for campaign advertisements. In contrast, the McCain campaign pursued a more traditional strategy. Assuming that much of its base was secure, it focused attention on the states that had been decided by narrow margins in the past two elections. McCain's decision to agree to limits on his spending in return for federal financing also contributed to his defeat, since it resulted in an inadequate amount of resources devoted to voter mobilization.

For Additional Review

Some observers say that in the United States, the campaigning never stops. Look on the web for presidential hopefuls. Also read about the financial statistics of recent elections at www.fec.gov. This information could be very helpful on a free-response question on the AP Government and Politics: United States Exam.

Multiple-Choice Questions

1. An ad that compares Barack Obama's health care proposals with John McCain's health care proposals would be a
(A) spot ad.
(B) contrast ad.
(C) negative ad.
(D) inoculation ad.
(E) positive ad.

2. The U.S. Supreme Court ruled that the provisions of the Bipartisan Campaign Reform Act that eliminated soft money
(A) were unconstitutional.
(B) infringed on the First Amendment's guarantee of freedom of speech.
(C) were valid because the government's interest in reducing corruption overrode concerns about limiting free speech.
(D) were null and void because improper procedural maneuvers prevented the president from exercising his veto authority.
(E) were political issues that were not the purview of the Supreme Court to review.

3. The phase of a campaign that involves a competition between the parties' nominees to determine who will hold office is called the
(A) wedge campaign.
(B) nomination campaign.
(C) general election campaign.
(D) executive campaign.
(E) primary campaign.

4. Which of the following is an example of voter canvassing?
(A) going door-to-door to solicit votes
(B) fundraising activities
(C) campaign rallies
(D) televised debates
(E) campaign ads

4. An unintended result of the Bipartisan Campaign Reform Act (BCRA) of 2002 was the increasing role of
(A) 527s.
(B) a candidates own wealth as a source of campaign funds..
(C) hard money.
(D) bundling.
(E) matching funds.

5. The goal of the Federal Election Campaign Act was to
(A)   make delegate selection easier.
(B)   make campaigns more fair and transparent.
(C)   enforce party discipline.
(D)   cause a realignment.
(E)   limit the impact of the media.

6.   New media refers to
(A)   television ads purchased for a campaign.
(B)   TV, radio, or newspaper coverage of the campaign.
(C)   the Internet and related technology that blends news coverage and paid ads.
(D)   "cross-media" advertising on busses and at ballparks.
(E)   cable television.

7.   The communications director is responsible for
(A)   writing letters to campaign volunteers.
(B)   purchasing cell phones, computers, BlackBerrys, and other electronic devices for the campaign.
(C)   the candidate's overall media strategy.
(D)   briefing the candidate on the day's news.
(E)   All of the above.

8.   The individual on a candidate's staff whose job it is to travel with the candidate and coordinate the campaign is known as the
(A)   chief of staff.
(B)   communications director.
(C)   campaign manager.
(D)   campaign consultant.
(E)   media consultant.

9.   An ad designed to counteract an anticipated attack ad before the initial attack occurs is called a/an
(A)   contrast ad.
(B)   inoculation ad.
(C)   spot ad.
(D)   countermeasures ad.
(E)   preemptive ad.

1. Discuss how campaigns deal with news media coverage of their campaigns and how they use advertising. What strategies do they employ in dealing with news coverage? What types of campaign advertising are there and what distinguishes them from each other? What types of free media are there and what do candidates do to take advantage of them?

2. Discuss how money is used in political campaigns and attempts to control money in campaigns. Explain what efforts have been made since the 1970s to diminish the potential for corruption of the electoral process through campaign donations and what obstacles have occurred.

ANSWERS AND EXPLANATIONS

Multiple-Choice Questions

- **1. (B) is correct.** Contrast ads compare the records and proposals of the candidates, with a bias toward the sponsor.

- **2. (C) is correct.** In *McConnell* v. *Federal Election Commission* (2003), the Supreme Court held that the government's interest in preventing corruption overrides the free speech rights to which the parties would otherwise be entitled. Therefore, it found that BCRA's restrictions on soft-money donations and political advertising did not violate free speech rights.

- **3. (C) is correct.** The general election decides which party's nominee wins the office being sought.

- **4. (A) is correct.** Voter canvassing refers to the process by which a campaign reaches individual voters, either by door-to-door solicitation or by telephone.

- **5. (A) is correct.** 527 groups are able to advertise for an issue and thus enable some to get around the restrictions of the Bipartisan Campaign Reform Act (BCRA) of 2002.

- **6. (B) is correct.** The goal of the Federal Election Campaign Act was to make campaigns more fair and transparent.

- **7. (C) is correct.** New technologies, such as the Internet, that blur the line between paid and free media sources are known as new media.

- **8. (C) is correct.** The communications director is the person who develops the overall media strategy for the candidate, blending free press coverage with paid TV, radio, and mail media.

- **9. (C) is correct.** The campaign manager is the individual who travels with the candidate and coordinates the many different aspects of the campaign.

- **10. (B) is correct.** The Democrats mandate minority participation at the national convention and Republicans have made efforts to include minorities.

Free-Response Questions

This rubric provides examples of many, but not all, of the possible correct responses to the free-response questions.

1. Campaign advertising refers to political advertisements purchased for a candidate's campaign. Media coverage of a campaign has traditionally meant coverage of a campaign by the news media, although increasingly candidates gain free media exposure by appearing on TV talk and comedy shows such as *The Tonight Show with Jay Leno, The Late Show with David Letterman*, and *The Daily Show with John Stewart*. Presidential debates can also be considered a free media opportunity. In recent years, campaigns have begun to use new technologies, such as the Internet, (referred to as new media) that blur the line between paid and free media sources.

   Campaigns go to great lengths to deal with news coverage. One strategy is to isolate the candidate from the press, thus reducing the chances that reporters will have negative incidents to highlight in their coverage. The campaign tries to control the message it sends via media coverage through spin, putting forward the most favorable possible interpretation for their candidate (and the most negative for their opponent) on any situation occurring during the campaign. The press secretary, the campaign official charged with interacting and communicating with journalists on a daily basis, is the frontline of spinning the campaign's message. Campaigns also arrange activities designed to include brief, clever quotes called sound bites, which are staged with appealing backdrops so that they will be covered on the television news and in the newspaper. When all else fails, campaigns can resort to TV talk and comedy shows such as *The Tonight Show with Jay Leno, The Late Show with David Letterman*, and *The Daily Show with John Stewart*, which give candidates an opportunity to present their views and answer questions in a less critical forum.

   There are several types of campaign advertisements. Positive advertising on behalf of a candidate stresses the candidate's qualifications, family, and issue positions, without reference to the opponent. Negative advertising on behalf of a candidate attacks the opponent's platform or character. Contrast ads compare the records and proposals of the candidates, with a bias toward the sponsor. Inoculation advertising attempts to counteract an anticipated attack from the opposition before the attack is launched. Advertising done on television and radio is done in the form of spot ads, television advertising on behalf of a candidate that is broadcast in a 60-, 30-, or 10-second duration. Producing these ads is the responsibility of the campaign's media consultant.

2. Money is needed to pay for a variety of campaign activities, including paying staffers and consultants, logistical expenses of the campaign, and advertising for the campaign. It is the lifeblood of a campaign. This means that campaigns have to spend great effort soliciting donations.

Several attempts have been made to restrict any potential corrupting influence on the candidates. The Federal Election Campaign Act (FECA) was passed in the 1970s. It tried to make campaigns more fair and transparent. The law enacted disclosure requirements and established the Presidential Public Funding Program, which provides partial public funding for presidential candidates who meet certain criteria, and created the Federal Election Commission (FEC). The FEC is an independent federal agency tasked with enforcing the nation's election laws.

The FECA did nothing to regulate soft money, money funneled by individuals and political committees through state and local parties. After great debate, an attempt to address the issue of soft money and other loopholes that had been found in the FECA was made in 2002 with the Bipartisan Campaign Reform Act (BCRA) of 2002. This was a multifaceted attempt to limit the influence of donated money on campaigns. It supplanted most of the provisions of the Federal Election Campaign Act, banned soft money, and placed restrictions on several types of advertising. It was immediately challenged in court. In two rulings, the Supreme Court clarified the parameters of how the BCRA could operate.

In *McConnell* v. *Federal Election Commission* (2003), the Supreme Court held that the government's interest in preventing corruption overrides the free speech rights to which the parties would otherwise be entitled and, thus, found that BCRA's restrictions on soft-money donations and political advertising did not violate free speech rights. In *Federal Election Commission* v. *Wisconsin Right to Life* (2007), the Supreme Court invalidated BCRA's strict ban on genuine issue ads during the "blackout" period, on the grounds that the timing of the ad does not automatically designate it as electioneering. Efforts to restrict campaign financing have been hampered by an earlier court decision, *Buckley* v. *Valeo* (1976), which stipulated that no limit could be placed on the amount of money candidates can spend from their own families' resources, since such spending is considered a First Amendment right of free speech.

CHAPTER 15

The News Media

A free press is a necessary component of a democratic society because it informs the public, giving them the information they need to choose their leaders and influence the direction of public policy. In fact, the American media have been called the "fourth branch of government" because their influence is often as great as that of the three constitutional branches. However, this term is misleading because the American media are composed of many competing private enterprises.

Roots of News Media in the United States

- **Mass media:** The entire array of organizations through which information is collected and disseminated to the general public.

- **News media:** Media providing the public with new information about subjects of public interest.

- **Print media** is the traditional form of mass media, comprising newspapers, magazines, newsletters, and journals.

- **Partisan press:** Initially, news media was overtly partisan and newspapers were really just organs of political parties.

- **Penny press:** Starting in the 1830s with the *New York Sun*, more profit-oriented media emerged. They sought to expand their audience by freeing themselves from the grip of a single political party and were the forerunners of modern newspapers, which rely on mass circulation and commercial advertising to produce profit.

- **Yellow journalism** was a form of newspaper publishing in vogue in the late 19th century that featured pictures, comics, color, and sensationalized, oversimplified news coverage developed to obtain the mass circulation necessary to maximize profit.

- **Muckraking** was a form of journalism in vogue in the early 20th century that was concerned with reforming government and business conduct. Although similar in tone to yellow journalism, the focus was issue-oriented and often involved investigative reporting and a higher standard of factual accuracy.

- **Broadcast media** is made up of television, radio, cable, and satellite services.

- **Radio news:** The first type of broadcast media, radio introduced the idea of nationwide networks of programming and provided the country with more centralized sources of news. Although increasingly eclipsed by television in the 1950s, radio regained popularity with the development of AM talk radio in the mid-1980s. Controversial radio host Rush Limbaugh began the trend with his unabashed conservative perspective. Today, talk radio is overtly partisan.

- **Television news:** By the 1970s, television had replaced print and radio as the nation's chief news provider, with almost two-thirds of Americans getting their news primarily from television. Broadcast networks have steadily lost market share to cable channels in all aspects of TV viewing, and news is no exception. Cable and satellite providers give consumers access to a less glitzy and more unfiltered source of news with C-SPAN, a basic cable channel that offers gavel-to-gavel coverage of congressional proceedings, as well as major political events when Congress is not in session. It also produces some of its own programming. A recent development in television news is the growth in popularity of comedy news programs like *The Daily Show with Jon Stewart* and Stephen Colbert's *Colbert Report*—a satire of FOX News's *The O'Reilly Factor*—which dedicate their entire programs to poking fun at world leaders and current issues. One study conducted by the Annenberg Public Policy Center of the University of Pennsylvania revealed comedy programs actually inform viewers as well as entertain them.

- **New media** are technologies, such as the Internet, that blur the line between media sources and create new opportunities for the dissemination of news and information. These include websites of traditional broadcast and print media. Blogs and social networking sites are also examples of new media. Usage of new media has grown significantly in the last several years.

- **Blogs** are web-based journal entries that provide an editorial and news outlet for citizens. Information made public on blogs has been picked up by mainstream news outlets, revealing how the new media provide unprecedented opportunities for the flow of information.

Current News Media Trends

- **Media consolidation:** The dynamics of private sector business push media firms toward consolidation in order to reap the benefits that come from larger market shares and fewer large-scale competitors. Unlike traditional industries, where the primary concern associated with consolidation is the manipulation of prices (which is made possible by monopolies or near-monopolies), the consolidation of the media poses a far greater potential risk. Should the news media become dominated by a few megacorporations, the fear is that these groups could limit the flow of information and ideas that form the very essence of a free society and make democracy possible. While it is unlikely that profit-driven media chains would intentionally manipulate the news in favor of specific political perspectives, it is possible that market forces, aimed at expanding market shares and pleasing advertisers, might lead to greater focus on sensational issues, news as entertainment, and avoidance of issues that might bore or alienate their audiences.

- **Use of experts:** Journalists cover such a variety of subjects that they cannot possibly have expertise in all of them, so the news media employ expert consultants to explain issues. These experts, also referred to as pundits, or the more derogatory term "talking heads," are hired to discuss the dominant issues of the day. There may be biases in the commentary of these experts, but it is the hope that a diversity of expert opinion is reflected on each subject throughout the media.

- **Narrowcasting** is the targeting of media programming to specific populations within society.

- **Citizen journalism** is the collecting, reporting, and analyzing of news content by members of the public who are not professional journalists.

Rules Governing the News Media

- **Journalistic standards:** The heaviest restrictions placed on reporters do not come from government regulations, but from the industry's own professional norms and each journalist's level of integrity. Oversight is also provided by editors, who are ultimately responsible for the accuracy of the news they produce.

  - **On background:** Information provided to a journalist that will not be attributed to a named source.

  - **Deep background:** Information provided to a journalist that will not be attributed to any source.

  - **Off the record:** Information provided to a journalist that will not be released to the public.

  - **On the record:** Information provided to a journalist that can be released and attributed by name to the source.

- **Government regulation of the electronic media:** The U.S. government regulates the electronic component of the media. Unlike radio or television, the print media are exempt from most forms of government regulation, although even print media must not violate community standards (for instance, obscenity). The reason for the difference in treatment between types of media is that the airwaves used by the electronic media are considered public property and are leased to private broadcasters by the federal government.

- **Telecommunications Act of 1996:** This deregulated whole segments of the electronic media in hopes of providing an optimal balance of competing corporate interests, technological innovations, and consumer needs. The result of this deregulation was the sudden merger of previously distinct kinds of media in order to create a more "multimedia" approach to communicating information and entertainment. This paved the way for the creation of multimedia corporations such as Viacom, Time Warner, and Comcast.

- **Content regulation** is the government's attempts at controlling the substance of the mass media.

- **Equal time rule** is the rule that requires broadcast stations to sell airtime equally to all candidates in a political campaign, if they choose to sell airtime to any candidates.

How the News Media Cover Politics

- **Press release:** A document offering an official comment or position.

- **Press briefing:** A relatively restricted session between a press secretary or aide and the press.

- **Press conference:** An unrestricted session between an elected official and the press.

Toward Reform: News Media Influence, News Media Bias, and Public Confidence

- **Media effect** is the influence of news sources on public opinion. In most cases, the press has surprisingly little effect on what people believe. To put it bluntly, people tend to see what they want to see. The media have a greater influence on political independents than on strong partisans, and they have a greater impact on topics far removed from the lives and experiences of readers and viewers. News reports can probably shape public opinion about foreign affairs fairly easily. Yet, media claims about domestic issues, such as rising prices, neighborhood crime, or child rearing, may have relatively little effect, since most citizens have personal experience and well-formed ideas about these subjects.

- **Agenda setting** is the ongoing process of forming the list of issues to be addressed by government.

- **Framing** is the process by which a news organization defines a political issue and consequently affects opinion about the issue.

- **Media bias to the left:** To this day, journalists are substantially Democratic in party affiliation and voting habits, progressive and antiestablishment in political orientation, and to the left of the general public on many economic, foreign policy, and social issues. Indeed, a 2007 survey revealed that, whereas 36 percent of the general public describes themselves as being ideologically conservative, only 8 percent of those in the national media would do the same. At the same time, the majority of national journalists—53 percent—describe themselves as moderate, while only 39 percent of Americans describe themselves in the same way.

- **Media bias to the right:** Some scholars argue that corporate interests play a significant role in what journalists report, and that they may counter any liberal leanings of reporters. Other analysts have argued that a conservative bias in the media is even more pervasive. They point to the elite background of the typical journalist, who tends to be white, male, highly educated, and relatively affluent. As a result, many of these journalists may unconsciously ignore reporting on issues that are important to racial and ethnic minorities, the poor, and others who might be critical of government and big business.

- **Dynamics of contemporary media bias:** It seems that much of the more recent media bias is intentional and a response to increasing fragmentation and competition among media. One-sided media, a type of narrowcasting, is gaining in popularity as networks intentionally market a one-sided message to secure a competitive edge in niche markets. Not all networks are forthright with their leanings, however. For example, the moniker for Fox News is "fair and balanced," while the reporting has a distinctly conservative bias. Ultimately, however the deepest bias among political journalists is the desire to get a good story and win ratings. News people know that if they report on a story with spice and drama, it will increase their audience. The fear of missing a good story shapes how media outlets develop headlines and frame their stories.

- **Public confidence in the media:** Americans' general assessment of the news media is considerably unfavorable, and has been in a downward trend since the 1980s. According to a 2009 survey by the Pew Research Center for the People and the Press, a majority of the public gives the media low ratings on a number of indicators. Pew found that just 29 percent of respondents said news organizations get the facts straight, and 63 percent believed the press was often inaccurate.

For Additional Review

Over a period of a few days, watch a variety of television news shows on different channels and critique them. How much attention is given to different kinds of issues? Do you detect any bias? For each news segment, think about what is not said, or which angles might be overlooked.

Multiple-Choice Questions

1. Which of the following best describes newspaper coverage under yellow journalism?
(A) dull
(B) thorough
(C) comprehensive
(D) sensationalized
(E) government propaganda

2. What is narrowcasting?
(A) the tendency of the media to frame political events using well-established stereotypes
(B) the tendency for the media to focus on domestic events rather than international events
(C) the increasing reliance of the media on political pundits
(D) targeting media programs at specific segments of the population
(E) political coverage that is superficial

3. Those who think the media has a conservative bias point to
(A) the fact that most journalists are registered Republicans.
(B) the corporate interests of the companies who own the media outlets.
(C) the influence of Hollywood elites on broadcast news and Rupert Murdock on print media.
(D) the fact that those who write the stories are usually conservative.
(E) all of the above.

4. When a journalist interviews someone on "deep background," the journalist is
(A) taking a big chance that the information may be incorrect.
(B) guaranteeing that the source will not be identified in any way.
(C) pledging not to name the source publicly, but might reference the source vaguely.
(D) promising the information will never be released to the public.
(E) actually breaking the law and violating the First Amendment.

5. Why do the media typically have little influence on public opinion?
(A) The media are required to present both sides of a story, leaving little room to influence public opinion.
(B) The media are owned by the same corporations that conduct public opinion polls.
(C) People tend to ignore all political information from the media due to its well-known biases.
(D) Public opinion is static and seldom changes.
(E) Typically, people only pay attention to media coverage that is consistent with their own political preferences.

6. Partisan newspapers gave way to
(A) broadcast media.
(B) the penny press.
(C) yellow journalism.
(D) Fox News.
(E) new media.

7. What is agenda setting?
(A) the ability of the media to influence public opinion about which issues the government should address
(B) the tendency to remember only those news stories that are consistent with one's predispositions
(C) the ability of the media to influence the public's opinions on issues
(D) the media's focus on scandal and corruption
(E) the public's ability to determine which issues the media covers

8. Which of the following is an example of citizen journalism?
(A) *The Colbert Report*
(B) the Drudge Report
(C) public opinion polls
(D) network affiliates
(E) blogs

9. Researchers found that if a news story about a Ku Klux Klan rally was presented as free speech, viewers were generally tolerant of the rally. However, if the story was presented as a law and order issue, public tolerance for the rally decreased. This is an example of
(A) agenda setting.
(B) minimal effects.
(C) convalescing.
(D) prior restraint.
(E) framing.

10. The deepest bias among political journalists is
(A) the desire to produce content that will gain the highest ratings or readership.
(B) to promote a liberal agenda.
(C) to provide accurate, even if boring, information to the public.
(D) to promote a conservative agenda.
(E) to create fame and celebrity for the journalist.

Free-Response Questions

1. Discuss the evolution of news media form and style in the United States. Include what type of media most of people get their news from, and how this has changed over time. Also, discuss the changes in the tone of the news media.

2. Discuss the rules that govern the media. Explain what rights government has to regulate the media and what protections the media have from government and legal action.

ANSWERS AND EXPLANATIONS

Multiple-Choice Questions

- **1. (D) is correct.** Yellow journalism involved increasing newspaper sales by writing stories with sensationalized coverage and dubious accuracy.

- **2. (D) is correct.** This is the definition of narrowcasting. Each of the other answers refers to a different concept.

- **3. (B) is correct.** There is a general sense that corporate America leans to the right politically. Since much of the media is privately owned by large corporate entities, it would seem that the employees would have to follow the more conservative ideas of management and ownership, even if the employee's own views were more left of center.

- **4. (B) is correct.** When a subject tells a reporter that he or she is providing the information on deep background, the expectation is that no source will be attributed to that information in final publication.

- **5. (E) is correct.** Studies show that people tend to ignore media information that is inconsistent with their existing beliefs or personal experiences.

- **6. (B) is correct.** The correct order of a media developments timeline based on this question would be: partisan press, penny press, yellow journalism, broadcast media, Fox News, new media.

- **7. (A) is correct.** This is the definition of agenda setting. Each of the other answers refers to a different concept.

- **8. (E) is correct.** Citizen journalism involves the collecting, reporting, and analyzing of news content by members of the public who are not professional journalists. Blogs allow anyone to post news and analysis and/or opinion of it to the world through the Internet.

- **9. (E) is correct.** "Framing" is when a news organization defines a political issue, often influencing public opinion about it. In the example, framing the rally as a free speech issue led people to support the rally, just as they support free speech. On the other hand, framing the story as an issue of law and order portrays the protesters as disruptive, and the public tends to oppose disruptions to the public order.

- **10. (A) is correct.** The media depend on an audience for success, and even survival. This compels them to seek out stories that will attract viewers or readers. While the dynamics of narrowcasting sometimes result in slanting a story ideologically to capture higher ratings within a certain market, the underlying motivation is high ratings, more than promotion of an ideological agenda, although the effect can be the promotion of an ideological agenda.

Free-Response Questions

This rubric provides examples of many, but not all, of the possible correct responses to the free-response questions.

1. When the country began, the only kinds of news media were traditional forms of mass media, like newspapers, magazines, newsletters, and journals. They were overtly partisan, and in many ways merely organs of political parties. Starting in the 1830s with the *New York Sun*, a more profit-oriented media called the penny press emerged. It sought to expand readership (and hence revenue) by appealing to a broader audience, and relied on mass circulation and commercial advertising to produce profit. Competition for readers led to the development of yellow journalism, a form of newspaper publishing in vogue in the late 19th century that featured pictures, comics, color, and sensationalized, oversimplified news coverage. Within a generation of the heyday of yellow journalism, a movement similar in tone, but more positive in focus, known as muckraking developed. Muckraking was concerned with reforming government and business conduct.

    Print media began to have competition from a new form of media called broadcast media starting in the early 1920s. Starting with radio, and later including television, broadcast media changed the form and organization of news media. Radio introduced the idea of nationwide networks of programming, and provided the country with more centralized sources of news. This trend continued with the rise of television news. By the 1970s, television had replaced print and radio as the nation's chief news provider, with almost two-thirds of Americans getting their news primarily from television.

    Today, there are two related trends in the evolution of news media. The first is switching to new technologies such as the Internet and cable TV, often referred to as new media. The overall effect of new media has been to diversify types of news media available to people in both form and tone. Cable and satellite providers give consumers access to a less glitzy and more unfiltered source of news, as well as access to entertainment-style news through comedy news programs like *The Daily Show with Jon Stewart* and *The Colbert Report*. One study conducted by the Annenberg Public Policy Center of the University of Pennsylvania revealed that comedy programs actually inform viewers, as well as entertain them. New media has also allowed the development of a strategy called narrowcasting, the targeting of media programming at specific populations within society. One might argue that this trend began in radio media with the development of AM talk radio in the mid-1980s. Controversial radio host Rush Limbaugh began the trend with his unabashed conservative perspective. Talk radio today is overtly partisan and aimed at audiences that are similarly inclined.

    The other trend has been toward media consolidation, in which more of the nation's media are controlled by fewer organizations. The dynamics of private sector business push media firms toward consolidation in order to reap the benefits that come from larger market shares and fewer large-scale competitors. Unlike traditional industries, where the primary concern associated with consolidation is the manipulation of prices made possible by monopolies or near-monopolies, the consolidation of the media poses a far greater potential risk. Should the news media become dominated by a few megacorporations, the fear is that these groups could limit the flow of information and ideas that form the very essence of a free society and that make democracy possible. While it is unlikely that profit-driven media chains would intentionally manipulate the news in favor of specific political perspectives, it is possible that market forces, aimed at expanding market shares and pleasing advertisers, could lead to greater focus on sensational issues, news as entertainment, and avoidance of issues that might bore or alienate their audiences.

2. The media is guided by several sets of rules and standards. In general, the heaviest restrictions placed on reporters do not come from government regulations, but from the industry's own professional norms and each journalist's level of integrity. Oversight is also provided by editors, who are ultimately responsible for the accuracy of the news they produce. Beyond that, however, government policy and court decisions impose rules on media operations.

The U.S. government regulates the electronic component of the media. Unlike radio or television, the print media are exempt from most forms of government regulation, although even print media must not violate community standards (for instance, obscenity). The reason for the difference in treatment of different types of media is that the airwaves used by the electronic media are considered public property, and are leased to private broadcasters by the federal government. The equal time rule is an example of this: This rule requires broadcast stations to sell airtime equally to all candidates in a political campaign, if they choose to sell it to any.

Government power to regulate interstate commerce had allowed the government to regulate the degree of centralization in media industries. The Telecommunications Act of 1996 significantly revised many of these regulations in hopes of providing an optimal balance of competing corporate interests, technological innovations, and consumer needs. The result of this deregulation was the sudden merger of previously distinct kinds of media in order to create a more "multimedia" approach to communicating information and entertainment. This paved the way for the creation of multimedia corporations such as Viacom, Time Warner, and Comcast.

The ability of the government to engage in "content regulation" (attempts at controlling the substance of the mass media), is severely constrained by the freedom of the press clause of the First Amendment to the Constitution. Despite this seeming absolute prohibition, the government has periodically tried to engage in content regulation. The Supreme Court has rendered a number of decisions in order to clarify what protections the media have against government regulation and the use of courts against the media. In *New York Times Co.* v. *Sullivan* (1964) the Supreme Court concluded that "actual malice" must be proved to support a finding of libel against a public figure. The actual malice rule has made it very difficult for public figures to win libel cases. *New York Times Co.* v. *U.S.* (1971)

established that the government, except under extremely rare and confined circumstances, cannot impose prior restraints on the press—that is, the government cannot prohibit the publication of a news story. Protecting the press from government was deemed essential because, as Justice Hugo Black noted, "only a free and unrestrained press can effectively expose deception in the government."

CHAPTER 16

Interest Groups

One of the most pronounced political trends in the last few decades is the rise of interest groups. An interest group is an organized group that tries to influence public policy. Today there are more than 20,000 of these private organizations in Washington and in state capitals. Interest groups represent bodies of people with shared interests who lobby legislators on their behalf. In this sense, they are a natural part of a democracy. However, Americans tend to view them with skepticism because, most often, the language of influence is money.

Roots of the American Interest Group System

- **Social capital:** The myriad relationships individuals enjoy that facilitate the resolution of community problems through collective action.

- **Civic virtue:** The tendency to form small-scale associations for the public good.

- **Interest group**: A collection of people or organizations that tries to influence public policy.

- **Pluralist theory:** The theory that political power is distributed among a wide array of diverse and competing interest groups.

- **Disturbance theory:** The theory that interest groups form in part to counteract the efforts of other groups.

- **Transactions theory:** The theory that public policies are the result of narrowly defined exchanges among political actors.

- **Collective good**: Something of value that cannot be withheld from a nonmember of a group, for example, a tax write-off or a better environment.

- **Population ecology theory:** The theory that the life of a political organization is conditional on the density and diversity of the interest group population in a given area.

- **Public interest group:** An organization that seeks a collective good that benefit group members and nongroup members alike. Today, civil liberties groups, environmental groups, good government groups, peace groups, church groups, groups that speak out for those who cannot (such as children, the mentally ill, or animals), and even MoveOn.org are examples of public interest groups.

- **Economic interest group:** A group with the primary purpose of promoting the financial interests of its members.

- **Earmark:** Funds that an appropriations bill designates for a particular purpose within a state or congressional district.

- **Political action committee (PAC):** This is a federally regulated, officially registered fundraising committee that represents interest groups in the political process.

The Development of American Interest Groups

- **First interest groups in the U.S.:** It was not until the 1830s, as communications networks improved, that the first national groups emerged. Many of these groups were single-issue groups deeply rooted in the Christian religious revivalism that was sweeping the nation. Concern with humanitarian issues such as temperance (total abstinence from alcoholic beverages), peace, education, slavery, and women's rights led to the founding of numerous associations dedicated to solving these problems.

- **Rise of business interest groups:** After the Civil War, business interests groups began to play even larger roles in both state and national politics, and they began to formally lobby government for legislation favorable to their interests. This is really the beginning of formal organized interest group activity on the part of the business community.

- **Lobbyist:** This is an interest group representative who seeks to influence legislation that will benefit his or her organization or client through political persuasion. A lobbyist's effectiveness depends largely on his or her reputation for fair play and provision of accurate information. Lobbyists who give false or misleading information quickly lose credibility and access, a lobbyist's two most important tools.

- **The Progressive Era (1890–1920):** This period was in many ways a combination of the return of the grassroots activism of the first interest groups and the lobbying of business interest groups. A host of interest groups emerged in the Progressive Era to put forth their vision for how to deal with the problems caused by rapid industrialization, an influx of immigrants, monopolistic business practices and the problems they created, such as crime, poverty, widespread political corruption, and squalid and unsafe working conditions.

- **Organized labor:** Until the creation of the American Federation of Labor (AFL) in 1886, there was no real national union activity. The AFL brought skilled workers from several trades together into one stronger national organization for the first time. Organized labor really gained solid legal ground as an interest group with the passage of the Clayton Act, which allowed unions to organize free from prosecution, and also guaranteed their right to strike—a powerful weapon against employers.

- **Trade association** is a group that represents a specific industry.

- **The rise of the interest group state:** During the 1960s and 1970s, the Progressive spirit reappeared with the rise of public interest groups. Generally, these groups devoted themselves to representing the interests of African Americans, women, the elderly, the poor, and consumers, or to working on behalf of the environment. These groups tended to advocate more liberal policy positions in representing these interests. Two major new public interest groups, Common Cause and Public Citizen, formed in this period and have a tremendous effect on government policy.

- **Common Cause** is a good-government group that acts as a watchdog over the federal government. It has effectively challenged aspects of the congressional seniority system, urged the passage of sweeping campaign financing reforms, and played a major role in the enactment of legislation, authorizing federal financing of presidential campaigns. It continues to lobby for accountability in government and for more efficient and responsive governmental structures and practices.

- **Public Citizen** is the collection of groups headed by Ralph Nader that tries to enforce government accountability on the private sector to provide safe products and services to consumers.

- **Conservative religious and ideological groups:** Conservatives, concerned at the success of some of the liberal public interest groups, responded by forming religious and ideological groups that became a potent force in U.S. politics. In 1978, Reverend Jerry Falwell founded the first major new religious group, the Moral Majority. The Moral Majority was widely credited with assisting in the election of Ronald Reagan as president in 1980 as well as with the defeats of several liberal Democratic senators that same year. Pat Robertson, a televangelist, formed the Christian Coalition in 1990. Since then, it has grown in power and influence. The Christian Coalition played an important role in the Republicans winning control of the Congress in 1994. It also lobbies Congress and the White House.

What Do Interest Groups Do?

- **Lobbying** is the activity of a group or organization that seeks to influence legislation and persuade political leaders to support the group's position. All three branches of government, even the judiciary, can be the targets of lobbying.

- *Amicus curiae* **briefs:** When a case a group is interested in but not actually sponsoring comes before a court, the organization often will file an *amicus* brief—either alone or with other like-minded groups—to inform the justices of the group's policy preference, generally offered in the guise of legal arguments.

- **Grassroots lobbying:** As the term implies, grassroots lobbying is a form of interest group activity that prompts individuals to contact their representatives directly in an effort to affect policy.

- **Protest and radical activism:** An occasional, though highly visible, tactic used by some groups is protest activity. Some animal rights activists, such as People for the Ethical Treatment of Animals (PETA), and some prolife groups, such as Operation Rescue, at times rely on illegal protest activities to draw attention to their causes. Some radical groups post the names of those they believe to be engaging in wrongful activity on the web, along with their addresses and threats. As a result, some groups have faced federal terrorism charges.

- **Recruitment and endorsement of candidates:** Some interest groups recruit, endorse, and/or provide financial or other forms of support for political candidates. For example, EMILY's List (supports prochoice Democratic women candidates) and its Republican counterpart, the Wish List, recruit and train candidates in addition to contributing to their campaigns.

- **GOTV efforts:** Many interest groups believe they can influence public policy by putting like-minded representatives in office. To that end, many groups across the ideological spectrum launch massive get-out-the-vote (GOTV) efforts. These include identifying prospective voters and getting them to the polls on Election Day.

- **Publicizing ratings of candidates:** Many liberal and conservative ideological groups rate candidates to help their members (and the general public) evaluate the voting records of members of Congress. These ratings are often published and distributed in the form of "voter guides" from the interest group.

What Makes Interest Groups Successful?

- Political scientists have studied several phenomena that contribute in varying degrees—individually and collectively—to particular groups' successes.

    - **Leaders:** The role of an interest group leader is similar to that of an entrepreneur in the business world.

    - **Patrons and funding:** A person who finances a group or individual activity is a patron. Without patrons, few public interest groups could survive their initial start-up period.

    - **Members:** Organizations usually are composed of three kinds of members. At the top are a relatively small number of leaders who devote most of their energies to the single group. The second tier of members generally is involved psychologically as well as organizationally. They are the workers of the group—they attend meetings, pay dues, and chair committees to see that things get done. In the bottom tier are the rank and file members who don't actively participate. They pay their dues and call themselves group members, but they do little more. Most group members fall into this last category.

- **The collective good** is something of value that cannot be withheld from a nonmember of a group, for example, a tax write-off or a better environment.

- **The free rider problem** is when potential members fail to join a group because they can get the benefit, or collective good, sought by the group without contributing the effort.

Toward Reform: Regulating Interest Groups and Lobbyists

- **Lobbying Disclosure Act of 1995:** This requires lobbyists to register with the clerk of the House and the secretary of the Senate, report their clients and issues and the agency or house they lobby, and estimate the amount they are paid by each client. These reporting requirements make it easier for watchdog groups or the media to monitor lobbying activities.

- **Honest Leadership and Open Government Act of 2007** is lobbying reform that bans gifts to members of Congress and their staffs, toughened disclosure requirements, and increased time limits on moving from the federal government to the private sector.

- **Ethics in Government Act** was enacted in the wake of the Watergate scandal. This act attempted to curtail questionable moves by barring members of the executive branch from representing any clients before their agency for one year after leaving governmental service.

For Additional Review

Make a table of several interest groups that have made the headlines recently. First define the interests of each one. Then evaluate them in terms of size, intensity, and financial resources. Was each group successful in influencing policy?

Multiple-Choice Questions

1. Disturbance theory posits that
(A)   groups form to counter the activities of other groups.
(B)   groups regularly compete for scarce resources.
(C)   disturbed people often are the entrepreneurs behind the formation of groups.
(D)   citizens need governmental support to succeed.
(E)   all interest groups promote the public good.

2. Labor unions and trade associations are examples of what type of interest group?
(A)   grassroots
(B)   single-issue
(C)   public
(D)   economic
(E)   occupational

3. Pluralist theory holds that
(A) interest group intensity places pressure on members of Congress.
(B) the large number of groups slows down the policymaking process.
(C) it is common for one group to rapidly split up into other groups.
(D) many groups compete for and share power.
(E) salient issues cause a plurality of groups to form.

4. Which of the following is a conservative interest group?
(A) MoveOn.org
(B) AARP
(C) ACLU
(D) Christian Coalition
(E) NAACP

5. Which of the following did the Clayton Act do?
(A)   It allowed labor unions to form and guaranteed their right to strike.
(B)   It established open shop laws.
(C)   It granted vast swaths of land to the Central Pacific Railroad.
(D)   It allowed Standard Oil to drill on publicly owned land in Pennsylvania.
(E)   It required interest groups to share their membership lists with the government.

6. What is a voter guide?
(A)   instructions distributed by local election boards on how to use voting technology
(B)   candidates' positions on issues important to the interest group that distributes them
(C)   lists of candidates officially endorsed by interest groups
(D)   descriptions of the job experiences of candidates distributed by public interest groups
(E)   calendars distributed by interest groups that contain the dates of upcoming elections

7. Which of the following statements accurately describe methods interest groups employ to influence policymaking?
I.   Class action lawsuits allow interest groups to sue in the name of a larger section of the public.
II. Interest groups meet with judges about cases that affect their policy area.
III. Interest groups make almost all of their PAC contributions to incumbents rather than challengers.
IV. Lobbyists use their policy expertise to make themselves indispensable to politicians.
V. Interest groups pay committee members to review proposed legislation from a legislative point of view.
(A) III only
(B) I and IV only
(C) II and V only
(D) I, III, and IV only
(E) II, IV, and V only

8. The activities of groups and organizations that seek to influence legislation and persuade political leaders to support a group's positions is most accurately called
(A)   political participation.
(B)   patronage.
(C)   lobbying.
(D)   testimony.
(E)   "politics by other means."

9.   A lobbyist's effectiveness depends on
(A)   a reputation for honesty and fair play.
(B)   his or her ability to play up to legislators' egos.
(C)   the resources available for bribing members of Congress.
(D)   giving legislators false and misleading information.
(E)   *A, B,* and *D* are all correct answers.

10. Interest groups lobby the federal courts through
(A)   direct, open contact with judges and justices.
(B)   contributions to judicial reelection campaigns.
(C)   filing *amicus curiae* briefs.
(D)   paying bonuses to judges to make decisions favored by the interest group.
(E)   impeaching unpopular judges.

Free-Response Questions

1.   Discuss the methods that interest groups use to influence the political process. Be clear in your discussion of which methods are aimed at which actors in the political process. Include as actors the general public, legislators, executive branch officials, and judges.

2.   Discuss the evolution of interest group formation in the United States. What types of interest groups first formed, which groups followed, and what sparked their formation? Close by discussing some of the main interest groups that exist today and what their causes and activities are.

ANSWERS AND EXPLANATIONS

Multiple-Choice Questions

- **1. (A) is the answer.** Disturbance theory suggests that groups form anytime there is a disturbance in a political system. The activities of one group can cause such a disturbance, giving rise to the formation of competing groups.

- **2. (D) is the answer.** The primary purpose of an economic interest group is to promote the financial interests of its members. Labor unions work for the interest of their workers, while trade associations work to advance the economic good for the firms in their industry; hence both would be examples of economic interest groups.

- **3. (D) is the answer.** Pluralists argue that political power is distributed among a wide array of diverse and competing interest groups.

- **4. (D) is the answer.** Pat Robertson, a televangelist, formed the Christian Coalition in 1990. Since then, it has grown in power and influence and played an important role in the Republicans winning control of the Congress in 1994. It continues to play a major role today. The NAACP focuses on civil rights issues, the ACLU on free speech issues. Although they are not overtly partisan in their focus, they are considered left of center. MoveOn is an avowedly left-of-center interest group. AARP is an organization dealing with senior citizen's issues, often at odds with conservative proposals to reform Social Security and Medicare.

- **5. (A) is the answer.** Although primarily an antitrust law, the Clayton Act also contains provisions that allow unions to organize free from prosecution and also guarantees their right to strike, a powerful weapon against employers, earning it the epithet the "Magna Carta of organized labor" by AFL president, Samuel Gompers.

- **6. (B) is the answer.** One way interest groups engage in election activities is to rate candidates. Issuing voter guides is the method through which they generally publicize those ratings.

- **7. (D) is the answer.** Interest groups frequently file class action lawsuits in an attempt to reverse policy decisions. They also solidify their relationships with members of Congress by channeling most of their campaign contributions to incumbents. Interest groups also know that policymakers are more easily influenced if they must rely on a lobbyist for information and advice about a policy.

- **8. (C) is the answer.** Lobbying is defined in the root of the question. Each of the other answers refers to a different concept.

- **9. (A) is the answer.** A lobbyist's effectiveness depends largely on his or her reputation for fair play and provision of accurate information. As one member of Congress noted: "It doesn't take very long to figure out which lobbyists are straightforward, and which ones are trying to snow you…. If anyone ever gives me false or misleading information, that's it—I'll never see him again." Without credibility with and access to members of Congress, a lobbyist is doomed.

- **10. (C) is the answer.** An *amicus curiae* brief (literally "friend of the court") is a tool used by interest groups to lobby the federal court system when a case the group is interested in, but not actually sponsoring, comes before a court. The brief expresses the group's policy preference, generally offered in the guise of legal arguments.

Free-Response Questions

This rubric provides examples of many, but not all, of the possible correct responses to the free-response questions.

1. Lobbying is the primary activity that interest groups engage in to influence the different branches of government.

   Influencing legislators sometimes starts from the very beginning with some interest groups because they become involved in the campaigns that elect members. Some interest groups recruit, endorse, and/or provide financial or other forms of support for political candidates. To influence those already elected, lobbyists will meet with members and try to put forth the group's position. They must do it in an honest and straightforward manner, otherwise they risk losing credibility and possibly even access to the member, which would eliminate their ability to continue to influence her or him. The same postelection processes and dynamics are in play for lobbying the executive branch officials that make regulations and policies that might be of interest to the group.

   Interest groups try to attain their goals through the courts by filing lawsuits, and again, lobbying. Lobbying the courts is primarily done through *amicus curiae* briefs. When a case the group is interested in, but not actually sponsoring, comes before a court, the organization will often file an *amicus* brief—either alone or with other like-minded groups—to inform the justices of the group's policy preference, generally offered in the guise of legal arguments.

   In terms of trying to get political participation of the average citizen, interest groups engage in several activities. A fundamental step is to mobilize and inform voters. Mobilizing voters is done through massive get-out-the-vote (GOTV) efforts. These include identifying prospective voters and getting them to the polls on Election Day. Informing voters is done through supporting candidate advertising efforts and publicizing ratings of candidates through "voter guides" from the interest group.

   As a further step to influence the process, group often try to spark grassroots lobbying efforts. As the term implies, grassroots lobbying is a form of interest group activity that prompts individuals to contact their representatives directly in an effort to affect policy. An occasional, though highly visible, tactic used by some groups is protest activity. Some animal rights activists, such as People for the Ethical Treatment of Animals (PETA), and some prolife groups, such as Operation Rescue, sometimes resort to illegal protest activities to draw attention to their cause. Some radical groups post threatening messages along with the names and addresses of those they believe to be engaging in wrongful activity on the web. As a result, some groups have faced federal terrorism charges.

2. It was not until the 1830s, as communications networks improved, that the first national groups emerged. Many of these groups were single-issue groups deeply rooted in the Christian religious revivalism that was sweeping the nation. Concern with humanitarian issues such as temperance (total abstinence from alcoholic beverages), peace, education, slavery, and women's rights led to the founding of numerous associations dedicated to solving these problems.

As the country industrialized and more businesses began to have a national reach, business interests groups began to formally lobby government for legislation favorable to their interests. This is really the beginning of formal organized interest group activity on the part of the business community.

In the last decades of the 19th century, as the country experienced rapid industrialization, an influx of immigrants, and the rise of monopolistic businesses, more attention had to be paid to problems such as crime, poverty, widespread political corruption, and squalid and unsafe working conditions, which are associated with those developments. This gave rise to the Progressive Era (1890–1920), which was in many ways a combination of the return of the grassroots activism of the first interest groups and the lobbying of business interest groups. A host of interest groups emerged in the Progressive Era to put forth their visions for how to deal with the problems. The Progressive Era saw the emergence of organized labor as a potent force once its activities were legalized by the Clayton Act, which allowed unions to organize free from prosecution and also guaranteed their right to strike, a powerful weapon against employers. It also saw the formation of trade associations—groups that represents a specific industry—like the Chamber of Commerce and the National Association of Manufacturers.

During the 1960s and 1970s, the Progressive spirit reappeared in the rise of public interest groups. Generally, these groups devoted themselves to representing the interests of African Americans, women, the elderly, the poor, and consumers, or to working on behalf of the environment. These groups tended to advocate more liberal policy positions in representing these interests. Two major new public interest groups, Common Cause and Public Citizen, formed in this period and have a tremendous effect on government policy. Common Cause is a good-government group that acts as a watchdog over the federal government, has effectively challenged aspects of the congressional seniority system, urged the passage of sweeping campaign financing reforms, and played a major role in the enactment of legislation authorizing federal financing of presidential campaigns. It continues to lobby for accountability in government and for more efficient and responsive governmental structures and practices. Public Citizen is a collection of groups headed by Ralph Nader, which enforces government accountability in the private sector in order to provide safe products and services to consumers.

As disturbance theory predicts, the success of these more liberal interest groups sparked a reaction among conservatives, who responded by forming religious and ideological groups that became a potent force in American politics. In 1978, Reverend Jerry Falwell founded the first major new religious group, the Moral Majority. The Moral

Majority was widely credited with assisting in the election of Ronald Reagan as president in 1980, as well as with the defeats of several liberal Democratic senators that same year. Pat Robertson, a televangelist, formed the Christian Coalition in 1990. Since then, it has grown in power and influence. The Christian Coalition played an important role in the Republicans winning control of the Congress in 1994. The Christian Coalition also lobbies Congress and the White House. The success of these groups sparked the formation of broad-based liberal interest groups like Moveon.org, which makes use of new media to advance their cause.

CHAPTER 17

Domestic Policy

Domestic policy is a term that designates a broad and varied range of government programs designed to provide the citizens of a nation with protection from poverty and hunger, to improve their health and physical well-being, to enable transportation, to maintain a healthy and livable environment, and otherwise enable them to lead more secure, satisfying, and productive lives. In short, domestic policies are intended to enhance quality of life through the establishment of societal conditions that allow citizens to pursue happiness and feel secure. These policies are meant to benefit all segments of society, but they often focus on the less fortunate members who find it more difficult to provide for themselves and their families.

Roots of Public Policy: The Policy-Making Process

- **Public policy:** An intentional course of action or inaction followed by government in dealing with some problem or matter of concern. As such, they are authoritative and binding on people.

- There are several theories that explain the formation of public policy:

  - **Elite theory** suggests that societies are divided into elites and masses. The elite, or "chosen few" make the important decisions in society. The elites have power to make and implement policy, while the masses simply respond to the desires of the elites. Elite theorists believe that an unequal distribution of power in society is normal and inevitable.

  - **Bureaucratic theory:** According to bureaucratic theory, all institutions, governmental and nongovernmental, have fallen under the control of a large and ever-growing bureaucracy that carries out policy using standardized procedures. This growing complexity of modern organizations has empowered bureaucrats, who become dominant as a consequence of their expertise and competence. Eventually, the bureaucrats wrest power from others, especially elected officials.

  - **Interest group theory** suggests that interest groups control the governmental process. According to this theory, there are so many potential pressure points in the three branches of the federal government, as well as at the state level, that interest groups can step in on any number of competing sides. The government then becomes the equilibrium point in the system as it mediates among competing interests.

  - **Pluralist theory** holds that political power is distributed among a wide array of diverse and competing interest groups. As such, no single elite group could ever gain monopoly control over any substantial area of policy and participants in every political controversy get something. Thus, each has some impact on how political decisions are made. Nevertheless, what is good for the public at large is often lost.

- There are seven steps in the policymaking process:

1. **Problem recognition** is the identification of an issue that disturbs the public and leads to a call for governmental intervention. There is usually not a single, accepted definition of a problem. Indeed, political struggle often occurs at this stage because the way the problem is defined determines what sort of action is appropriate. Public policies themselves may even be viewed as problems or the causes of other problems.

2. **Agenda setting** is government recognition that a problem is worthy of consideration for governmental intervention and the constant process of forming the list of issues to be addressed by government.

   - **Agenda** is a set of issues to be discussed or given attention.

   - **Systemic agenda** includes all public issues that are viewed as requiring governmental attention; a discussion agenda.

   - **Governmental (institutional) agenda** is the changing list of issues to which governments believe they should address themselves.

3. **Policy formulation** identifies alternative approaches to addressing the problems placed on government's agenda. It is the crafting of appropriate and acceptable proposed courses of action to ameliorate or resolve public problems. Policy formulation may be undertaken by various players in the policy process: the president, presidential aides, agency officials, specially appointed task forces and commissions, interest groups, private research organizations ("think tanks"), and legislators and their staffs.

4. **Policy adoption** is the approval of a policy proposal by the people with requisite authority, such as a legislature or chief executive. This approval gives the policy legal force.

5. **Budgeting** is the allocation of resources to provide for the proper implementation of public policies. A policy can be nullified by a refusal to fund or by grossly inadequate funding.

6. **Policy implementation** is the process of carrying out public policy through governmental agencies and the courts. Most policies are implemented by administrative agencies, which are authorized to use a number of techniques to implement the public policies within their jurisdictions. Some are enforced in other ways. Product liability and product dating are two examples. Product liability laws are typically enforced by lawsuits initiated in the courts by injured consumers or their survivors. State product-dating laws are implemented more by voluntary compliance when grocers take out-of-

date products off their shelves or when consumers choose not to buy food products after the use-by dates stamped on them expire.

- **Authoritative techniques** for policy implementation rest on the notion that people's actions must be directed or restrained by government in order to prevent or eliminate activities or products that are unsafe, unfair, evil, or immoral.

- **Incentive techniques** for policy implementation encourage people to act in their own best interest by offering payoffs or financial inducements to get them to comply with public policies.

- **Capacity techniques** provide people with information, education, training, or resources that will enable them to participate in desired activities. The assumption underlying the provision of these techniques is that people have the incentive or desire to do what is right but lack the capacity to act accordingly. Job training might help able-bodied people to find work, and accurate information on interest rates will enable people to protect themselves against interest-rate gouging.

- **Hortatory techniques** encourage people to comply with policy by appealing to people's "better instincts" in an effort to get them to act in desired ways. The "Just Say No" anti-drug campaign, and the use of highway signs displaying slogans like "Don't Be a Litterbug" are examples of hortatory techniques.

7. **Policy evaluation** is the process of determining whether a course of action is achieving its intended goal and what other effects it might be having. It may also try to determine whether a policy is being fairly or efficiently administered.

The Evolution of Health Policy

Governments in the United States have long been active in the health care field. Local governments began to establish public health departments in the first half of the 19th century, and state health departments followed in the second half. Public sanitation and clean water programs, pasteurization of milk, and immunization programs greatly reduced the incidence of infectious and communicable diseases.

- The government is active in health policy in a number of ways:

- **Medicare** is the federal program established in the Lyndon B. Johnson administration that provides medical care to elderly Social Security recipients.

- **Medicaid** is an expansion of Medicare; this program subsidizes medical care for the poor.

- The Obama administration's Patient Protection and Affordable Care Act established government-run health insurance exchanges to ensure that all Americans would have access to health care coverage. These exchanges, which will not be fully implemented until 2014, are financed by a number of taxes and fees.

- Between 2010 and 2018, the act will expand Medicaid eligibility and subsidize insurance premiums for low-income Americans. It also provides incentives for businesses to offer health insurance—a very costly proposition for many employers. Finally, it prevents health insurance companies from denying Americans coverage on the basis of preexisting conditions.

- Public reaction to the Patient Protection and Affordable Care Act has been mixed.

- The majority of Americans believe that the legislation will lead to significant changes in the American health care system, but only 37 percent of Americans believe that these changes will improve the system.

- As many as 20 states have already sued or announced that they will sue the federal government to block implementation of the policy. These states argue that the act is an infringement on states' reserved powers, which are granted to them under the Tenth Amendment of the U.S. Constitution.

- **Public health:** In addition to funding large portions of the nation's health care costs, government plays a major role in managing the growth of both infectious and chronic disease. Public health officials also use vaccines in the adult population to manage the spread of diseases such as influenza (the flu). While not requiring citizens to receive flu shots, the government recommends that high-risk groups (infants and senior citizens) receive immunizations and also subsidizes vaccines for low-income populations.

The Evolution of Education Policy

Education reform in the United States has focused on three central values of American democracy: social and political order, individual liberty, and social and political equality.

- In America's earliest days, individual colonies were responsible for establishing their own education policies.

- Education was seen as a good way of instilling the moral values of the community in future generations by focusing on character traits and basic skills such as reading, writing, and arithmetic.

- Liberal policy reformers emphasized the need to promote equality through educational opportunity and adopted many of Dewey's principles about education and freedom.

- In *Brown* v. *Board of Education* (1954), the Supreme Court unanimously ruled that separate educational facilities for black and white students were inherently unequal.
- The Civil Rights Act promoted equality of opportunity for all Americans and the Elementary and Secondary Education Act concentrated primarily on policies that would advance equality of opportunity for children.

- Conservative policy reformers emphasized the issues of economic freedom in educational choices.
  - Conservatives argue for the privatization of elementary and secondary education, allowing individuals the freedom to choose what and what not to purchase.

- **The No Child Left Behind Act** is an educational reform passed in 2002 that employs high standards and measurable goals as a method of improving American education.

  - There are four main pillars of the No Child Left Behind Act: (1) results-oriented accountability, (2) flexibility in funding, (3) best practices, and (4) school choice.

  - Two popular ways to implement school choice policy are vouchers and charter schools:

    - **Vouchers** are certificates issued by the government that may be applied toward the costs of attending private or public schools.

    - **Charter schools** are semipublic schools founded by universities, corporations, or concerned parents that have open admission but may also receive private donations to increase the quality of education.

The Evolution of Energy and Environmental Policy

Energy and environmental policies in the United States are prone to cycles that contain dramatic shifts in public attention over time.

- **The Foundations of Energy Policy:** The United States first paid serious attention to developing energy policy in the early 1970s after dramatic price increases in imported oil, upon which the country had grown dependent. A new cabinet department, the Department of Energy, was created in 1977 to oversee energy policy.

- **Corporate Average Fuel Efficiency (CAFE) standards** began in 1975 as a means of improving the gas mileage of automobiles in the United States. Under CAFE, automakers are required to meet average fuel efficiency standards for the fleet of cars that they sold in the United States.

- **Strategic Petroleum Reserve:** Congress established the Strategic Petroleum Reserve in 1975 as part of the Energy Policy and Conservation Act. The Strategic Petroleum Reserve holds about two months of inventory that can be accessed under a presidential order.

- **The Energy Tax Act** of 1977 gave tax breaks to individuals and companies that used alternative energy sources and penalized inefficient use of energy by establishing a "gas-guzzler tax" on cars that did not reach the minimum miles-per-gallon (MPG) threshold.

- **The foundations of environmental policy:** As America was being forced to confront energy as a national concern in the 1970s, the issue of the environment was also moving into a prominent role in the national discourse. Americans' growing concerns about environmental conditions led to the first Earth Day in 1970, when millions of the nation's citizenry took part in marches and rallies demanding greater government action to protect the environment. Although momentum on environmental issues slowed considerably in the 1980s with the Reagan administration, recent concerns over global warming and another round of steep oil price increases have brought the issue to prominence again. The Obama administration has vowed to take significant action regarding both energy and environmental issues, which, because of greenhouse gases and global warming, are increasingly considered tandem problems.

- **Environmental Protection Agency (EPA)** was created by executive order in December 1970. The EPA assembled many federal environmental programs under one independent executive branch agency, with the agency administrator reporting directly to the president.

- **Clean Air Act of 1970** is the law that established the primary standards for air quality in the United States. A revised version was passed in 1990.

- **Energy and Environmental Policy Hibernates:** Momentum on environmental issues slowed considerably in the 1980s with the Reagan administration. Reagan reduced government intervention in energy and environmental policy.

  o Reagan's 1981 National Energy Policy Plan ended the price and allocation controls on crude oil and petroleum products that had been established in the 1970s.

  o Reagan also did not seek to renew tax breaks for alternative energy purchases or maintain government financial support for many alternative fuel research projects.

- During the George H.W. Bush and Clinton administrations of the late 1980s and 1990s, energy and environmental policies largely remained off the governmental agenda.

  o Among the cornerstones of the proposed George W. Bush energy policy were plans to allow drilling in Alaska's Arctic National Wildlife Refuge, relaxing rules for the placement of new electrical transmission lines, research into reprocessing nuclear fuel, and greater funding and support for clean coal initiatives.

o After 9/11, American troops headed to war in Iraq and the impact of the national dependence on oil became apparent. Demands for new measures to make the nation more energy independent grew, and Congress began to more aggressively assemble a legislative response to the country's energy needs.

o The calls for more a comprehensive energy policy were also fueled by the increasing concerns about global warming.

- **Global warming** is the increase in global temperatures due to carbon emissions from burning fossil fuels such as coal and oil.

- Since the 1980s, scientists have warned that burning fossil fuels contributes to increased levels of greenhouse gases in the atmosphere, which in turn lead to higher global temperatures. These higher temperatures have a number of significant impacts on the planet, such as melting polar ice caps, rising sea levels, prolonged droughts, more intense storms, major habitat destruction, and species extinction.

Toward Reform: Ongoing Challenges In Domestic Policy

- Health Policy: As medical technology advances, citizens live longer. But this increased life span increases health care costs as the demand for long-term care, prescription drugs, and costly medical procedures rise. These rising costs place a significant burden on individuals and insurance companies, as well as the state and federal governments in the form of Medicare and Medicaid.

  - The rising cost of health care is a serious governmental problem for a number of reasons. First, under the Patient Protection and Affordable Care Act of 2010, at least some of these health care costs will be shouldered by or through the government's insurance exchanges when they are fully implemented in 2014. Second, these rising costs coupled with the rising number of beneficiaries and shrinking number of workers are projected to produce budget shortfalls for the Medicare program as early as 2020. Among the policy proposals to address this problem are raising the Medicare tax on workers or increasing the age of eligibility for beneficiaries. Neither of these proposals is a popular policy solution.

- Education Policy: Implementation of the No Child Left Behind Act remains controversial.

  - Critics claim that the reform:

    - Places too much emphasis on standardized testing as a means of measuring student achievement, ignoring many nonmeasurable but equally important aspects of student learning.

    - Encourages teachers to "teach to the test" rather than helping students to learn analytical thinking skills.

    - Force schools and teachers to sacrifice education in subject areas that are untested, such as science, civics, art, or music.

    - Nationalizes elementary and secondary education, which is best administered by state and local governments.

    - Contains federal mandates for state and local governments, but little funding to help with policy implementation.

- As a result of the criticisms, the National Education Association and its affiliates filed a lawsuit charging that the act was unconstitutional because it required state and local governments to spend their own funds to comply with federal legislation. The courts disagreed.

- President Barack Obama proposed ending the yearly benchmarks and report cards, in order to focus on college and career readiness. The administration has also proposed funding education through competitive federal grant programs, rather than a formula based on student achievement on standardized tests.

- **Energy and Environmental Policy**: Americans have become much more interested in the availability of alternative energy sources. However, fossil fuels still dominate the energy field in the United States so it will take significant efforts to move alternative fuels into the mainstream.

  - Many state governments have begun to adopt Renewable Portfolio Standards (RPS) that require set amounts of electricity to be generated from alternative sources.

  - States and the federal government have also used their fiscal powers to increase the adoption of alternative energy technologies and to encourage citizens to become more environmentally friendly, or "green."

For Additional Review

Make a list of the incomes security programs mentioned in this chapter. Sort them by whether they are means-tested or entitlement programs. Look up the nearest local office of each of them. (Going to the website of the agency that oversees them and looking for its listing of local field offices is probably the best starting place). Write down the location of the nearest offices of each along with a brief description of the assistance each program provides and who is eligible to receive it.

1. The exchanges in the Patient Protection and Affordable Care Act of 2010, will be fully implemented in
(A) 2011.
(B) 2014.
(C) 2018.
(D) 2020.
(E) 2023.

2. In 1993, under the provisions of the Clean Air Act, an emissions trading system was created and the first sales of allowances for the discharge of sulfur dioxide were held. This illustrates which stage of the public policy process?
(A) agenda setting
(B) policy evaluation
(C) budgeting
(D) policy adoption
(E) implementation

3. Implementation of which of the following policies employs an incentive technique?
(A) consumer products must meet certain safety requirements
(B) the license of a radio station can be revoked for broadcasting obscenities
(C) public universities cannot discriminate against women
(D) farmers receive subsidies for growing wheat
(E) job training to assist able-bodied citizens in finding work

4. The crafting of appropriate and acceptable proposed courses of action to ameliorate or resolve public problems is called
(A)   agenda initiation.
(B)   public administration.
(C)   policy adoption.
(D)   policy restitution.
(E)   policy formulation

5. An intentional course of action followed by government in dealing with problems or matters of concern is called
(A)   policy formulation.
(B)   social welfare policy.
(C)   policy administration.
(D)   public administration.
(E)   public policy.

6. The changing list of issues that governmental officials believe they should address is called a
(A)   policy agenda.
(B)   governmental agenda.
(C)   systematic agenda.
(D)   legislative agenda.
(E)   policy addendum.

7. Which of the following programs provides medical care to elderly Social Security recipients?
(A) Old Age, Survivors, and Disability Insurance
(B) veterans disability benefits
(C) Medicare
(D) Medicaid
(E) the National Health Service

8.   Due to the steep rise in oil prices in the early 1970s, energy policy
(A) was put on the backburner.
(B) was placed on the governmental agenda.
(C) began to focus on renewable energy over fossil fuels.
(D) relied almost exclusively on renewable portfolio standards to increase domestic production.
(E) was declared a "national security event" that enabled the president to tap into the Strategic Petroleum Reserve.

9.   Which of the following is NOT a theory to explain the formulation of public policy in the United States?
(A) elite theory
(B) bureaucratic theory
(C) realignment theory
(D) pluralist theory
(E) interest group theory

10. The first step of the policy process is
(A)   problem recognition.
(B)   agenda setting.
(C)   policy implementation.
(D)   policy evaluation.
(E)   policy formulation

1. Discuss the various theories of the policymaking process. According to each theory, which groups influence the making of policy? Compare each theory's conclusions about the group that it assumes is the primary policymaker.

2. List and briefly describe the stages of the policymaking process. Use energy policy as a case study and discuss the specific actions that illustrate each stage of the policymaking process in the creation of the current U.S. energy policy.

ANSWERS AND EXPLANATIONS

Multiple-Choice Questions

- **1.** (B) is the answer. The primary purpose of the Patient Protection and Affordable Care Act is to establish government-operated health insurance exchanges to ensure that all Americans would have access to health care coverage. These exchanges will not be fully implemented until 2014.

- **2. (E) is the answer.** Policy implementation is the process of carrying out public policy through governmental agencies and the courts. Actually creating an emissions trading system and selling allowances for the discharge of sulfur dioxide is carrying out the policies set forth in the Clean Air Act.

- **3. (D) is the answer.** Incentive techniques for policy implementation encourage people to act in line with government policy by offering payoffs or financial inducements. Subsidies for growing wheat is an example of a financial inducement.

- **4. (E) is the answer.** The root of the question is the definition of policy formulation. Each of the other answers refers to a different stage in the policy process.

- **5. (E) is the answer.** Public policy is defined in the root of the question. Each of the other answers refers to a different concept.

- **6. (B) is the answer.** Governmental agenda is defined in the root of the question. Each of the other answers refers to a different concept.

- **7. (C) is the answer.** Medicare is the federal program established in the Lyndon B. Johnson administration that provides medical care to elderly Social Security recipients. Medicaid is the government program that subsidizes medical care for the poor. Old Age, Survivors, and Disability Insurance is another name for Social Security. The National Health Service is the government-operated healthcare system in Britain.

- **8. (B) is the answer.** The governmental agenda is the changing list of issues which government believes it should address. Prior to the steep rise in oil prices and concomitant Arab oil embargo demonstrating America's vulnerability to heavy reliance on imported oil, energy policy was not an issue most government leaders thought needed to be on the governmental agenda, but changes in the early 1970s worked to put it there.

- **9. (C) is the answer.** Realignment theory is related to political parties and the interest groups that comprise them, the rest of the choices are theories of policy formulation.

- **10. (A) is the answer.** The correct order of stages in the policymaking process is: problem recognition, agenda setting, policy formulation, policy adoption, budgeting, policy implementation, and policy evaluation.

Free-Response Questions

This rubric provides examples of many, but not all, of the possible correct responses to the free-response questions.

1. All societies are divided into elites and masses. According to elite theory, the chosen few or elite make the important decisions in society. The elites have power to make and implement policy, while the masses simply respond to the desires of the elites. This results in elites having a disproportionate influence in society and almost complete control over policy.

   According to bureaucratic theory, organizations of any but the smallest size need the routine and standardized procedures provided by bureaucracy to function effectively. This growing complexity of modern organizations empowers bureaucrats, who become dominant as a consequence of their expertise and competence. Eventually, the bureaucrats wrest power from others, especially elected officials.

   According to interest group theory, interest groups—not elites or bureaucrats—control the governmental process. The noted interest group theorist David B. Truman believed that there are so many potential pressure points in the three branches of the federal government, as well as at the state level, that interest groups can step in on any number of competing sides. The government then becomes the equilibrium point in the system as it mediates among competing interests.

   Pluralist theory suggests that political power is distributed among a wide array of diverse and competing interest groups. For example, Robert Dahl argues that political resources in the United States are scattered so widely that no single elite group could ever gain monopoly control over any substantial area of policy. According to political scientist Theodore Lowi, participants in every political controversy get something; thus, each has some impact on how political decisions are made. Lowi contends that governments in the United States rarely say no to any well-organized interest, noting that all organized interests receive some benefits.

Two of the theories, pluralist theory and interest group theory, see interest groups having the dominant influence on policymaking, although they suggest ultimately that the state decides which interest group objectives will be achieved. Bureaucratic theory contends that it is the bureaucrats within the state that ultimately make the policies because they are about the only ones who fully grasp the complexities of implementing and evaluating policy. Both perspectives could be correct, however, with bureaucrats deciding exactly how the pluralistic policy objectives of different (and perhaps competing) interest groups will be met. Unless one assumes that bureaucrats are not part of the elite posited by elite theory, then bureaucratic theory and elite theory see different groups making policy. Even if one accepts elite theory's contention that it is the elites of the country who control decision-making, and through that policymaking, that is still compatible with the perspective of interest group theory and pluralist theory in that an elite-controlled state serves as the broker between the diverse, pluralistic competing interest groups that are trying to affect policy.

2. The first step in the policymaking process is problem recognition. This involves identification of an issue that disturbs the public and leads to a call for governmental intervention. In the case of energy policy, the hardships caused by both the steep increases in petroleum prices and the vulnerability that Americans felt as a result of the Arab Oil Embargo helped the public recognize that the country needed a new energy policy.

    Once this was recognized, energy policy moved into the next stage in the policymaking process—agenda setting. In this stage, reducing reliance on imported petroleum is placed on the governmental agenda, the list of issues to which governments believe they should address themselves.

    The next stage, policy formulation, is key. In this stage, policymakers come up with alternative approaches to addressing the problems placed on government's agenda. In the case of energy policy, one policy that was formulated was the Corporate Average Fuel Efficiency (CAFE) standards. In 1975, as a means of improving the gas mileage of automobiles in the United States, Congress decided to regulate the gas mileage of the entire line of cars made by each automaker. Collectively, a fleet could not exceed certain miles-per-gallon standards. Under CAFE, automakers were required to meet average fuel efficiency standards for the fleet of cars they sold in the United States.

    Then there is policy adoption, the approval of a policy proposal by the people with requisite authority. In the energy policy example, this would involve bureaucrats in the Department of Energy drafting the CAFE Standards. Closely related to creation of the standards is the next stage in the policymaking process—budgeting, which is the allocation of resources to provide for the proper implementation of public policies. A policy can be nullified by a refusal to fund or by grossly inadequate funding.

    Next is the stage of policy implementation, the process of carrying out public policy through governmental agencies. This would involve monitoring the performance of automakers to make sure they were adhering to the limits imposed by the CAFE Standards.

Lastly is the stage of policy evaluation, the process of determining whether a course of action is achieving its intended goal and what other effects it might be having.

CHAPTER 18

Economic Policy

The U.S. government and economy have always been closely entwined. The American economy is based on the principles of **capitalism** and **laissez-faire,** but in practice it is a **mixed economy** because the government plays a regulatory role. The regulatory role is evidenced by the activities of agencies like the **Securities and Exchange Commission (SEC),** which regulates stock fraud, and through the passage of laws such as the **minimum wage** law. The economic concerns of the government are changing due to the growth of **multinational corporations,** which have created a global economy.

Roots of Economic Policy

- **The 19th century move to an industrial economy:** Although the U.S. economic system is a mixed free-enterprise system characterized by the private ownership of property, private enterprise, and marketplace competition, the national government has long played an important role in fostering economic development through its policies on taxes, tariffs, the use of public lands, and the creation of a national bank. Once the industrial revolution began to hit full force in the late 1800s, new problems caused by industrialization became apparent, including workplace accidents and disease, labor–management conflict, unemployment, and the emergence of huge corporations that could exploit workers and consumers. Another problem was the hardship that resulted from downturns in the business cycle, which became more severe in the new industrial society. In these downturns, people lose their jobs and income, and the economy experiences a low or even negative growth rate. Disturbed by the problems resulting from industrialization, many people turned to government for help. At the same time, however, businesses and conservatives who had welcomed government intervention to aid economic development in the early decades of the 19th century, such as tariffs that provided protection from foreign competitors, now insisted that the market be allowed to regulate itself without government involvement. This debate over the role of government and the role of markets still goes on today.

- **Business cycles** are fluctuations between growth and recession, or periods of "boom and bust," and are an inherent part of modern capitalist economies.

- **Laissez-faire** is a French term meaning "to allow to do, to leave alone." It is a hands-off governmental policy that is based on the belief that government involvement in the economy is wrong.

- **The Interstate Commerce Act in 1887** was the first major government effort to regulate business. It was sparked by growing concern over the power of the railroads and resulted in the creation of the Interstate Commerce Commission (ICC), which would ensure that railroad rates would be "just and reasonable."

- **The Sherman Antitrust Act of 1890** prohibits all restraints of trade, including price-fixing, bid-rigging, and market allocation agreements. It also prohibits all monopolization or attempts to monopolize, including domination of a market by one company or a few companies.

- **The Progressive Era** was a reform movement that in part sought to bring corporate power under the control of government and make it more responsive to democratic ends. A wave of economic and business regulation to accomplish that was implemented under the Progressives, and much of it is still with us today.

- **The Pure Food and Drug Act and the Meat Inspection Act (both 1906):** These laws prohibited adulteration and mislabeling of food and drugs, set sanitary standards for the food industry, and marked the beginning of consumer protection as a major responsibility of the national government.

- **The Federal Reserve Act (1913)** created the Federal Reserve System to regulate the national banking system and to provide for flexibility in the money supply in order to better meet commercial needs and combat financial panics.

- **The Federal Trade Commission (FTC) Act and the Clayton Antitrust Act of 1914** strengthened antitrust policy. The FTC Act created the Federal Trade Commission and authorized it to prevent "unfair methods of competition," including price discrimination, exclusive dealing contracts, and corporate mergers that lessened competition. These statutes, like the Sherman Antitrust Act, sought to prevent businesses from forming monopolies. Also, recall that it was a provision of the Clayton Act that legalized unions and their activities like striking and picketing.

- **The Sixteenth Amendment** authorized the national government "to lay and collect taxes on incomes, from whatever source derived" without being apportioned among the states. Personal and corporate income taxes have since become the national government's major source of general revenues. Income taxes and particularly the tax burden have also been a source of continued political controversy.

- **Interventionist state** is an alternative to the laissez-faire state; the government takes an active role in guiding and managing the private economy. It was a result of the Depression and New Deal that the laissez-faire state was replaced with an interventionist state.

- **Federal Deposit Insurance Corporation (FDIC)** created federally administered bank deposit insurance (up to a maximum amount per account).

- **The Securities Act (1933)** required that prospective investors be given full and accurate information about the stocks or securities being offered to them.

- **The Securities Exchange Act (1934)** created the Securities and Exchange Commission (SEC), an independent regulatory commission. The SEC was authorized to regulate the stock exchanges, enforce the Securities Act, and reduce the number of stocks bought on margin.

- **Agricultural subsidies:** The overall effect of the New Deal agricultural legislation was to protect farmers through extensive government subsidies and price support programs. This is still the basis of American agricultural policy.

- **National Labor Relations Act (or the Wagner Act):** This statute guaranteed workers' rights to organize and bargain collectively through unions of their own choosing. The act prohibited a series of "unfair labor practices," such as discriminating against employees because of their union activities. The National Labor Relations Board (NLRB) was created to carry out the act and to conduct elections to determine which union, if any, employees wanted to represent them. Unions prospered under the protection provided by the Wagner Act.

- **The Fair Labor Standards Act (FLSA) of 1938** intended to protect the interests of low-paid workers. The law set a minimum wage workers could be paid and a standard workweek of 40 hours. If workers worked over the 40 hours, the FLSA required that they be paid overtime.

- **Economic regulation** is government regulation of business practices, industry rates, routes, or areas serviced by particular industries. Economic regulation is usually tailored to the conditions of particular industries, such as railroads or stock exchanges.

- **Social regulation** is government regulation of the quality and safety of products as well as the conditions under which goods and services are produced. Social regulation strives to protect and enhance the quality of life.

- **Deregulation** is a reduction in market controls (such as price fixing, subsidies, or controls on who can enter the field) in favor of market-based competition. Advocates of deregulation contended that regulation often encouraged lack of competition and monopolistic exploitation, discrimination in services, and inefficiency in operation of regulated industries.

- **The Airline Deregulation Act of 1978** is a good example of deregulation. This law completely eliminated economic regulation of commercial airlines over several years. Although many new passenger carriers flocked into the industry when barriers to entry were first removed, they were unable to compete successfully with the existing major airlines. Consequently, there are now fewer major carriers than under the regulatory regime, although new airlines continue to emerge.

- **Fiscal policy:** The deliberate use of the national government's taxing and spending policies to maintain economic stability. Examples include federal government policies on taxes, spending, and debt management, intended to promote the nation's macroeconomic goals, particularly with respect to employment, price stability, and growth.

- **John Maynard Keynes** was an influential British economist who argued that deficit spending by a government could supplement the total or aggregate demand for goods and services, especially during recessions. There is a level of total or aggregate spending at which the economy will operate at full employment. Total spending is the sum of consumer spending, private investment spending, and government spending. If consumer and business spending does not create demand sufficient to cause the economy to operate at full employment, then the government should make up the shortfall by increasing spending in excess of revenues. This was essentially what Keynes recommended for the national government during the Great Depression. If inflation is the problem confronting policy makers, then government can reduce demand for goods and services by reducing its expenditures and running a budget surplus. With adoption of Keynes's views, the government had essentially assumed responsibility for economic stability.

- **Discretionary fiscal policy** involves deliberate decisions by the president and Congress to run budget surpluses or deficits. This can be done by increasing or decreasing spending while holding taxes constant, by increasing or cutting taxes while holding spending stable, or by some combination of changes in taxing and spending. There remains a serious partisan division over tax politics. By and large, Republicans have remained steadfast supporters of tax cuts, while Democrats have remained committed to tax revenues as the means of funding government programs.

- **Effects of globalization:** Many believe that reducing trade barriers and increasing economic interaction with other countries has, on balance, had a beneficial impact on the U.S. economy because the competition created by free trade limits price increases on American goods and services, thereby benefiting consumers. In addition, free trade expands the market for high-quality American products that are in demand in the global economy. On the other hand, a number of analysts have warned of globalization's impact on income distribution. Globalization appears to further segment the market into economic winners and losers. During the 1990s, Fortune 500 companies achieved huge gains, yet many of those gains appeared to come at the expense of smaller businesses and workers. In 1999, analysts found that the average real after-tax income of the middle 60 percent of Americans was lower than it was in 1977.

- **Gross domestic product (GDP)** is the total market value of all goods and services produced in a country during a year.

  - **The budget process:** The primary purpose of the federal budget is funding government programs, but manipulating the budget can also be used as part of fiscal policy to stabilize the economy and to counteract fluctuations. The budget runs for a single fiscal year, beginning on October 1 of one calendar year and running through September 30 of the following calendar year. The fiscal year takes its name from the calendar year in which it ends; thus the time period from October 1, 2008 through September 30, 2009 is designated fiscal year (FY) 2009. The president sends a budget proposal to Congress in January or February of each year. Article I of the Constitution provides that "no money shall be drawn from the Treasury, but in consequence of appropriations made by law." Congress and its legislative committees (such as those on resources, education and educational opportunities, and national security) may authorize spending on programs, but it is Congress and the appropriations committees in each chamber that actually provide the funding needed to carry out these programs. Congress often modifies the president's budget request.

- **How the federal government raises and spends money:** The federal government raises money from a variety of sources, with individual income taxes and social insurance and retirement receipts representing over 80 percent of the funds received. Most government spending is directed toward national defense and human resources.

- **Office of Management and Budget (OMB)** was created to assist the president and handle the details of budget preparation. Acting in accordance with presidential decisions on the general structure of the budget, the OMB provides the various departments and agencies with instructions and guidance on presidential priorities to help them in preparing their budget requests. The departments and agencies then proceed to develop their detailed funding requests. The OMB reconciles the discrepancies between presidential and agency preferences, but it should be remembered that the OMB's mission is to defend the presidential budgetary agenda.

- **The Congressional Budget Office (CBO)** is a professional staff of technical experts who assist the budget committees and provide members of Congress with their own source of budgetary information, making them more independent of the OMB.

- **Major budget conflicts:** Conflict often develops between Congress and the president over the details of the budget and its overall dimensions, such as the size of the deficit, the balance between military and domestic spending, and international agreements affecting domestic economics. Uncertainty also arises over the political feasibility of funding very specific initiatives.

- **Federal budget deficit** is the amount by which federal expenditure exceeds federal revenue.

- **The budget deficit and the debt:** While deficits have long been recognized for their potentially negative impact on economies, acceptance of Keynesian economic perspectives since the 1930s has led some economists to justify federal deficits as a means of stimulating economic growth in periods of decline. In contrast to state governments, the federal government (because of its size and macroeconomic responsibilities) legitimizes deficit spending. It is believed that such spending is needed from time to time to stimulate economic recovery and keep vital social and defense-related expenses intact. Deficits are justified in times of recession; however, they are criticized if they are viewed as "structural" or built into the economy even in times of prosperity.

- **Inflation** is a rise in the general price levels of an economy.

- **Monetary policy** is a form of government regulation in which the nation's money supply and interest rates are controlled.

- **The Federal Reserve System** was created in 1913 to adjust the money supply to the needs of agriculture, commerce, and industry. The Federal Reserve System comprises the Federal Reserve Board (FRB—formally, the Board of Governors of the Federal Reserve System; informally, "the Fed"), the Federal Open Market Committee (FOMC), the 12 Federal Reserve Banks in regions throughout the country, and other member banks. Formally, the FRB has much independence from the executive branch, ostensibly so that monetary policy will not be influenced by political considerations.

- **Board of Governors:** In the Federal Reserve System, this is a seven-member board that sets member banks' reserve requirements, controls the discount rate, and makes other economic decisions. The president appoints (subject to Senate confirmation) the seven members of the Board of Governors, who serve 14-year, overlapping terms. The president can remove a member for stated causes, but this has never occurred. The president designates one board member to serve as chair for a four-year term, which runs from the midpoint of one presidential term to the midpoint of the next to ensure economic stability during a change of administrations. The current chair is Ben Bernanke.

- **Reserve requirements** are government requirements that a portion of member banks' deposits must be retained to back loans made. If the Fed lowers the discount rate, more money is available for loans, and economic growth is encouraged. If inflation were occurring because economic growth was too rapid, the Fed could raise the discount rate and make credit less available, slowing economic growth and reducing inflation.

- **Discount rate** is the rate of interest at which member banks can borrow money from their regional Federal Reserve Bank. Lowering the discount rate encourages local member banks to increase their borrowing from the Fed and extend more loans at lower rates. This expands economic activity, since when rates are lower, more people should be able to qualify for large purchases by taking out car loans or housing mortgages. As a consequence of cheaper interest rates, more large durable goods (such as houses and cars) should be produced and sold. As with reserve requirements, raising the discount rate is a way to slow economic growth that is occurring too rapidly and causing economic instability because of high inflation.

- **Open market operations** are the buying and selling of government securities by the Federal Reserve Bank in the securities market. Fed purchases of securities from member banks in essence give the banks an added supply of money. This action increases the availability of loans and should decrease interest rates. Decreases in interest rates stimulate economic activity.

- **The FRB and the executive and legislative branches:** Although the public generally holds the president responsible for maintaining a healthy economy, he does not really possess adequate constitutional or legal authority to meet this obligation. The president shares responsibility for fiscal policy with Congress, and Congress authorizes the FRB to make monetary policy. In terms of pressing the Fed to adjust its monetary policy, presidential power is, at its best, "the power to persuade."

- **Income security programs** protect people against loss of income because of retirement, disability, unemployment, or death or absence of the family breadwinner. Programs that serve these functions have become increasingly expected by many citizens since the federal government began the first income security programs to help bring about economic stability during the Great Depression.

- **Social Security Act**: A 1935 law that established old age insurance; assistance for the needy, aged, blind, and families with dependent children; and unemployment insurance.

- **Entitlement programs**: Government benefits that all citizens meeting eligibility criteria—such as age, income level, or unemployment—are legally "entitled" to receive.

- **Non-means-tested programs**: Programs that provide cash assistance to qualified beneficiaries, regardless of income. Among these are Social Security and unemployment insurance.

- **Means-tested programs**: Programs require that people must have incomes below specified levels to be eligible for benefits. Among these are Supplemental Security Income (SSI), Temporary Assistance for Needy Families (TANF), Earned Income tax Credit (EITC), and Supplemental Nutrition Assistance Program (SNAP).

Toward Reform: Recession and Economic Recovery

- **Economic stability** is a situation in which there is economic growth, rising national income, high employment, and steadiness in the general level of prices.

- **Recession** is a short-term decline in the economy that occurs as investment sags, production falls off, and unemployment increases.

- **Fiscal Policy responses to recession of 2008**

- **Troubled Assets Relief Program (TARP**. Monies allocated to it are called TARP funds.) This was a $700 billion federal bailout package of the financial services industry. The plan was intended to reassure the financial markets by allowing the government to buy up the assets that had led to the crisis.

- **American Recovery and Reinvestment Act**: This legislation authorized the government to spend more than $787 billion on a variety of tax cuts and public works programs designed to stimulate the economy and to maintain and create jobs in transportation, education, health care, and other industries.

- **Monetary Policy responses to the recession of 2008**: Federal Reserve Board responded to the economic slowdown by lowering interest rates and engaging in large open-market operations and discount rate reductions to increase liquidity in the markets. Despite signs of an economic recovery in early 2010, the Fed has continued to keep interest rates low in the hopes of attracting borrowers who will inject money in to the market.

- **Income Security Policy:** The worsening economic conditions and rising unemployment have put pressure on the national and state governments to continue to administer income security programs, even as their rolls grow rapidly. The most severe consequences of this growth are for state budgets and the national deficit and debt. Recall that states must have balanced budgets—the amount of revenues must be equal to or greater than expenditure levels. For its part, the federal government has engaged in deficit spending in order to fund these and other programs, as well as to help states balance their budgets. The costs of these expenditures will not be fully realized for years, as the nation faces a growing national debt.

For Additional Review

Unemployment and inflation are two social consequences of economic downturns. Brainstorm a list of some other social problems that may arise as a result of these two situations. What other consequences might result from a poor economy? Can you think of anything consumers can do to avoid or alleviate these problems?

Multiple-Choice Questions

1. Which of the following best describes the doctrine of laissez-faire?
(A) an active government role in the economy to ensure widespread prosperity
(B) a hands-off approach to government involvement in the economy
(C) the philosophy that if it's worth doing, it's worth doing well
(D) the philosophy that if it's worth doing, it's worth doing poorly
(E) using fiscal policy to ensure sound monetary policies

2. Monetary policy refers to government control of
(A) the banking and computer industries.
(B) the money supply and interest rates.
(C) taxing and spending policies.
(D) equities and securities.
(E) bonds and deficits.

3. The purpose of antitrust policy, such as that set forth in the Sherman and Clayton Antitrust acts is to
(A) ensure competition and prevent monopolies.
(B) increase the amount of trust the public has in government.
(C) ensure a smooth relationship between the Federal Reserve Board and Congress.
(D) increase tax revenue from private corporations.
(E) reduce the likelihood of high unemployment.

4. A recession is
(A) a short-term decline in the economy that occurs as investment sags, production falls off, and unemployment increases.
(B) caused by high levels of government debt.
(C) a decrease in the amount of money in banks, which raises loan rates and discourages people from borrowing.
(D) a time when monetary policy is used to increase interest rates to keep people from going further into debt.
(E) a time of increasing amounts of imports that displace American workers.

5. Which of the following would be an example of fiscal policy?
(A) intentionally running a budget deficit to spur economic growth
(B) cutting the prime interest rate to encourage investment
(C) engaging in open market operations
(D) inflating the value of government assets to increase real estate prices
(E) purchasing consumers' credit card debt to prevent personal bankruptcies

6. Which of the following statements best describes the significance of the National Labor Relations Act?
(A) It prohibits labor unions within the federal bureaucracy.
(B) It guarantees workers the right to unionize and bargain collectively.
(C) It allows mediation to solve conflicts between public and private workers.
(D) It allows companies to disband labor unions after giving 30 days advanced notice.
(E) It prohibits labor unions from collecting union dues from federal workers.

7. Which of the following is an example of an income security program response to the recession of 2008?
(A) the Federal Reserve raising the Reserve Requirement
(B) the American Recovery and Reinvestment Act
(C) Troubled Assets Relief Program
(D) lowering interest rates and engaging in large open-market operations and discount rate reductions to increase liquidity in the markets.
(E) an increased federal deficit. The federal government has engaged in deficit spending in order to fund these and other programs, as well as to help states balance their budgets.

8. All of the following are affected by actions of the Federal Reserve Board EXCEPT
(A) the federal budget deficit.
(B) the money supply.
(C) interest rates.
(D) the availability of credit to consumers.
(E) the amount of money available for banks to loan.

9. The Fair Labor Standard Act (FLSA) of 1938 established
(A) a minimum wage.
(B) job classifications such as blue collar and white collar.
(C) official descriptions of different types of jobs.
(D) Unions.
(E) the minimum age at which a person could work.

10. A Federal Reserve open-market operation involves
(A) protecting people against loss of income because of retirement, disability, unemployment, or death or absence of the family breadwinner.
(B) government benefits that all citizens meeting eligibility criteria—such as age, income level, or unemployment—are legally "entitled" to receive.
(C) the buying and selling of government securities by the Federal Reserve Bank in the securities market.
(D) government requirements that a portion of member banks' deposits must be retained to back loans made.
(E) the setting of the rate of interest at which member banks can borrow money from their regional Federal Reserve Bank.

It is very unlikely that you would be asked to address one specific policy area in an AP free-response question. It is, however, important that you understand the public policymaking process in general and be able to draw appropriate examples from a variety of policy areas. The following questions will help you to prepare.

1. Economic policy involves deciding which government actions are necessary to maintain economic stability.

    a. Identify three types of economic policy.
    b. Describe the goals of economic policy pursued by the types of economic policy you discuss.
    c. Explain how the policies work to achieve those goals.

2. Congress and the president share responsibility in the budget process. Discuss the role of each in the process and what institutions they have created to handle their roles and what issues of conflict occur between them.

ANSWERS AND EXPLANATIONS

Multiple-Choice Questions

- **1. (B) is correct.** Laissez-faire is French for "to allow to do, to leave alone." In economic terms, it refers to the idea that government involvement in the economy is wrong.

- **2. (B) is correct.** Monetary policy is a form of government regulation in which the nation's money supply and interest rates are controlled to promote economic stability, as distinct from fiscal, in which tax rates and spending are used to promote economic stability.

- **3. (A) is correct.** Antitrust policy is designed to ensure competition in the marketplace and prevent monopolies. Antitrust policy is another example of the government's ability to be involved in the economy.

- **4. (A) is correct.** A recession is a short-term decline in the economy that occurs as investment sags, production falls off, and unemployment increases is known as a recession. It is not caused directly by high levels of government debt, increasing amounts of imports that displace American workers, or by a decrease in the amount of money in banks. It is also not a time when monetary policy is used to increase interest rates to keep people from going further into debt. Typically, the government tries to expand credit.

- **5. (A) is correct.** Fiscal policy involves government policies on taxes, spending, and debt management. It is used to promote the nation's macroeconomic goals, particularly with respect to employment, price stability, and economic growth. Running a deficit with the goal of encouraging economic growth would be fiscal policy.

- **6. (B) is correct.** The National Labor Relations Act, also known as the Wagner Act, is a 1935 law that guarantees workers the right to unionize and bargain collectively.

- **7. (E) is correct.** To maintain income security programs during the recession, a time of declining government revenue at all levels, the federal government has engaged in deficit spending in order to fund income security programs, as well as to help states balance their budgets as the cost of their contribution to these programs has gone up. Raising the Reserve Requirement would be an example of monetary policy response to the recession, while the American Recovery and Reinvestment Act and the Troubled Assets Relief Program are examples of fiscal policy responses.

- **8. (A) is correct.** The Federal Reserve Board has either direct or indirect influence over money supply, interest rates, the availability of credit to consumers and the amount of money available for banks to loans. It does not have control over the amount of money the government spends.

- **9. (A) is correct.** The FLSA established a minimum wage workers could be paid and a standard workweek of 40 hours. It did none of the things discussed in the other choices.

- **10. (E) is correct.** When the Federal Reserve engages in the buying and selling of government securities in the securities market, it is engaged in open market operations. Income security programs protect people against loss of income because of retirement, disability, unemployment, or death or absence of the family breadwinner. Government benefits that all citizens meeting eligibility criteria—such as age, income level, or unemployment—are legally "entitled" to receive are referred to as entitlements. The requirements that portions of member banks' deposits must be retained to back loans made are known as Reserve Requirements. The Discount Rate is the rate of interest at which member banks can borrow money from their regional Federal Reserve Bank.

Free-Response Questions

1.

a. Three types of economic policy are regulation of business, fiscal policy, and monetary policy.

b. Business regulation assumes two forms:

1. Economic regulation is government regulation of business practices, industry rates, routes, or areas serviced by particular industries. It is usually tailored to the conditions of particular industries, such as railroads or stock exchanges. The goal of this regulation is to preserve "economic fair play" between businesses within an industry and between those

businesses and theirs consumers. They do this by establishing and enforcing regulations that act as rules for economic fair play.

2. Social regulation is government regulation of the quality and safety of products as well as the conditions under which goods and services are produced. Social regulation strives to protect and enhance the quality of life. They do this in part by establishing standards for business to observe, but also by providing a framework for lawsuits that consumers and workers can use to enforce safe product and workplace standards.

c. Fiscal policy involves federal government use of policies on taxes, spending, and debt management to promote the nation's macroeconomic goals, particularly with respect to employment, price stability, and growth. It is in large measure shaped by the ideas of John Maynard Keynes, an influential British economist who argued that total spending is the sum of consumer spending, private investment spending, and government spending. If consumer and business spending does not create demand sufficient to cause the economy to operate at full employment, then the government should make up the shortfall by increasing spending in excess of revenues. This can be done by increasing or decreasing spending while holding taxes constant, by increasing or cutting taxes while holding spending stable, or by some combination of changes in taxing and spending. There remains a serious partisan division over tax politics.

d. Monetary policy involves government regulation in which the nation's money supply and interest rates are controlled in order to promote economic stability. This is done by the Federal Reserve System (FRS), which formally has much independence from the executive branch, ostensibly so that monetary policy will not be influenced by political considerations.

   The FRS has three primary tools that it uses to implement monetary policy. One is reserve requirements. These are government requirements that a portion of member banks' deposits must be retained to back loans made. If the Fed lowers the discount rate, more money is available for loans, and economic growth would be encouraged. If inflation were occurring because economic growth was too rapid, the Fed could raise the discount rate and make credit less available, slowing economic growth and reducing inflation. Another is the discount rate, the rate of interest at which member banks can borrow money from their regional Federal Reserve Bank. Lowering the discount rate would encourage local member banks to increase their borrowing from the Fed and extend more loans at lower rates. This would expand economic activity, since when rates are lower, more people should be able to qualify for large purchases by taking out car loans or housing mortgages. As a consequence of cheaper interest rates, more large durable goods (such as houses and cars) should be produced and sold. As with reserve requirements, raising the discount rate would be a way to slow economic growth that was occurring too rapidly and causing economic instability because of high inflation. The FRS can also use open-market operations, the buying and selling of government securities by the Federal Reserve Bank in the securities market. Fed purchases of securities from member banks in essence give the banks an added supply of money. This action increases the availability of loans and should decrease interest rates. Decreases in interest rates stimulate economic activity.

2. The primary purpose of the federal budget is funding government programs, but manipulating the budget can also be used as part of fiscal policy to stabilize the economy and to counteract fluctuations. The president sends a budget proposal to Congress in January or February of each year. Article I of the Constitution provides that "no money shall be drawn from the Treasury, but in consequence of appropriations made by law." Congress and its legislative committees (such as those on resources, education and educational opportunities, and national security) may authorize spending on programs, but it is Congress and the appropriations committees in each chamber that actually provide the funding needed to carry out these programs. Congress often modifies the president's budget request.

Presidents use the Office of Management and Budget (OMB) to handle the details of budget preparation. Acting in accordance with presidential decisions on the general structure of the budget, the OMB provides the various departments and agencies with instructions and guidance on presidential priorities to help them in preparing their budget requests. The departments and agencies then proceed to develop their detailed funding requests. The OMB reconciles the discrepancies between presidential and agency preferences, but it should be remembered that the OMB's mission is to defend the presidential budgetary agenda.

Congress has its own institution to help with the budget, the Congressional Budget Office (CBO). The CBO assists the budget committees and provides members of Congress with their own source of budgetary information so that they are more independent of the OMB.

Conflict often develops between Congress and the president over the details of the budget and its overall dimensions, such as the size of the deficit, the balance between military and domestic spending, and international agreements affecting domestic economics. Uncertainty also arises over the political feasibility of funding very specific initiatives.

CHAPTER 19

Foreign and Defense Policy

Foreign policy has become crucial to governmental affairs in the past century, as the United States made the transition from isolationist country to world superpower. In this global era of high-speed connections, brief but deadly missile strikes, and free trade, it is apparent that this policy area will continue to hold an important place on every politician's agenda and in the public's mind as well.

Roots of U.S. Foreign and Defense Policy

- **Foreign policy**: Encompasses how one country builds relationships with other countries in order to safeguard its national interest.

- **Defense policy**: Comprised of the strategies that a country uses to protect itself from its enemies.

- **Isolationism:** A national policy of avoiding participation in foreign affairs.

- **Embargo Act** was passed by Congress in 1807 to prevent U.S. ships from leaving U.S. ports for foreign ports without the approval of the federal government. President Thomas Jefferson believed that European states, embroiled in the continuing Napoleonic Wars, depended so much on U.S.-provided supplies and raw materials that they would accede to America's demands and respect the rights of neutral countries to trade. The policy failed, doing more damage to the American economy than the countries being targeted.

  Monroe Doctrine was President James Monroe's 1823 pledge that the United States would oppose attempts by European states to extend their political control into the Western Hemisphere. In reality, the Monroe Doctrine was a preference more than a policy, since the United States had little capability to enforce it. However, Great Britain also wanted to keep other European powers out of the Americas. The Royal Navy thus protected British interests and promoted U.S. preferences.

- **War of 1812** was the first war declared by the United States. It was fought over British violations of America's vision of the trading rights of neutral countries. It was a draw, with the peace reverting back to the prewar situation.

- **Tariffs** are taxes on imports used to raise government revenue and to protect infant industries. Congress passed the first protectionist tariff in 1816. High protectionist tariffs were the American norm well into the 20th century. While high tariffs protected the U.S. market for American producers, they also cut off foreign markets for American producers as foreign countries retaliated with their own high tariffs.

- **Manifest destiny** was the theory that the United States was divinely mandated to expand across North America to the Pacific Ocean. The United States fought a war with Mexico in pursuit of this policy and obtained roughly a quarter of the continental United States, extending from Texas to California up to Colorado, Utah, and Nevada.

- **Roosevelt Corollary** is the concept developed by President Theodore Roosevelt early in the 20th century that it was the United States' responsibility to ensure stability in Latin America and the Caribbean.

- **Interests beyond the Western Hemisphere:** The United States did not limit its economic ambitions to North America. By the mid-19th century, the United States concluded a commercial treaty with China and opened Japan to Western trade. As American economic interests in the Pacific expanded, so did U.S. interest in acquiring Pacific islands to support expansion. Thus, in the 1890s, the United States acquired the Hawaiian Islands, Midway Island, Wake Island, and part of Samoa.

- **Spanish–American War** was fought between the United States and Spain over Spanish policies and presence in Cuba. The United States won an easy victory, making the world take note of the United States as a rising power. Not only had the United States defeated an established European power, albeit one in decline, but it also acquired heavily populated overseas territories, Puerto Rico, the Philippines, Guam, and for a few years, Cuba. The United States had clearly become a colonial power.

- **Open Door Notes**: A proposal to the countries with spheres of influence in the late 19th century, calling upon them not to discriminate against other investors in their spheres of influence, including China. A major weakness of this strategy was that the Open Door Notes lacked any form of enforcement and thus were easily ignored. Nevertheless, it was the background for later American initiatives to have global trade operate on a more liberal basis, culminating in the World Trade Organization (WTO).

- **World War I:** Although the United States maintained neutrality for much of WWI, defending America's vision of the rights of neutral countries to trade ultimately led the U.S. to enter WWI. Even though the United States entered the war late, its armed forces and economic assistance swung the tide of victory to the Allies' side.

- **Collective security** is the concept that peace would be secured if all countries collectively opposed any country that invaded another.

- **League of Nations** was proposed by President Woodrow Wilson and created the peace treaty that ended World War I. It was an international governmental organization dedicated to preserving peace. Aside from some partisan reasons, many senators opposed the League because they believed membership in it went against traditional U.S. isolationism and unilateralism. The Senate thus refused to give the necessary two-thirds vote to ratify the Treaty of Versailles, which formalized the terms of the end of the war, and the United States never joined the League.

- **Smoot-Hawley Tariff** was a high tariff passed to try to protect the U.S. market for American producers during the Great Depression. Other countries responded by raising their tariffs, and overseas trade dropped to about one-third its former level. As the Great Depression of the 1930s worsened, some Americans concluded that isolationism and unilateralism were wrong. They argued that the depression was worse than it may have been because of the decline in trade brought about by high tariffs.

The United States as a World Power

- **Pearl Harbor** is a naval base in Hawaii, which was attacked by Japan on December 7, 1941, initiating America's entry into World War II.

- **World War II and its aftermath, 1941–1947:** The experience of WWII convinced many Americans that the United States had to be less isolationist and less unilateralist than before the war and had to involve itself in world affairs on a regular, sustained basis.

- **United Nations (UN)** is an international governmental organization created shortly before the end of World War II to guarantee the security of nations and to promote global economic, physical, and social well-being.

- **Bretton Woods System** is an international financial agreement signed shortly before the end of World War II that created the World Bank and the International Monetary Fund.

- **International Monetary Fund (IMF)** is an international governmental organization created shortly before the end of World War II to stabilize international financial relations through fixed monetary exchange rates.

- **World Bank** is an international governmental organization created shortly before the end of World War II to provide loans for large economic development projects.

- **General Agreement on Tariffs and Trade (GATT):** Post–World War II economic development program designed to help facilitate international trade negotiations and promote free trade.

- **The Cold War** is a period of tension and largely unarmed conflict between the Soviet Union and the United States from the end of WWII to the early 1990s. It was largely caused by the belief of many Americans that the Soviet Union was bent on dominating the world.

- **Truman Doctrine** was the U.S. policy initiated in 1947, providing economic assistance and military aid to countries fighting against Communist threats or political pressure.

- **Marshall Plan** was a postwar European recovery program, named after the secretary of state, George C. Marshall. It provided extensive U.S. aid to Western Europe after World War II.

- **Containment** was a strategy to oppose expansion of Soviet power, particularly in Western Europe and East Asia, using military power, economic assistance, and political influence.

- **North Atlantic Treaty Organization (NATO)** was the first peacetime military treaty the United States joined. NATO is a regional political and military organization that was created in 1949.

- **Cuban Missile Crisis** was the 1962 confrontation that nearly escalated into nuclear war between the United States and the Soviet Union. It was caused by Soviet deployment of medium range ballistic missiles in Cuba.

- **Vietnam War:** Between 1965 and 1973, the United States deployed up to 500,000 troops to Vietnam to try to prevent North Vietnam from taking over South Vietnam; the effort failed and was extremely divisive within the United States.

- **Détente** was the relaxation of tensions between the United States and the Soviet Union that occurred during the 1970s. Détente finally ended in 1979 when the Soviet Union invaded Afghanistan.

- **Human rights** policies are based on the belief that human beings have inalienable rights, such as freedom of speech and freedom of religion. Trying to support human rights across the globe—in part to contrast the United States with the Soviets, and swing neutral countries to America's side during the Cold War—was a policy promoted by the Carter administration.

- **End of the Cold War:** President Reagan accelerated the U.S. arms buildup and, in response to Soviet influence in developing countries, initiated an activist foreign policy. Eventually, internal weakness of the Soviet system, exacerbated by trying to keep up with Reagan activist foreign policy, caused the Communist governments in Eastern Europe and the Soviet Union to collapse, thus ending the Cold War.

- **Reagan Doctrine** was a policy that the United States would provide military assistance to anticommunist groups fighting against pro-Soviet governments.

- **Persian Gulf War:** The 1990 Iraqi invasion of Kuwait produced a new challenge. The Bush administration believed that the invasion threatened vital U.S. interests, and the United Nations passed a resolution authorizing the use of force to expel Iraq from Kuwait. Shortly after the U.S. Congress voted to support the use of military force against Iraq, the Persian Gulf War began in January 1991. In an attack called Operation Desert Storm, U.S. and allied forces defeated Iraq in a matter of weeks. The objective—expelling Iraq from Kuwait—had been achieved with few U.S. casualties.

- **Democratic enlargement** is a policy implemented during the Clinton administration, specifying that the United States would actively promote the expansion of democracy and free markets throughout the world.

- **North American Free Trade Agreement (NAFTA)** is an agreement that promotes free movement of goods and services among Canada, Mexico, and the United States.

- **World Trade Organization (WTO)** is an international governmental organization created in 1995 that manages multilateral negotiations to reduce barriers to trade and settle trade disputes.

- **Al-Qaeda** is a worldwide terrorist organization led by Osama bin Laden; it is responsible for numerous terrorist attacks against U.S. interests, including the 9/11 attacks at the World Trade Center and the Pentagon.

- **War on terrorism** was initiated by the Bush administration after the 9/11 attacks, to weed out terrorist operatives throughout the world using diplomacy, military means, improved homeland security, stricter banking laws, and other means. It was under this conflict that the U.S. led invasions of Afghanistan in 2001 and Iraq in 2003.

- **Taliban** is a fundamentalist Islamic government of Afghanistan that provided terrorist training bases for al-Qaeda.

- **The War in Iraq**: A broader foreign policy agenda emerged in President Bush's 2002 State of the Union Address. In this speech, Bush identified Iraq, North Korea, and Iran as an **"axis of evil"** that threatened American security interests. Movement to war with Iraq soon developed. The United States invaded Iraq in March 2003 and quickly defeated the Iraqi army. Clearly, the Bush administration did not plan for a long or contested occupation of Iraq, but the reality on the ground soon challenged this vision. American casualties began to rise. As of 2010, the deployment of U.S. troops continued, although these forces are scheduled to leave Iraq by 2011.

Foreign and Defense Policy Decision Making

- **The Constitution and foreign and defense policy:** The framers of the Constitution divided authority for many foreign and military policy functions between the president and Congress. The framers named the president commander in chief of the armed forces but gave Congress power to fund the army and navy and to declare war. The president has authority to negotiate and sign treaties, but treaties only take effect after the Senate ratifies them by a two-thirds majority.

- **The president** is preeminent in foreign and defense policy for several reasons. The president alone is in charge of all executive branch resources. The president has greater access to and control over information.

- **Department of State** is the chief executive branch department responsible for formulation and implementation of U.S. foreign policy.

- **Department of Defense** is the chief executive branch department responsible for formulation and implementation of U.S. military policy.

- **Joint Chiefs of Staff** is an advisory body to the president that includes the army chief of staff, the air force chief of staff, the chief of naval operations, and the marine commandant.

- **Department of Homeland Security** is a cabinet department created after the 9/11 attacks to coordinate domestic U.S. security efforts against terrorism. The department includes the Transportation Security Administration (TSA), the organization responsible for aviation security; the Federal Emergency Management Agency (FEMA), the primary federal disaster relief organization; Customs and Border Protection; the Coast Guard; the Secret Service; and immigration services and enforcement.

- **Central Intelligence Agency (CIA)** is an executive agency responsible for collection and analysis of information and intelligence about foreign countries and events.

- **Congressional oversight:** Congress oversees foreign and defense policy in many ways. Congress's oversight powers include the ability to conduct hearings on foreign and defense policy and to have the president and CIA inform congressional committees about covert operations.

- **Executive agreements:** Presidents can avoid the treaty process by using executive agreements, which, unlike treaties, do not require Senate approval.

- **Appropriations:** Congress has a key role in shaping foreign and defense policy through its power to appropriate funds, and it influences when and where the United States fights through its control of the budget. For example, in 1982, Congress used its appropriation power to limit U.S. involvement in Nicaragua, where the Reagan administration had been providing military aid to the Contras, a guerrilla group fighting the Sandinistas, the governing faction who were receiving aid from Cuba and the Soviet Union.

- **War Powers Act** was passed by Congress in 1973; the president is limited in the deployment of troops overseas to a 60-day period in peacetime (which can be extended for an extra 30 days to permit withdrawal), unless Congress explicitly gives its approval for a longer period.

- **Military-industrial complex** is the grouping of the U.S. armed forces and defense industries. President Eisenhower feared the military-industrial complex could become an increasingly dominant factor in U.S. politics with "potential for the disastrous rise of misplaced power."

Contemporary Challenges in Foreign and Defense Policy

- **Trade**: Countries adopt one of three basic approaches in constructing their international trade policy:

  - **Protectionism**: A trade policy wherein a country closes off its markets to foreign goods.

  - **Strategic trade policy:** A trade policy wherein governments identify key industries that they wish to see grow and enact policies to support this economic enlargement.

  - **Free trade system**: A system of international trade with limited government interference.

  - **North American Free Trade Agreement (NAFTA)**: Agreement that promotes free movement of goods and services among Canada, Mexico, and the United States.

  - **World Trade Organization (WTO)**: An international organization created in 1995 to supervise and open international trade.

  - **Trade with China**: The bilateral trade relationship between the United States and China has grown dramatically over the past three decades. By 2009, it was valued at $366 billion. This has made China the United States' second-largest trading partner, the single largest source of imports in the United States, and its third-largest export market. Two issues have been of particular concern to American policymakers when judging the impact of Chinese imports on the U.S. economy. The first is the loss of jobs that appears to be the result of the surge in Chinese imports. The second major issue involves health and safety problems associated with Chinese imports.

- **Immigration and Border Security**: The presence of large numbers of immigrants can be a source of international and domestic tension. The September 11 terrorist attacks dramatically altered citizens' views on immigration in the United States. Citizens repeatedly reaffirmed their belief in the need for a border fence and dramatic increases in the number of Border Patrol agents. Though additional patrolmen were hired almost immediately after the attacks, little progress was made on the fence until 2006, when President George W. Bush signed the Secure Fence Act. The project has proven to be controversial on a number of counts. It experienced significant cost overruns. Legal waivers were needed to circumvent the requirements of the Endangered Species Act, the Clean Water Act, the Clean Air Act, and the National Historic Preservation Act. States and communities along the border registered objections to the concept of a fence because of the negative impact it had on economic activity in their areas. In more recent years, concern over terrorists crossing the U.S.–Mexican border has been overtaken by a concern for mounting drug-related violence.

- **Terrorism**: Terrorism is violence for purposes of political intimidation. The common goal shared by Islamic terrorist groups has been to drive the United States out of the Middle East. Before 9/11, this wave of terrorist activity had produced a steady flow of attacks on the United States. Finally, the September 11, 2001 attacks compelled the United States to declare war on terrorism. The Islamic Fundamentalist group, Al Qaeda, has been the focus of much of this effort.

- **Promoting democracy in the Middle East** is a difficult task that can have unexpected consequences. In both the Palestinian Authority and Iraq, democratic elections have brought governments into power that had a strong anti-American bias.

- **Transnational threats to peace:** Terrorist organizations are an ever-evolving threat that are not easily contained or defeated with traditional military activities. Operating as nonstate actors, terrorists "blur the line between civilians and the military" and "confound war plans and diplomatic practices based upon enemies with fixed territory and political sovereignty."

Toward Reform: Rethinking American Power

The events of September 11, 2001 produced a consensus among Americans about the importance of a strong homeland defense and an effective prosecution of the war on terrorism. Nevertheless, the Bush administration's support of preemptive military action generated debate about how to address the future scope of U.S. involvement in world affairs: Since the United States is economically and militarily the most powerful country in the world, why should it limit its foreign and defense actions to only those that other countries and international organizations agree with? Proponents of the unilateralist approach argue that when American interests collide with those of the international community, the United States must be willing to engage in unilateral action in order to protect vital national interests—regardless of the level of opposition to those activities by other countries. They argue that preemptive military action in Iraq generated instability in the region, created greater hostilities with both our allies and adversaries, and did little to dampen the nuclear ambitions of Iran and North Korea. During his second administration, Bush moved away from unilateralism, making diplomatic overtures to Iran and emphasizing a multilateral approach in dealing with North Korea.

For Additional Review

Make a timeline of some of the most important foreign policy events of the 20th century. Note important political actors and briefly describe the consequences of each event.

Multiple-Choice Questions

1. The U.S. decision to continue with the planned invasion of Iraq even after failing to gain approval from the United Nations Security Council is an example of
(A) containment.
(B) isolationism.
(C) humanitarianism.
(D) unilateralism.
(E) deterrence.

2. Which of the following plays the dominant role in making American foreign policy?
(A) Senate Foreign Relations Committee
(B) president and the executive branch
(C) National Security Agency
(D) Joint Chiefs of Staff
(E) House Foreign Affairs Committee

3. All of the following contribute directly to the development of U.S. foreign policy EXCEPT
(A) the United Nations' General Assembly
(B) the Joint Chiefs of Staff
(C) the Central Intelligence Agency
(D) the State Department
(E) the Department of Defense

4. Congress exercises influence over foreign policy in which of the following ways?
I. declaring war
II. confirming ambassadors
III. appropriating money
IV. ratifying treaties
(A)   I only
(B)   III only
(C)   I, II, and III only
(D)   I, III, and IV only
(E)   All of the above

5. President Jimmy Carter differed from his Cold War predecessors in operating foreign policy according to the principles of
(A) isolationism.
(B) unilateralism.
(C) moralism.
(D) containment.
(E) Pragmatism.

6. All of the following can be used to characterize U.S. foreign policy at various times during the 20th century EXCEPT
(A) isolationism.
(B) unilateral disarmament.
(C) détente.
(D) containment.
(E) arms race.

7. The Constitution divided foreign policy powers between
(A) the Democrats and the Republicans.
(B) Congress and the Supreme Court.
(C) Congress and the president.
(D) the president and the Supreme Court.
(E) the states and the federal government.

8. Taxes on imports used to raise government revenue and to protect infant industries are
(A) domestication duties.
(B) excise taxes.
(C) revenue taxes.
(D) tariffs.
(E) embargo taxes.

9. Which of the following bureaucratic institutions has primary responsibility for advising the president about foreign and defense policy and events?
(A) Department of Defense
(B) National Security Agency
(C) Central Intelligence Agency
(D) National Security Council
(E) State Department

10. Which of the following is most consistent with the principle of isolationism?
(A) the Truman Doctrine
(B) the Marshall Plan
(C) the Bush Doctrine
(D) American involvement in the United Nations
(E) the Senate's refusal to join the League of Nations

Free-Response Questions

It is very unlikely that you would be asked to address one specific policy area in an AP free-response question. It is, however, important that you understand the public policymaking process in general and be able to draw appropriate examples from a variety of policy areas. The following questions will help you to prepare.

1. Explain the difference between a unilateral and a multilateral foreign policy. Discuss which periods in history the U.S. has followed each type of foreign policy. Analyze why the U.S. shifted between unilateral and multilateral policies.

2. Congress shares with the president constitutional authority over foreign and defense policy.

    a. Identify and describe four constitutionally derived powers Congress has in foreign policymaking.

    b. Identify and describe four constitutionally derived powers the president has in foreign policymaking.

    c. Identify and describe limitations on Congress in foreign policymaking.

ANSWERS AND EXPLANATIONS

Multiple-Choice Questions

- **1. (D) is correct.** Unilateralism is acting without consulting or support from others. Invading a country after being denied support by others can be seen as acting unilaterally.

- **2. (B) is correct.** The president is the chief initiator of foreign policy in the United States. The Constitution gives the president the power to lead the military and be the country's top representative in dealing with other countries. Presidents are aided in foreign policy decision making by several executive branch agencies including the State Department, the Department of Defense, the National Security Council, and the Central Intelligence Agency. These agencies ensure that the president has access to and control over the information needed to conduct America's foreign relations.

- **3. (A) is correct.** The UN General Assembly plays no direct role in formulating American foreign policy, while all the other choices aid the president in the conduct of foreign policy.

- **4. (E) is correct.** Congress exercises influence over foreign policy through its powers to declare war and appropriate funds. The Senate has the power to ratify treaties and confirm ambassadors to foreign nations.

- **5. (C) is correct.** President Carter differed from his Cold war predecessors by emphasizing support for human rights as the moral and proper course of action to follow. Moralism is the policy of emphasizing morality in foreign affairs, thus emphasizing human rights would be an example of moralism.

- **6. (B) is correct.** Although the U.S. has entered into several arms control agreements over the years, it has never had a foreign policy predicated on unilateral disarmament. The U.S. followed isolationism in the period between WWI and WWII. Détente was the policy toward the Soviet Union for most of the 1970s, replacing the more conflict-based policy of the nuclear arms race and attempts to use containment to prevent further Soviet expansion.

- **7. (C) is correct.** The Constitution divided authority for foreign and military policy functions between the president and Congress. The president is made commander in chief of the armed forces. but Congress has the power to fund the army and navy and to declare war. The president has authority to negotiate and sign treaties, but treaties only take effect after the Senate ratifies them by a two-thirds majority.

- **8. (D) is correct.** Tariff is defined in the root of the question. The other choices either refer to other types of taxes or are made up phrases.

- **9. (D) is correct.** Created in 1947, the National Security Council (NSC) is charged with the responsibility of advising the president about foreign and defense policy and events. The other agencies mentioned play other roles in the foreign policy process. The Department of Defense runs the military, the National Security Agency is in charge of gathering electronic intelligence, the Central Intelligence Agency is in charge of collecting human intelligence, analyzing all intelligence, and conducting the occasional covert operation, and the State Department is in charge of conducting negotiations and relations with other countries.

- **10. (E) is correct**. Isolationism is a policy of avoiding participation in foreign affairs. Refusing to join the League of Nations would be a way of avoiding participation in foreign affairs.

Free-Response Questions

This rubric provides examples of many, but not all, of the possible correct responses to the free-response questions.

1. Unilateralism is taking action without consulting or getting support from others. Multilateralism involves actions taken in cooperation with other states after consultation.

    Until Woodrow Wilson's attempt to create the League of Nations and ensure America's national security by collective security, the U.S. followed unilateralism. The country was following Washington's advice not to enter into "permanent alliances" with other powers and unilateralism seemed to work. The U.S. was not attacked while unilateralist and it was able to win substantial territory and empire by unilaterally seizing it from weaker countries.

Unilateralist pressure won out over Wilson's vision and it was not until the experience of WWII that the U.S. really followed principles of multilateralism. The horror of that conflict and the massive, coordinated effort necessary to prevail, convinced the U.S. that it needed to pursue multilateral policies. The U.S. followed multilateral policies until the 9/11 attacks, when the Bush administration, with its preemptive war doctrine, again returned to unilateralism. The Bush administration switched to a more unilateral policy when it saw that it did not have support from others to carry out the actions it wanted. The debate goes on in foreign policy today, which is better to achieve America's foreign policy goals, unilateral or multilateral action?

2.

a. Identify and describe four constitutionally derived powers Congress has in foreign policymaking.
   - Power to declare war.

   - Power of the purse. A president's national security agenda requires a willingness on the part of Congress to appropriate the necessary funds to support it.

   - Treaty ratification. Treaties that presidents negotiate with foreign countries must be approve by a two-thirds vote in the Senate.

   - Approval of key personnel. The secretaries of state and defense, the director of the CIA, and ambassadors to foreign nations must be confirmed by the Senate.

b. Identify and describe four constitutionally derived powers the president has in foreign policymaking.

   - Commander in chief. Because the framers wanted civilian control of the military, they made the president commander in chief of the armed forces. As commander in chief, the president controls where and how the military is deployed. The president also commands the vast arsenal of weapons of mass destruction.

   - Appointment power. The president selects the persons who serve in key foreign policy decision-making positions, like the secretaries of state and defense, the national security advisor, and the director of the CIA.

   - Diplomatic powers. The president alone extends diplomatic recognition to foreign governments. The president can also terminate relations with other countries and is responsible for choosing U.S. ambassadors to foreign countries.

   - Power to make treaties with other nations. The president has the sole power to negotiate treaties with other countries, although the Constitution requires the Senate to approve them by a two-thirds vote.

c. Identify and describe limitations on Congress in foreign policymaking.

- Congress is a relative large and decentralized institution, which makes it difficult to speak with one unified voice.

- There is a common perception that the Constitution vests foreign policy decision making solely in the president. This often makes it difficult for Congress to effectively assert itself in matters of foreign policy.

- Congress has to rely on the president for important intelligence information about other countries. This can sometimes result in Congress receiving misleading or wrong information, like the events that led up to the 2003 invasion of Iraqi.

Part III

Sample Exams with Answers and Explanations

On the following pages are two sample exams. They mirror the actual AP exam in format and question types. Set aside time to take these exams, timing yourself as you will be timed when you take the real test, to prepare yourself for your actual test-taking experience.

Government and Politics: United States
Section I

Time: 45 minutes
60 Questions

Directions: Each of the questions or incomplete statements below is followed by five suggested answers or completions. Select the one that is best in each case and then fill in the corresponding oval on the answer sheet.

1. Political action committees were created by campaign reform laws to

    (A) involve the public more directly in presidential campaigns.

    (B) regulate how groups such as business and labor contribute to campaigns.

    (C) finance challengers' campaigns to eliminate the advantages of incumbency.

    (D) pay for candidates' air time because it has become the most expensive feature in a campaign.

    (E) limit the influence of political parties over election outcomes.

2. All of the following are examples of entitlement programs EXCEPT

    (A) Social Security.

    (B) Medicare.

    (C) defense contracts.

    (D) veterans benefits.

    (E) agricultural subsidies.

Expenditures by PACs, 2008 Election

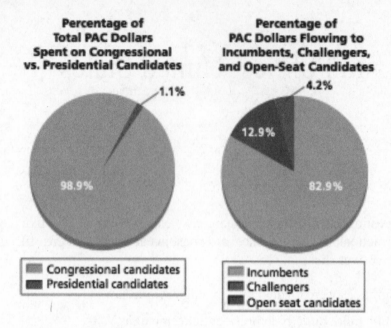

Source: Federal Election Commission, http://www.fec.gov; Center for Responsive Politics, http://www.opensecrets.org/lobby.

3. Which of the following generalizations is supported by the information in the figure above?

   (A) Incumbent presidential candidates are more likely than other candidates to receive campaign contributions.

   (B) Candidates for open seats collect the majority of campaign contributions.

   (C) Congressional candidates receive more campaign contributions than presidential candidates.

   (D) PACs spend very little money in congressional elections.

   (E) Open seat candidates and challengers are equally likely to receive campaign contributions.

4. Federal district courts are the only federal courts in which

   (A) the facts are presented by both parties in the case.

   (B) *amicus curiae* briefs are registered with the court.

   (C) the solicitor general appears for oral argument.

   (D) juries are impaneled to decide cases.

   (E) three judge panels decide the outcome of cases.

5. The government began to pursue civil rights in the 1950s when

   (A) Congress passed the Voting Rights Act.

   (B) civil rights activists marched on Washington to demand government action.

   (C) the Supreme Court declared public school segregation unconstitutional.

   (D) states agreed to discontinue their use of poll taxes as a means of preventing people from voting.

   (E) the president issued an executive order to desegregate all public transportation.

6. Which of the following statements about the president as commander in chief is true?

   (A) The president has the authority to declare war for up to 60 days without consulting Congress.

   (B) The president can decide if and when to use weapons of mass destruction in times of war.

   (C) Presidents with no prior military experience are not allowed to make major military decisions alone.

   (D) The president is required by law to consult with the Joint Chiefs of Staff before deploying the military.

   (E) The president is a nonvoting member of the Senate Armed Services Committee.

7. Interest groups play a role in the federal judicial process in all of the following ways EXCEPT by

   (A) giving campaign contributions to judicial nominees.

   (B) lobbying the Judiciary Committee about a judicial nominee.

   (C) filing *amicus curiae* briefs.

   (D) having their lawyers represent a plaintiff.

   (E) filing a class action suit.

8. Presidents exercise their influence over the ideology of federal courts by

   (A) trying to appoint only judges who agree with their ideology and political views.

   (B) ordering Congress to impeach judges who are too liberal or too conservative.

   (C) demoting judges to lower courts.

   (D) allowing them to hear only those cases on which they are likely to agree with the president's point of view.

   (E) meeting with members of the Senate Judiciary Committee when they are performing oversight.

9. The electoral votes of most states are allocated by which of the following methods?

   (A) Each party's candidate receives electoral votes based on his or her percentage of the state's popular vote.

   (B) Each elector chooses the candidate whom he or she feels is best suited to represent the needs of the state.

   (C) The winner of the popular election in the state receives 75 percent of the state's electoral votes and the loser receives 25 percent.

   (D) All of the state's electors cast their votes for whichever candidate won the state's popular vote.

   (E) The loser in the popular election receives one electoral vote and the winner receives the rest of the state's electoral votes.

10. Which of the following groups is most likely to vote in elections?

    (A) people under the age of 21

    (B) senior citizens

    (C) people without a college degree

    (D) people with no party affiliation

    (E) men with low-income jobs

11. The Supreme Court asserted which of the following principles in *Marbury* v. *Madison?*

    (A) The Fourteenth Amendment guarantees all individual freedoms under state laws.

    (B) Freedom of religion is guaranteed, but some religious practices may violate the establishment clause.

    (C) Under the Tenth Amendment, the federal government can regulate commerce among states.

    (D) The exclusionary rule must be upheld in all state court trials.

    (E) The Supreme Court has the power to declare laws passed by Congress unconstitutional.

12. In the process of political socialization, individuals

    (A) form their political beliefs.

    (B) participate in a direct democracy.

    (C) attend functions organized by political parties.

    (D) evaluate and select their representatives.

    (E) engage in political protest against a law.

13. The failure of the Articles of Confederation and necessity for a new Constitution were made evident by the

    (A) success of the American Revolution.

    (B) legislature's inability to select a president.

    (C) need for a bicameral legislature.

    (D) government's inability to subdue Shays's Rebellion.

    (E) excess of centralized power in the national government.

14. Voter turnout in the United States is low in part because

    (A) minority groups still struggle for the right to vote in Southern states.

    (B) registering to vote has become more difficult.

    (C) voters see little difference between the platforms of the two parties' candidates.

    (D) many low-income people are not able to pass the literacy test required to vote.

    (E) candidates do little to try to attract voters.

15. Which of the following statements is true about U.S. budget deficits?

    (A) The first federal budget deficit did not occur until the 1990s.

    (B) The Constitution requires a balanced federal budget.

    (C) Large budget deficits make the U.S. government more financially dependent on foreign investors.

    (D) Budget deficits have no practical effect on individual citizens.

    (E) The Democratic and Republican parties have agreed that the deficit issue should not become an issue in presidential campaigns.

16. Congress performs legislative oversight over executive departments by

    (A) hiring and firing department heads.

    (B) determining departments' budgets.

    (C) vetoing department proposals.

    (D) issuing impoundment bills.

    (E) coordinating department activities with the president.

17. Members of Congress most often vote according to

    (A) their own policy preferences.

    (B) the needs of their constituents.

    (C) their relationships with the president.

    (D) their party affiliations.

    (E) the ideology of their geographic region.

18. Which of the following is NOT specifically prohibited by the Constitution?

    (A) gender bias in the workplace

    (B) self-incrimination

    (C) slavery

    (D) a national religion

    (E) cruel and unusual punishment

19. The number of employees in the federal government grew most quickly in the

    (A) 2000s.

    (B) 1790s.

    (C) 1930s.

    (D) 1860s.

    (E) 1970s.

20. The largest federal expenditure is

    (A) national defense.

    (B) public education.

    (C) Social Security.

    (D) grants to the states.

    (E) political campaigns.

Entitlements and Discretionary Spending, 1963–2007

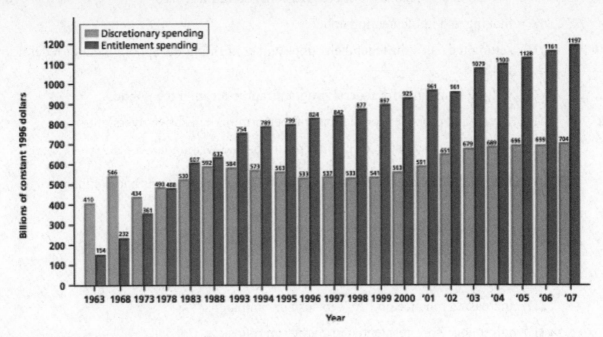

Source: United States Budget, Fiscal Year 2007, www.gpo.gov.

21. Which of the following are true of the data in the figure above?

   I. The government has always spent more on entitlements than on discretionary spending.

   II. Discretionary spending has declined over time.

   III. Entitlement spending has increased by more than 900 percent.

   IV. Entitlement and discretionary spending are at relatively equal levels.

   (A) III only

   (B) I and II only

   (C) II and III only

   (D) III and IV only

   (E) I and IV only

22. The two main responsibilities of congressional committees are

(A) making and implementing policies.

(B) setting the dates for federal elections and confirming the appointment of federal judges.

(C) writing guidelines for federal programs and educating the public.

(D) reviewing proposed legislation and performing legislative oversight.

(E) suggesting candidates for cabinet positions and writing tax codes.

23. All of the following are recent trends in presidential nominations and campaigns EXCEPT

(A) declining party identification among voters.

(B) increasing costs of campaigning.

(C) decreasing importance of national conventions.

(D) increasing reliance on PACs to sustain campaigns.

(E) infrequency of presidential primaries among states.

24. Single-issue groups, as opposed to other types of groups, represent people in the electorate who

(A) have little political access and influence.

(B) donate money to political campaigns.

(C) pressure candidates to be less ambiguous about their ideology.

(D) feel strongly about a certain cause.

(E) advocate campaign finance reform.

25. Which of the following presidential appointments requires Senate confirmation?

(A) National Security Council

(B) Chief of Staff

(C) White House Counsel

(D) Council of Economic Advisors

(E) The Secretary of State

26. According to the Constitution, the vice president

    (A) chairs all cabinet meetings.

    (B) is ineligible to run for president after two terms as vice president.

    (C) is the president of the Senate.

    (D) must be of the same party as the president.

    (E) is an ex officio member of the Council of Economic Advisors.

27. The Social Security program is endangered primarily because

    (A) the U.S. birth rate has increased dramatically over the past decade.

    (B) the program has lost public support in recent years.

    (C) the number of contributors to the program is growing at a much slower rate than the number of recipients.

    (D) large federal budget deficits have reduced the amount of tax revenue collected in support of the program.

    (E) the program has become more identified with racial minorities.

28. The Supreme Court has upheld which of the following in its interpretation of the freedom of speech?

    (A) All forms of speech, including obscenity, are protected under the First Amendment.

    (B) The government cannot under any circumstances censor information.

    (C) Protests against the government are not protected under the First Amendment.

    (D) Forms of symbolic speech are protected under the First Amendment.

    (E) Freedom of speech is guaranteed by federal law, but it does not have to be upheld by the states.

29. The rise of the primary election system has led to

    (A) the increasing role of political parties in presidential elections.

    (B) the public's more direct involvement in the election of the president.

    (C) a decline in media coverage of presidential campaigns.

    (D) a shift in power from national to state party organizations.

    (E) fewer candidates seeking each party's nomination.

30. Congress exercises influence over foreign policy in which of the following ways?

   I. declaring war

   II. confirming ambassadors

   III. appropriating money

   IV. ratifying treaties

   (F) I only

   (G) III only

   (H) I, II, and III only

   (I) I, III, and IV only

   (J) all of the above

31. Unlike members of the House of Representatives, senators can influence policy debates by

   (A) relying on partisan support.

   (B) calling for a vote.

   (C) using a filibuster.

   (D) forming a presidential coalition.

   (E) running televised ads.

32. Bureaucracies are often criticized as being undemocratic because

   (A) they are not directly accountable to the people.

   (B) they utilized a merit system for hiring.

   (C) citizens tend to have low opinions of them.

   (D) the courts have no influence over their actions.

   (E) they are overly influenced by campaign contributions.

33. All of the following influence the selection of federal judges and Supreme Court justices EXCEPT

   (A) campaign contributions.

   (B) partisanship.

   (C) ideology.

   (D) experience.

   (E) judicial philosophy.

34. A president can be removed from office in which of the following ways?

    (A) The Supreme Court rules that he is incompetent or has violated the law.

    (B) In a recall, citizens can vote to remove the president from office.

    (C) The House votes to impeach him, and the Senate tries and convicts him.

    (D) The Senate votes to impeach him, and the Supreme Court tries the president.

    (E) Both houses of Congress vote to remove the president by a simple majority.

Presidential Approval Ratings Since 1981

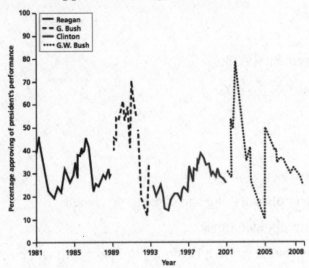

Source: Roper Center, University of Connecticut.

35. All of the following statements accurately describe the data in the graph EXCEPT:

    (A) Most presidents experience a drop in public approval ratings over their terms.

    (B) George Bush and George W. Bush lost the most public approval during their presidencies.

    (C) Ronald Reagan maintained the highest average popularity.

    (D) Presidents maintain the approval of a majority of the public most of the time.

    (E) Presidents enjoy their highest levels of popularity in times of crisis.

36. Proponents of the pluralist theory argue that

    (A) interest group growth is almost unlimited.

    (B) interest group growth depends on the carrying capacity of the environment.

    (C) groups form only for economic reasons.

    (D) interest groups rarely form as a result of political disturbances.

    (E) interest groups are significantly limited by the free rider problem.

37. The government institution responsible for the drawing of congressional district lines is the

    (A) state's governor.

    (B) Senate Committee on Governmental Affairs.

    (C) state's legislature, or its delegated body.

    (D) House Rules Committee.

    (E) Department of the Interior.

38. Third parties rarely last in the American system because

    (A) they encourage moderation in policymaking and discourage change.

    (B) they offer voters no choice among ideologies.

    (C) the rules of the U.S. political system make it hard for third parties to win elections.

    (D) they deal with unimportant issues and political figures.

    (E) citizens are more likely to be independents than to affiliate with a party.

39. The media has the most influence over which of the following aspects of the presidential selection process?

    (A) the way electoral votes are distributed

    (B) the outcome of the popular election

    (C) who decides to run for office

    (D) the outcome of primary elections

    (E) the party's national convention

40. The framers' distrust of the public when writing the Constitution is best illustrated by the

   (A) Electoral College.

   (B) Bill of Rights.

   (C) process of electing members of the House of Representatives.

   (D) creation of a bicameral legislature.

   (E) ability to amend the Constitution.

41. Congress increased the power of the federal government to enforce regulations in employment by passing the

   (A) Fourteenth Amendment.

   (B) Civil Rights Act of 1964.

   (C) Fifteenth Amendment.

   (D) Equal Rights Amendment.

   (E) Voting Rights Act of 1965.

42. The Hatch Act helps maintain a nonpartisan bureaucracy because it

   (A) creates a federal commission on which half the members are Democrats and half are Republican.

   (B) ensures that federal employees are hired based on merit.

   (C) requires all federal employees to register to vote as independents.

   (D) requires all federal agencies to have staffs that are balanced along party lines.

   (E) prohibits government employees in their official capacities from active participation in partisan politics.

43. In *Miranda* v. *Arizona,* the Supreme Court ruled that persons accused of a crime

   (A) cannot be denied bail.

   (B) have the right to a fair trial.

   (C) have rights during police questioning.

   (D) have equal protection under the law.

   (E) cannot be searched illegally.

44. The principle that the Constitution gives states all powers neither granted to the federal government nor denied the states refers to .

(A) states' rights.

(B) reserved powers.

(C) federal supremacy.

(D) concurrent powers.

(E) federalism.

45. Critical elections tend to occur under which of the following circumstances?

(A) when a third-party candidate wins some electoral votes

(B) after a presidential scandal has been exposed in the media

(C) when the United States engages in a military operation

(D) after a serious domestic crisis alters the political agenda

(E) when one of the parties suffers a major defeat in a congressional election

46. Which of the following statements is true about Congress's influence over Supreme Court decision making?

(A) Congress can pass laws to prohibit judicial activism.

(B) The Senate can filibuster court decisions.

(C) Congress has significant control over the court's appellate jurisdiction.

(D) The Senate can decide which cases the Supreme Court will hear. /

(E) District court judges are reviewed by Congress every 10 years.

47. Which of the following statements are true of political parties?

I. The United States has a multiparty system.

II. The electorate is becoming increasingly independent of political parties.

III. The use of television advertising allows candidates more independence from their political parties.

IV. Political party organizations are exercising greater control over the choice of candidates.

(A) II only

(B) III only

(C) II and III only

(D) I, III, and IV only

(E) II, III, and IV only

48. Each of the following helps explain the incumbency advantage of members of Congress EXCEPT

   (A) the franking privilege.

   (B) the pattern of campaign contributions.

   (C) casework.

   (D) the low standing of Congress in public opinion.

   (E) name recognition.

49. Implementation of public policy is most successful when

   (A) the goals of the policy and the authority of the implementers are clear.

   (B) there is a court order mandating compliance with the policy.

   (C) the executive branch has precleared the policy with the federal judiciary.

   (D) multiple agencies and bureaucrats are involved.

   (E) the policy originated in the executive branch as opposed to the legislative branch.

50. Interest groups differ from political parties in which of the following ways?

   (A) Interest groups link the public to the political process.

   (B) Interest groups pursue general policy goals in the political arena.

   (C) Interest groups do not run candidates for election.

   (D) Interest groups are not allowed to play any part in political campaigns.

   (E) Interest groups unite politicians with the same political ideology.

51. Which of the following is true of relationships between the president and Congress?

   (A) Presidents usually have little success in forming presidential coalitions in Congress.

   (B) Presidents work most with minority party leaders to win minority support.

   (C) Policy gridlock results when the president's party is not the majority in Congress.

   (D) Members of Congress almost always vote in favor of presidential initiatives.

   (E) Presidents usually have closer relationships with members of the House than they do with senators.

52. The elderly fare better than the poor in social welfare budget battles for which of the following reasons?

   (A) The Constitution requires a certain amount of spending for the elderly but not the poor.

   (B) Most social services for the elderly come from state governments.

   (C) Lobbyists representing the poor are not allowed to make campaign contributions.

   (D) The elderly are more organized and better represented politically than the poor.

   (E) There are more elderly people in the U.S. than there are poor people.

53. Which of the following statements accurately describes iron triangles?

   (A) Iron triangles are composed of members of the military-industrial complex, Congress, and the Defense Department.

   (B) Iron triangles are formed in specific policy areas to advance policies among groups that benefit each other mutually.

   (C) Iron triangles are formed to generate support for presidential proposals in Congress.

   (D) Iron triangles help coordinate policy among the executive, legislative, and judicial branches.

   (E) Iron triangles help perform policy implementation among the local, state, and federal levels of government.

54. Which of the following statements represent a prevalent myth about the federal bureaucracy?

   I. The bureaucracy is growing bigger and bigger each year.

   II. Most federal bureaucrats work in Washington, D.C.

   III. Citizens are generally dissatisfied with the bureaucracy.

   IV. The bureaucracy makes government inefficient and cumbersome.

   (A) I only

   (B) IV only

   (C) I and II only

   (D) II, III and IV only

   (E) All of the above

55. The establishment clause, as interpreted by the Supreme Court, prevents

(A) states from passing laws that conflict with federal laws.

(B) the government from violating the rights of individuals.

(C) Congress from exercising any powers beyond those necessary to execute the law.

(D) gender discrimination in the workplace.

(E) government entanglement with religion.

56. *Regents of the University of California* v. *Bakke* is a Supreme Court case that addressed

(A) affirmative action.

(B) prayer in school.

(C) the rights of the accused.

(D) the right of privacy.

(E) desegregation through busing.

57. One of a president's most powerful tools for gaining support of his proposals is

(A) his financial resources.

(B) executive privilege.

(C) "going public" to sway public opinion.

(D) senatorial courtesy.

(E) his cabinet.

58. Which of the following statements accurately describes traditional Republican Party economic positions?

I. Republicans place greater emphasis on full employment than Democrats.

II. Republicans tend to worry about inflation more than Democrats.

III. Republican economic positions tend to appeal to the working class and unions.

IV. Republicans tend to favor higher income tax rates.

(A) I only

(B) II only

(C) II and III only

(D) I and IV only

(E) I, II, and III only

59. Members of Congress are more likely to vote according to their personal ideology when

(A) the issue is not well known by their constituents.

(B) they are up for reelection.

(C) the piece of legislation was introduced by the president.

(D) they are on the committee responsible for the piece of legislation.

(E) interest groups have been actively involved with the piece of legislation.

60. In the era of globalization, which of the following presidential powers is becoming more important?

(A) vetoing legislation

(B) negotiating executive agreements

(C) declaring war

(D) authorizing the use of weapons of mass destruction

(E) appointment of Supreme Court justices

END OF SECTION I.

IF YOU FINISH BEFORE TIME IS CALLED, YOU MAY CHECK YOUR WORK ON THIS SECTION.

DO NOT GO ON TO SECTION II UNTIL YOU ARE TOLD TO DO SO.

Government and Politics: United States
Section II

Time: 100 minutes

Directions: You have 100 minutes to answer all four of the following questions. It is suggested that you take a few minutes to plan and outline each answer. *Spend approximately one-fourth of your time (25 minutes) on each question.* Illustrate your essay with substantive examples where appropriate. Make certain to number each of your answers as the question is numbered below.

1. In the American democracy, political parties use two different systems for selecting delegates to the national party conventions that nominate presidential candidates.
    a. Explain how caucuses select delegates to the national convention.

    b. Explain how primaries select delegates to the national convention.

    c. Discuss one consequence of "frontloading" the delegate selection process.

2. The mass media have a major effect on politics in the United States. Media have both positive and negative consequences for the political process.

    a. Identify and describe two positives effects that the media have on the political process.

    b. Identify and describe two negative effects that the media have on the political process.

How a President Affects the Federal Judiciary

President	Appointed to Supreme Court	Appointed to Courts of Appeals[a]	Appointed to District Courts[b]	Total Appointed	Total Number of Judgeships[c]	Percentage of Judgeships Filled by President
Johnson (1963–1969)	2	40	122	164	449	37
Nixon (1969–1974)	4	45	179	228	504	45
Ford (1974–1977)	1	12	52	65	504	13
Carter (1977–1981)	0	56	202	258	657	39
Reagan (1981–1989)	3	78	290	368	740	50
Bush (1989–1993)	2	37	148	185	825	22
Clinton (1993–2001)	2	66	305	373	841	44
G. W. Bush (2001–2009)[d]	2	57	287	344	866	40

Source: "Imprints on the Bench," *CQ Weekly Report* (January 19, 2001): 173. Reprinted by permission of Copyright Clearance Center on behalf of Congressional Quarterly, Inc. Updated by authors.

3. The above table shows data on presidential appointments to the federal judiciary. Using this information and your knowledge of U.S. politics, answer the following questions.

   a. Discuss the criteria presidents use to make judicial appointments.

   b. Which presidents have had the greatest impact on the federal bench? Discuss two reasons why this is the case.

   c. Which presidents have had the greatest impact on the Supreme Court? Why are these appointments particularly important?

4. The Tenth Amendment reserves for the states all powers neither denied nor designated to the federal government in the Constitution. For decades, this afforded states a good deal of freedom in writing their state laws. However, the ratification of the Fourteenth Amendment allowed the Supreme Court to exercise its authority over the states in an attempt to advance the civil liberties of all Americans.

   a. What provision of the Fourteenth Amendment has been used by the Supreme Court to exercise its authority over the states for the purpose of advancing civil liberties?

   b. Identify two areas in which civil liberties protections have been extended to the states, and discuss the specific case that accomplished this task in each area.

ANSWERS AND EXPLANATIONS

Practice Test 1

Section I

- **1. (B) is correct.** Political action committees were created by the Federal Election Campaign Act of 1974 to regulate how much business, labor, and other groups could contribute to a candidate's election. Through them, the federal government can better regulate campaign financing because all PACs must register with the Federal Election Commission and report all of their spending activities to the government and the public.

- **2. (C) is correct.** Entitlement programs are a form of mandatory spending because everyone entitled to the benefits of the program must be paid. Congress cannot control these expenditures unless it changes the eligibility requirements of the program, which it is unlikely to do unless such measures are absolutely necessary. Defense contracts clearly do not fit this definition.

- **3. (C) is correct.** The pie chart on the left shows that nearly 99 percent of funds spent by PACs is spent in congressional races.

- **4. (D) is correct.** There are no juries in the courts of appeals, the Supreme Court, or any other federal court.

- **5. (C) is correct.** The Supreme Court's 1954 landmark decision in *Brown* v. *Board of Education* was a dramatic reinterpretation of what the Constitution required. Following this decision, the court, Congress, and the executive took steps to advance civil rights.

- **6. (B) is correct.** As commander in chief of military forces, the president decides if and when American armed forces use weapons of mass destruction in times of war.

- **7. (A) is correct.** Interest groups do attempt to influence the appointment of federal judges, but not by giving campaign contributions. The process of filling judgeships is far removed from the public—the only means of influence they have is influencing the election of the president and members of the Senate, who, in turn, choose judges.

- **8. (A) is correct.** Presidents work hard to seek and appoint judges who agree with their own political ideologies. Not only would such judges be more likely to favor the president's agenda, they would also (because they have no term limit) continue to influence policy long after the president's term has ended. The appointment of Supreme Court justices is a golden opportunity for presidents, but it is also one that is highly scrutinized by Congress.

- **9. (D) is correct.** Most states award their electoral votes in a "winner-take-all" system. Whichever candidate wins the popular vote in the state receives all of that state's electoral votes. One criticism of the electoral system is that this gives larger states an unfair advantage because they have more electors than smaller states.

- **10. (B) is correct.** Senior citizens have a high voter turnout rate. Young people, low-income citizens, those without college degrees, or those without party affiliations are much less likely to turn out and vote.

- **11. (E) is correct.** In the 1803 case of *Marbury* v. *Madison,* the Supreme Court under Chief Justice John Marshall first asserted its power of judicial review. Judicial review allows the Supreme Court, whose responsibility is to interpret the Constitution, to declare laws passed by Congress unconstitutional. This power helped solidify the system of checks and balances among the three branches of government.

- **12. (A) is correct.** Political socialization is the process through which citizens learn about government and form their political beliefs. Family, school, the media, and religion play major parts in influencing how people see the government and with which party they identify themselves.

- **13. (D) is correct.** Shays's Rebellion occurred when a group of Massachusetts farmers raided several courthouses in protest of the government's foreclosure of their farms. Under the Articles of Confederation, the national government was not able to raise a militia to stop the group, and so the rebellion was an embarrassing failure for the new government. It served as the final proof that the government established by the Articles lacked centralized power and legitimacy.

- **14. (C) is correct.** People who have not voted often cite the generally indistinguishable ideologies of the candidates of the two parties as one major reason for their inaction. This perception may be partly the result of the media's focus on the campaign game rather than on the two candidates' platforms, but it is also due to the fact that, because there are only two major parties in the United States, each one must remain near the center of the political spectrum to win elections.

- **15. (C) is correct.** Large budget deficits make the U.S. government more financially dependent on foreign investors, other governments, and individuals. Foreign investors currently hold one-fifth of the U.S. national debt.

- **16. (B) is correct.** One of the ways Congress oversees the activities of the departments in the executive branch is by determining their budgets. Each department submits its budget proposal to the president, who in turn coordinates them and submits his proposal to Congress. Congress makes the final decision about how much each department can spend on its programs and activities.

- **17. (D) is correct.** Members of Congress do sometimes vote according to their own ideology. However, they most often vote according to their party affiliations. In doing so, they may presume that the constituents who elected them as a Democrat or

Republican probably agree with that party's political ideology. By voting along the party line, they may also be voting according to their constituency's preferences.

- **18. (A) is correct.** Gender discrimination is not specifically addressed in the Constitution or its amendments. However, it is prohibited by law as a form of civil rights discrimination.

- **19. (C) is correct.** The number of employees of the federal government grew most quickly during President Franklin D. Roosevelt's New Deal, a series of economic recovery measures passed during the 1930s.

- **20. (C) is correct.** In the past few decades, Social Security has become the largest federal expenditure. It alone accounts for nearly a quarter of all expenditures.

- **21. (A) is correct.** Entitlement spending has increased exponentially since 1963; today it encompasses a majority of the federal budget. No other statements are true.

- **22. (D) is correct.** Congressional committees play an important role in the legislative process. They review and assess bills for their feasibility and consequences, and they either revise or kill them. If they pass a bill on to the floor, they make a recommendation for it, and many other congresspeople are likely to vote according to the recommendation. The other major function of a committee is to perform oversight of all the federal departments and agencies under its jurisdiction. Committees do this by setting agencies' budgets and by assessing their performance and activities in committee hearings.

- **23. (E) is correct.** The use of presidential primaries has been increasing, not decreasing. Almost every state now holds a primary election. These have, in turn, led to a much longer campaign season and have added significantly to the cost of campaigning. They make the nomination of presidential candidates a process that involves voters directly, at least in some states.

- **24. (D) is correct.** Single-issue groups attract people who feel very strongly about one particular issue. These issues, such as abortion or gun control, often incite emotional responses. Single-issue groups pressure senators and representatives to vote according to that one issue, and members themselves often vote for political officials based solely on their stand on the issue.

- **25. (E) is correct.** Because they are members of the president's cabinet, the Senate must confirm nominees for secretary of state. The National Security Council, the chief of staff, the White House counsel, and the Council of Economic Advisors are considered to be part of the president's personal staff of advisors and are not required to be approved by the Senate.

- **26. (C) is correct.** The Constitution assigns vice presidents the relatively minor tasks of presiding over the Senate and voting in case of a tie among the senators.

- **27. (C) is correct.** The Social Security dilemma is that the number of Social Security contributors (the workers) is growing slowly, while the number of recipients (the retired) is growing rapidly.

- **28. (D) is correct.** In the 1989 case of *Texas* v. *Johnson,* the Supreme Court determined that flag burning, a form of symbolic speech, is protected under the First Amendment. Symbolic speech is that which communicates nonverbally; participating in parades or protests is another form of symbolic speech.

- **29. (B) is correct.** Primary elections give voters the opportunity to participate more directly in the presidential election process. In their state's primary election, people can nominate either a candidate or delegates pledged to that candidate. This process circumvents the traditional role of political parties in the nomination process, especially when a blanket primary is used.

- **30. (E) is correct.** Although the president is the chief initiator of foreign policy in the U.S., Congress exercises influence over foreign policy through its powers to declare war, appropriate funds, ratify treaties, and confirm ambassadors to foreign nations. Congress has full authority over all military expenditures, including foreign aid and the budgets of the State Department, the Department of Defense, and the CIA.

- **31. (C) is correct.** Only senators have the ability to use a filibuster to hold up debate on a bill. The Senate imposes no restrictions on the length of time for debate over a piece of legislation, so senators are free to talk as long as it takes for their colleagues to lose interest and choose not to vote on the bill. Southern senators made effective use of the filibuster during debates over civil rights legislation.

- **32. (A) is correct.** Although they make vital decisions and perform essential services for government and the people, bureaucrats are not directly accountable to citizens the way the president and Congress are. This has led to the criticism that the bureaucracy is an undemocratic branch of government.

- **33. (A) is correct.** There is no evidence that campaign contributions to presidential races are a major factor in determining a presidents' nominees for federal judgeships.

- **34. (C) is correct.** The Constitution sets forth the process of removing a president from office. First, the House votes to impeach the president. Then the Senate tries the president, with the chief justice of the Supreme Court presiding. The Senate must reach a two-thirds vote to remove the president from office. Only two presidents have been impeached, but neither was removed from office through this process.

- **35. (D) is correct.** This statement is false; approval ratings for these presidents rarely topped 50 percent. Most of these occasions were short-lived and in times of crisis. All of the other statements are true and can be inferred from the figure.

- **36. (A) is correct.** Pluralists believe that interest group growth within the political system is almost unlimited. This is in sharp contrast to the transactions and population ecology perspectives.

- **37. (C) is correct.** State legislatures have the task of drawing congressional district lines for their state. Every 10 years, the population count of the national census determines how many House seats each state receives. If seats must be reapportioned or redistricted, the state legislature, or a body it designates, redraws district lines.

- **38. (C) is correct.** The winner-take-all system used in American legislative elections and in apportioning most states' Electoral College votes makes it very hard for third parties to win substantial representation in government, even when citizens agree with their policy platforms.

- **39. (D) is correct.** One of the major criticisms held against the primary system is that it allows the media too much influence over election results, particularly in the early primaries. Media attention skews the results by branding winners and losers so early in the campaign process that losers have little chance to score victories in later primaries.

- **40. (A) is correct.** The authors of the Constitution were a group of elite intellectuals who distrusted leaving government too much in the hands of the uneducated masses. Therefore, they arranged for the president to be chosen by the Electoral College, a group of chosen electors, rather than by the public at large. Although today citizens cast individual votes for president, the Electoral College still casts the final vote. In fact, Al Gore won the popular vote in the 2000 election but lost the presidency because of the distribution of electoral votes.

- **41. (B) is correct.** By passing the Civil Rights Act of 1964, Congress outlawed discrimination in the workplace. Consequently, the Justice Department was granted authority to enforce equality in employment and to pursue violators of the Civil Rights Act.

- **42. (E) is correct.** The Hatch Act, originally passed in 1939 and amended most recently in 1993, prohibits civil service employees from actively participating in partisan politics while on duty. The act was intended to help ensure a fair and impartial bureaucracy and to protect bureaucrats from coercion on the part of superiors or political appointees.

- **43. (C) is correct.** The Supreme Court enhanced the rights of the accused in its decision in *Miranda* v. *Arizona*. This decision required that all people arrested for a crime be informed of their rights before questioning.

- **44. (B) is correct.** The Tenth Amendment articulates the reserved powers of the states. All powers not denied by the Constitution or specifically designated to the federal government are held by the states. Many states have used this principle of reserved powers to their advantage, particularly in the case of civil rights. Many Supreme Court cases of the twentieth century focused on limiting the power of states to make laws that conflict with federal law.

- **45. (D) is correct.** Most critical elections follow a serious domestic problem that significantly alters the political landscape. The Great Depression is one such crisis that generated a critical election. Republicans lost power to a new coalition of Democrats that included workers, minority groups, and Southerners.

- **46. (C) is correct.** In many instances federal courts' jurisdiction derives from Congress and not the Constitution. The Constitution provides Congress with the discretion to determine which category of cases appellate courts may hear.

- **47. (C) is correct.** Political parties are losing power because both candidates and voters have come to rely less on them. Because candidates can address voters directly through television, the public does not have to fall back on party identification to choose candidates. At the same time, candidates who use television do not need their party to help attract voters as much as in the past.

- **48. (D) is correct.** More than 90 percent of all congressional incumbents seeking reelection win. This occurs in spite of the fact that people hold a low opinion of Congress as an institution.

- **49. (A) is correct.** If the goals of a policy are not clear to those who have to implement it, and if those who have to implement lack the authority to act definitively, then the policy in question is not likely to be well implemented or received.

- **50. (C) is correct.** The chief difference between interest groups and political parties is that interest groups do not run candidates for office, though they may endorse them. Running candidates for office is the primary function of political parties.

- **51. (C) is correct.** The relationship between the president and Congress tends to be strained when the president's party is not the majority party in Congress. The two often have conflicting policy goals and work together less often than do a president and Congress of the same political party. Policy gridlock has occurred more frequently in recent years because this kind of divided government has been more common.

- **52. (D) is correct**. The elderly fare better than the poor in social welfare budget battles because they are more organized, more politically active, and better represented than the poor. The elderly are also widely considered to be among the deserving poor.

- **53. (B) is correct.** Iron triangles are unofficial political entities composed of interest groups, agencies, and legislative committees that are all concerned with the same policy area. Each group helps the others to help itself in the policy arena. For example, interest groups lobby committee members for larger agency budgets so that the interest groups will benefit from the agency's money.

- **54. (E) is correct.** All of these statements are false or misleading. The federal bureaucracy is not growing bigger and bigger each year. Only about 12 percent of federal bureaucrats work in Washington, D.C. With more than 245,000 federal employees, California leads the nation in the number of federal bureaucrats. Most citizens are generally satisfied with the service they receive from the bureaucracy.

- **55. (E) is correct.** The establishment clause, located in the First Amendment of the Constitution, establishes the separation of church and state in all levels of government. Religious qualifications cannot be imposed on public officials, and the government cannot regulate, restrict, or endorse religious worship.

- **56. (A) is correct.** Both cases dealt with the constitutionality of affirmative action. In *Bakke,* the Supreme Court upheld the principle of affirmative action but banned the use of quotas to establish racial diversity.

- **57. (C) is correct.** A president relies heavily on the power of public opinion because, with the backing of the public, members of Congress have little recourse but to support him as well. This power has grown in recent decades, as presidents have been able to communicate directly with the public through television.

- **58. (B) is correct.** Republicans tend to worry about inflation more than Democrats do. Republicans generally try to prevent inflation, even at the risk of rising unemployment.

- **59. (A) is correct.** Because their constituents usually are familiar with only the most publicized issues, members of Congress have many opportunities to vote according to their own ideology on smaller, less publicized issues. In theory, because they were elected by people who share their ideology, representatives and senators would still be voting according to the wishes of their constituents.

- **60. (B) is correct.** In the recent era of globalization, the president, as chief diplomat, has both increasing power and responsibility as the nation's negotiator of treaties and executive agreements. Many of today's agreements focus on expanding free trade among nations around the world.

Free-Response Questions

This rubric provides examples of many, but not all, of the possible correct responses to the free-response questions.

1.

a. Explain how caucuses select delegates to the national convention.

In some states, delegates are chosen for the national conventions by caucuses. Caucuses are small, statewide meetings where members of political parties meet (i.e., caucus) to discuss and debate their party's nominees for the presidency. Individuals attending the caucus vote for their preferred candidates. Candidates are awarded delegates to the state and national party conventions based on the number of votes they receive.

b. Explain how primaries select delegates to the national convention.

In some states, delegates are elected for the national party conventions in a primary vote. In states that have primaries, voters go to the poll to vote for a particular candidate. When people vote for the presidential candidate they prefer, they are most often voting for a delegate to the state or national convention who, at the convention, is obligated to vote for the candidate they represent.

c. Discuss one consequence of "frontloading" the delegate selection process.

Frontloading is when several states hold their primary or caucus early in the primary election cycle. With frontloading, one candidate often is able to gain an insurmountable lead in the delegate count long before primaries and caucuses are held in other states. Frontloading has led to a race to the front of the line, with many states moving their primaries or caucuses to earlier dates.

2.

a. Identify and describe positive effects that the media have on the political process.

- Citizens have access to important information about candidates for public office, elected officials, and public policy.

- Through investigative reporting the media perform a watchdog role for the political process. In this role the media uncover governmental fraud, waste, and abuse and help voters hold public officials accountable for their actions.

b. Identify and describe negative effects that the media have on the political process.

- The media tend to provide superficial coverage of complex public policy issues.

- Because mass media outlets tend to be owned by profit seeking corporations, the choice of what news they cover might be influenced by how well it will sell rather than how important it is to the public.

- The media (especially television) are biased towards stories that generate good pictures.

3.

a. Discuss the criteria presidents use to make judicial appointments.

- Presidents use a number of criteria to guide their judicial appointments. Among these are competence, ideology, rewards, pursuit of political support, religion, and demographic characteristics. These include race, ethnicity, and gender.

b. Which presidents have had the greatest impact on the federal bench? Discuss two reasons why this is the case.

- Among all presidents, Nixon, Reagan, and Clinton have filled the greatest percentage of judgeships. They all appointed more than 44 percent of sitting judges. Carter also had a significant impact for a one-term president, appointing 39 percent of judges.

- The presidents that had the greatest impact all served for more than one term, giving them more opportunities to make appointments.

- Political circumstances worked in their favor. For example, during the Carter administration, the number of federal judgeships was drastically increased. The same can be said for the Reagan administration.

c. Which presidents have had the greatest impact on the Supreme Court? Why are these appointments particularly important?

- President Nixon had the greatest impact on the Supreme Court, appointing four justices during his term in office. President Reagan was also able to appoint three Supreme Court justices.

- These appointments are particularly important because the Supreme Court is the highest court in the land and has the final say on the constitutionality and legality of all laws and policies in the United States. In addition, there are only nine justices who serve on this court, making each extraordinarily powerful. Altering just one justice, let alone four, can have a significant impact on the decisions of the court and the direction of the country.

4.

a. What provision of the Fourteenth Amendment has been used by the Supreme Court to advance civil liberties?

- The due process clause of the Fourteenth Amendment was used to make the provisions of the federal Bill of Rights applicable to state governments.

b. Identify two areas in which civil liberties protections have been extended to the states, and discuss the specific case that accomplished this task in each area.

- **Freedom of speech** (*Gitlow* v. *New York*)

- **Freedom of press** (*Near* v. *Minnesota*)

- **Right to privacy** (*Griswold* v. *Connecticut*)

- **Right to counsel in felony cases** (*Gideon* v. *Wainwright*)

Government and Politics: United States
Section I

Time: 45 minutes
60 Questions

Directions: Each of the questions or incomplete statements below is followed by five suggested answers or completions. Select the one that is best in each case and then fill in the corresponding oval on the answer sheet.

1. In which of the following elections are voters allowed to choose candidates from either party for different offices?

    (A) open primary

    (B) initiative

    (C) closed primary

    (D) blanket primary

    (E) recall election

2. All of the following play a role in an impeachment of the president, EXCEPT

    (A) court of appeals.

    (B) Judiciary Committee.

    (C) U.S. House of Representatives.

    (D) chief justice of the United States.

    (E) U.S. Senate.

3. Popular elections are held for all of the following governmental offices EXCEPT

    (A) senator.

    (B) president.

    (C) federal judge.

    (D) member of the House of Representatives.

    (E) governor.

4. In general, Democrats are more likely than the Republicans to advocate for which of the following?

(A) lower tax rates

(B) reduced spending for social services

(C) prayer in public schools

(D) increased military spending

(E) affirmative action programs

Congressional Party Unity Scores, 1959-2007

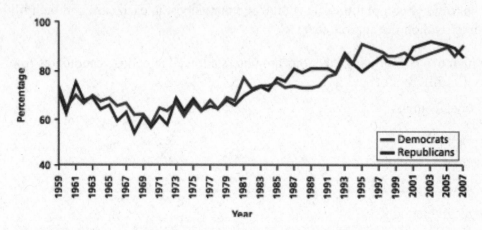

Source: *Congressional Quarterly Almanacs* (Washington, DC: CQ Press).

5. Which of the following conclusions may be drawn about congressional party unity based on the data in the graph above?

(A) Republicans always have higher party unity than Democrats.

(B) Party unity has declined from 1960s levels.

(C) The unity of the two parties generally tracks closely.

(D) Democrats always have higher party unity than Republicans.

(E) Unity is higher in the Senate than the House.

6. The elastic clause grants Congress the authority to

   (A) amend the president's budget proposal as it sees fit.

   (B) make any laws that enable it to carry out its assigned responsibilities.

   (C) raise taxes.

   (D) create any number of legislative committees and subcommittees.

   (E) reapportion seats based on the nation's changing population.

7. The most common way that ordinary citizens participate in politics is by

   (A) participating in political protests.

   (B) writing letters to the editor of a local newspaper.

   (C) voting in elections.

   (D) contacting their elected representatives.

   (E) joining an interest group.

8. The Constitution authorizes Supreme Court justices to be appointed for life for which of the following reasons?

   (A) to shield judges from political influence and pressure

   (B) to reward judges for their distinguished careers

   (C) to create a strong relationship between the Court and Congress

   (D) to allow politicians to use the patronage system

   (E) to limit the power of presidents to appoint judges too frequently

9. One common criticism of the media's participation in politics is

   (A) media bias in favor of outsiders and third parties.

   (B) media focus on the Supreme Court to the exclusion of the other branches.

   (C) media live and uncensored coverage of committee hearings.

   (D) media tendency to focus more on personalities than issues.

   (E) media failure to shape the public agenda through its news coverage.

10. Which of the following groups is the least likely to participate in politics?

   (A) 65- to 75-year-olds

   (B) high school graduates

   (C) women

   (D) Protestants

   (E) 18- to 25-year-olds

11. Which of the following statements about the budgetary process is true?

(A) The president submits a budget proposal to Congress, which ultimately decides how to allocate money.

(B) The president assigns a spending minimum and maximum to each agency in the executive branch.

(C) Interest groups have little influence over this aspect of policymaking.

(D) The Office of Management and Budget handles the entire budgetary process.

(E) Committees submit their internal budget requests to the Congressional Budget Office.

12. According to the Supreme Court's decision in *Lemon* v. *Kurtzman* (1971) which of the following is true about public aid to church-related schools?

(A) Any use of public funds for church-related schools violates the separation of church and state doctrine.

(B) Only local governments may allocate public money to church-related schools.

(C) Public aid to church-related schools must be matched by an equal amount of privately raised funds.

(D) Public aid to church-related schools must have a primary effect that neither advances nor inhibits religion.

(E) Religious schools are not allowed to receive any public funds.

13. Which of the following powers are granted to Congress by the Constitution?

I.   appropriate money

II. confirm justices

III. send troops into war

IV. enforce laws

V.   regulate commerce

(A) I and IV only

(B) II and III only

(C) III and V only

(D) I, II, and V only

(E) III, IV, and V only

14. Which of the following elevated the level of constitutional scrutiny for gender-based claims?

    (A) Fifteenth Amendment

    (B) *Craig* v. *Boren.*

    (C) *Hernandez* v. *Texas.*

    (D) Nineteenth Amendment

    (E) Civil Rights Act of 1964.

15. In which of the following cases is a congressional candidate most likely to be elected?

    (A) If he or she has a good television presence

    (B) When a state has just gained seats due to reapportionment

    (C) If he or she is new to politics

    (D) After a critical election for the presidency

    (E) If he or she is an incumbent

16. Which of the following is true of iron triangles?

    (A) An iron triangle is composed of the president, the Speaker of the House, and the chief justice.

    (B) Iron triangles inhibit the policy process by interfering with the debate over a piece of legislation.

    (C) Iron triangles help unify the three branches of government in pursuit of a single, clear policy agenda.

    (D) Iron triangles help advance legislation and implementation in a particular policy area.

    (E) Iron triangles rarely form in government at the federal level because they lack sufficient resources for sustainability.

17. Which of the following is a grassroots lobbying technique?

    (A) an interest group official meets with a federal judge

    (B) a lobbyist drafts a bill for a House committee

    (C) a coalition of interest groups files an *amicus curiae* brief before the Supreme Court

    (D) an interest group organizes its constituents to email and call members of Congress

    (E) a corporate executive meets with a White House official

18. A voter's choice of candidate is influenced most by

    (A) campaign finance laws.

    (B) political advertisements.

    (C) party identification.

    (D) the media.

    (E) radio talk shows.

19. Many Supreme Court cases of the 1960s involved issues of

    (A) gender discrimination.

    (B) economic regulation.

    (C) constitutional powers of the president.

    (D) rights of the accused.

    (E) campaign finance reform.

20. If the Supreme Court rules that a newly passed law is unconstitutional, Congress can

    (A) ask the president to appoint new justices.

    (B) try to amend the Constitution to override the Supreme Court's interpretation.

    (C) appeal the court's decision to the Senate Judiciary Committee.

    (D) issue a referendum to allow the public to vote on the Supreme Court's decision.

    (E) vote to override the Supreme Court's decision.

21. Which of the following are types of elections held in the U.S.?

    I. runoff election

    II. national primary

    III. general election

    IV. initiative

    V. referendum

    (A) III only

    (B) II and III only

    (C) I, II and III only

    (D) I, III, IV, and V only

    (E) all of the above

22. If the House and Senate pass two different versions of a bill,

   (A) the Senate version has seniority and is sent to the president.

   (B) the Supreme Court chooses the better version.

   (C) the two versions are sent to a conference committee to work out a compromise bill.

   (D) the president has the authority to choose which version he will sign into law.

   (E) each house must amend its bill and take another vote.

23. One tool that allows the president to sidestep congressional approval of his diplomatic duties is the

   (A) power to negotiate treaties.

   (B) authority to enter into executive agreements.

   (C) ability to send troops into war.

   (D) freedom to appoint ambassadors.

   (E) privilege of receiving foreign diplomats.

24. Which of the following is an accurate statement about the caseload of the Supreme Court?

   (A) Only a small portion of cases seeking review are heard by the Supreme Court.

   (B) The Senate Judiciary Committee requires the court to hear certain types of cases.

   (C) The justices have very little say over the composition of their docket.

   (D) The solicitor general is responsible for assigning cases to the Supreme Court.

   (E) The Supreme Court attempts to hear every case appealed to it.

25. The Supreme Court has extended federal supremacy over state laws through its interpretation of the

   (A) Tenth Amendment.

   (B) just compensation clause.

   (C) First Amendment.

   (D) Fourteenth Amendment.

   (E) establishment clause.

26. Which of the following is an incumbent's greatest advantage during an election?

(A) automatic endorsement from the president

(B) a clean political record

(C) name recognition

(D) more campaign resources and funding

(E) a large number of undecided voters in the constituency

27. Television has had which of the following effects on government?

(A) It has helped lower the cost of campaigning.

(B) It has forced candidates to rely more heavily on their parties.

(C) It has caused a decrease in party unity in Congress.

(D) It has increased the president's ability to use the bully pulpit.

(E) It has made the judiciary more accessible.

527 Groups, 2008 Election

Committee	Expenditures	Pro-Democratic	Pro-Republican
Service Employees International Union	$25,058,103	✔	
America Votes	$19,672,551	✔	
American Solutions Winning the Future	$17,470,711		✔
The Fund for America	$11,514,130	✔	
EMILY's List	$10,349,746	✔	
GOPAC	$8,100,840		✔
College Republican National Committee	$6,458,084		✔
Citizens United	$5,238,329		✔
Alliance for New America	$4,890,620	✔	
Working for Working Americans	$2,049,833	✔	
Gay & Lesbian Victory Fund	$5,145,721	✔	
Club for Growth	$4,246,547		✔

Source: www.opensecrets.org/527s/527cmtes.php.

28. The data in the table above supports which of the following statements?

(A) Spending by 527 groups has grown between 2006 and 2008.

(B) Democratic Party committees are more likely to form 527s than Republican Party committees.

(C) Most 527 groups spend about $20 million per election cycle.

(D) 527 groups were formed to circumvent the Bipartisan Campaign Reform Act.

(E) 527 groups favor Democrats over Republicans.

29. What happens if no presidential candidate receives an Electoral College majority?

   (A) The election is decided by the U.S. House of Representatives.

   (B) The winner is decided by a conference of the state governors.

   (C) A runoff election is held to determine the winner.

   (D) The U.S. Supreme Court determines the winner.

   (E) The winner is decided by a vote of superdelegates.

30. Which of the following is a trend in American elections?

   (A) Fewer candidates are seeking elective office.

   (B) Campaigns are becoming less expensive to run.

   (C) Political pundits are becoming more influential.

   (D) Fewer citizens are making financial contributions to candidates.

   (E) More states are allowing early voting.

31. Article II of the Constitution grants the president power to do all of the following EXCEPT

   (A) authorize troop movements during war.

   (B) appropriate funds for agencies.

   (C) veto proposed legislation.

   (D) appeal to Congress and make legislative requests in a state of the union address.

   (E) establish or discontinue relations with foreign governments.

32. The Civil Rights Act of 1964 articulated which of the following?

   (A) the requirement that all public schools desegregate

   (B) a prohibition on states instituting poll taxes or literacy tests when administering elections

   (C) the illegality of discrimination in employment and public accommodations

   (D) the creation of the Justice Department to investigate civil rights violations

   (E) the right of all Americans, regardless of race or gender, to vote in federal elections

33. Which of the following statements accurately describes the procedure of debate in the House?

(A) The Rules Committee determines the order in which bills will be heard and the length of debate for each one.

(B) Representatives who are introducing a bill are allowed the privilege of unlimited debate.

(C) The Speaker and the sergeant at arms together determine the schedule of debate.

(D) The minority party is allowed an automatic 10 minutes of debate time to refute legislation introduced by the majority party.

(E) Only members of the party whose representative introduced the bill are allowed time on the floor to discuss it.

34. Which of the following statements characterize the relationship between congressional committees and federal agencies?

I. Committees play a role in appropriating funds for each agency to spend during the year.

II. Agencies regulate committees by holding hearings to assess their performance.

III. Committees perform oversight of the agencies that fall under their jurisdiction.

IV. Both committees and agencies can be influenced by the lobbying efforts of interest groups.

(A) II only

(B) III only

(C) I and III only

(D) II and IV only

(E) I, III, and IV only

35. In *Texas* v. *Johnson,* the Supreme Court determined that

(A) the drawing of unreasonable school district lines cannot be used as a means of integrating schools.

(B) symbolic speech is protected under the First Amendment.

(C) affirmative action quotas are unconstitutional.

(D) the death penalty is not a form of cruel and unusual punishment.

(E) obscenity is not protected by the First Amendment.

36. Which of the following is usually a result of a critical election?

    (A) party dealignment

    (B) divided government

    (C) policy implementation

    (D) party realignment

    (E) policy gridlock

37. A weakness of the Articles of Confederation was that the government was unable to

    (A) remain a democracy.

    (B) be recognized by foreign governments.

    (C) represent the views of the various states.

    (D) centralize its powers.

    (E) make decisions through a legislative process.

38. The Federal Reserve Board oversees which of the following policy areas?

    (A) social welfare policy

    (B) foreign policy

    (C) monetary policy

    (D) health care policy

    (E) domestic policy

39. Which of the following is a major difference between the Democratic and Republican parties?

    (A) The Democratic Party campaigns fairly, but the Republican Party does not.

    (B) A wider variety of groups in the electorate vote for Republican candidates.

    (C) The Republican Party is much older than the Democratic Party.

    (D) The Republican Party endorses raising taxes, whereas the Democratic Party favors cutting taxes.

    (E) The Democratic Party has a more liberal ideology, whereas the Republican Party has a more conservative ideology.

U.S. Defense Spending, 1940–2012

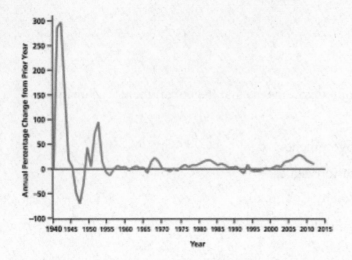

Source: Harold W. Stanley and Richard G. Niemi, eds., *Vital Statistics on American Politics, 2007–2008* (Washington, DC: CQ Press, 2008). Reprinted by permission.

40. The graph indicates that

   (A) defense spending changes dramatically from year to year.

   (B) in most years, defense spending conforms to a model of incremental change.

   (C) the most varied period of defense spending has been from 2000 to present.

   (D) defense spending is lower today than during World War II.

   (E) defense spending is rising as a percentage of the federal budget.

41. A unitary system of government is one in which

   (A) an executive, legislative, and judicial branch share equal powers.

   (B) political officials are elected by the public in a popular election.

   (C) legislative committees and federal agencies work together to make and implement policy.

   (D) more than one level of government oversees a body of people.

   (E) all power resides in a central government.

42. The rise of the Social Security system has had which of the following effects on the federal budget?

(A) It has led to cutbacks in defense spending and the building of new weapons.

(B) It has become the largest federal expenditure.

(C) It has increased Americans' trust in a government that provides for all Americans.

(D) It has caused income tax rates to double since its initiation.

(E) It has discouraged senior citizens from participating in politics.

43. The federal bureaucracy handles all of the following activities EXCEPT

(A) issuing rules and regulations.

(B) holding hearings to obtain information about proposed policies.

(C) implementing policies passed by Congress.

(D) appropriating funds to pay for federal government programs.

(E) acting as a quasi-judicial body.

44. Members of Congress are most likely to endorse a president's proposal when

(A) one party holds the majority in Congress by only a slim margin.

(B) the congressional session is nearing its end.

(C) the president has a high public approval rating.

(D) the issue at hand is not well publicized.

(E) it involves amending the federal tax codes.

45. Which of the following is a basic weakness inherent in the presidency?

(A) Except in military affairs, presidents must rely on the support of other people to influence policy decisions.

(B) Because they are limited to only two terms, presidents rarely have enough time to achieve any of their policy goals.

(C) Media attention focuses heavily on the president, which leads the public to hold him accountable and, in turn, deprives him of power.

(D) The president is commander in chief, yet he cannot act in military situations without congressional approval.

(E) Because the Electoral College officially elects the president, presidents usually lack legitimacy among the electorate.

46. Despite their influence over the political agenda, interest groups may be seen as democratic institutions in that they

(A) help voters decide how to cast their ballots in an election.

(B) fund campaigns through political action committees.

(C) run advertisements to generate public support for a presidential proposal.

(D) promote equal representation of citizens' political beliefs.

(E) represent the concerns of groups in the electorate in the political arena.

47. The power of the president has expanded for which of the following reasons?

   I. increasing globalization

   II. the shift toward candidate-centered politics as a result of television

   III. the use of primaries in presidential elections

   IV. the easing of tensions among social groups as a result of the civil rights movement

(A) II only

(B) IV only

(C) I and II only

(D) III and IV only

(E) I, II, and III only

48. Which of the following is true of federal systems of government?

(A) The central government completely regulates the activities of state governments.

(B) Citizens vote for central government officials only.

(C) The central government shares power with the states.

(D) Most democracies are federal systems.

(E) Federal systems tend to have just two major political parties.

49. The House of Representatives differs from the Senate in all of the following ways EXCEPT

(A) House seats are distributed according to each state's population, whereas each state has the same number of senators.

(B) House debates are scheduled, whereas the Senate allows unlimited debate.

(C) representatives tend to act more independently, whereas senators usually vote according to party lines.

(D) power is distributed more hierarchically in the House than it is in the Senate.

(E) senators have the ability to filibuster, but representatives do not.

50. An American citizen's approval of the president depends most heavily on

(A) the president's ability to stand up to Congress.

(B) whether the president is of the same party with which the citizen identifies himself or herself.

(C) whether the president has balanced his attention to foreign and domestic policy.

(D) how accessible the president is to members of the public.

(E) the media's bias in favor of or against the president.

51. One way the executive branch may attempt to influence the outcome of a Supreme Court case is by

(A) filing an *amicus curiae* brief.

(B) selecting which justices will hear the case.

(C) having the solicitor general preside over the justices.

(D) requesting the chief justice to meet with the president.

(E) issuing an opinion on the case.

52. The president may exercise authority over the federal bureaucracy in all of the following ways EXCEPT by

(A) advising cabinet members and agency heads on department activities.

(B) proposing budgets for each department to Congress.

(C) appointing department secretaries who share his political goals.

(D) creating or dismantling agencies and departments.

(E) holding hearings on the departments' activities and performance.

53. In some states, citizens can participate directly in lawmaking by

(A) appointing legislators to committees.

(B) presenting a budget proposal in the state legislature.

(C) approving legislation through referenda.

(D) writing letters to the governor.

(E) setting the requirements for who can run for office.

54. Which of the following is a true statement about the Voting Rights Act of 1965?

   (A) It resulted in increased discrimination against women voters.

   (B) It allowed literacy tests to be administered as a prerequisite for voting.

   (C) It gave the states more control over federal elections.

   (D) It was the first voting rights law to pass Congress with no opposition.

   (E) It resulted in dramatic increases in the number of African American voters.

55. In a state that has six electoral votes, the Republican candidate wins the popular vote by 54 to 46 percent. The electoral votes would most likely be allocated in which of the following ways?

   (A) The Republican and Democrat would each get three electoral votes.

   (B) The Republican would get five electoral votes, and the one electoral vote reserved for a third-party candidate would go unused.

   (C) The Republican would get four electoral votes, and the Democrat would get two.

   (D) The Republican would get six electoral votes.

   (E) The Republican would get five electoral votes, and the Democrat would get one.

56. Members of Congress

   (A) must be 35 years old.

   (B) are redistricted after every election cycle.

   (C) rarely represent a political party.

   (D) are older, more white, and more male than the average citizen.

   (E) may serve no more than 12 years in office.

57. The president exercises influence over policymaking most by

   (A) vetoing legislation passed by Congress.

   (B) setting the congressional agenda.

   (C) introducing legislation for debate.

   (D) participating in committee hearings.

   (E) appointing party leaders in both houses of Congress.

58. Which of the following sets of states has the most Electoral College votes?

(A) California, New York, and Texas

(B) Iowa, New Hampshire, and South Carolina

(C) Florida, New Jersey, and Ohio

(D) Maine, Massachusetts, and Vermont

(E) North Carolina, Oregon, and Pennsylvania

59. If there are candidates from more than one party on a ballot, you may be voting in a(n)

I. open primary

II. closed primary

III. blanket primary

IV. general election

(A) I only

(B) I and III only

(C) I, III, and IV only

(D) III and IV only

(E) IV only

60. Which of the following is the presiding officer of the U.S. Senate?

(A) Speaker

(B) majority leader

(C) majority whip

(D) chief clerk

(E) vice president

END OF SECTION I.

IF YOU FINISH BEFORE TIME IS CALLED, YOU MAY CHECK YOUR WORK ON THIS SECTION.

DO NOT GO ON TO SECTION II UNTIL YOU ARE TOLD TO DO SO.

Government and Politics: United States
Section II

Time: 100 minutes

Directions: You have 100 minutes to answer all four of the following questions. It is suggested that you take a few minutes to plan and outline each answer. *Spend approximately one-fourth of your time (25 minutes) on each question.* Illustrate your essay with substantive examples where appropriate. Make certain to number each of your answers as the question is numbered below.

1. The writers of the Constitution favored the ideals of democracy, yet they feared putting too much power in the hands of the people.

   a. Identify TWO changes from the original Constitution that increased the democratic nature of government.

   b. Explain how each of the two factors identified in *a* has resulted in a more democratic nation.

2. Incumbent members of Congress have a tremendous advantage over challengers in elections.
   a. Identify three possible sources of the incumbency advantage.

   b. Describe how the items you identified in *a* work to incumbents' advantage.

   c. The many advantages notwithstanding, incumbents do sometimes lose elections. Identify and explain two reasons why incumbents tend to lose elections.

Race and Ethnicity in America, 1967–2008

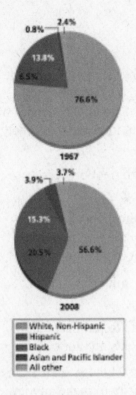

Source: U.S. Census Bureau, Statistical Abstract of the United States

3. The above graph details how the composition of the American population has changed over the last 40 years.

   Using the data above and your knowledge of U.S. government and politics, identify and explain THREE ways that these shifting populations will have an impact on government and politics.

4. During the budgetary process, Congress weighs revenues and expenditures to determine how to allocate money within the federal government. Social spending has become a major component of the federal budget in recent decades, but in some cases Congress is not able to adjust spending for it.

   a. Identify TWO items in the budget that cannot usually be amended during the budgetary process.

   b. For each one, explain why spending is not cut.

END OF EXAMINATION

ANSWERS AND EXPLANATIONS

Practice Test 2

Section I

- **1. (D) is correct.** In a blanket primary, candidates of all parties are listed on the ballot. A voter may choose a candidate from one party for one office and a candidate from another party for a different office. This is called ticket splitting. Two consequences of ticket splitting are a decline in the power of political parties and an increase in divided government.

- **2. (A) is correct.** The court of appeals plays no role in the impeachment process.

- **3. (C) is correct.** Federal judges are not elected by the public—they are appointed by the president and confirmed by the Senate. This process is intended to insulate them from the political pressures of campaigning so that, in office, they are free to make unbiased decisions without having to return favors or worry about reelection.

- **4. (E) is correct.** Democrats more than Republicans tend to favor minority rights polices like affirmative action.

- **5. (C) is correct.** Generally speaking, the party unity scores of the Republican and Democratic parties in Congress move together. The other statements are not true.

- **6. (B) is correct.** Located in Article I of the Constitution, the elastic clause enumerates the implied powers of Congress. It gives the legislature full authority to make any laws "necessary and proper" to carry out those responsibilities assigned to it by the Constitution.

- **7. (C) is correct.** Voting is the most common way people express their political views. By participating in an election, voters choose those candidates whom they feel agree with their political beliefs, and these candidates therefore act on their behalf in government.

- **8. (A) is correct.** Supreme Court justices are granted life terms on the condition that they remain in good conduct. This allows them to make judicial decisions objectively without the pressures of political influence. They do not have to appeal to the public or represent any one interest if they are guaranteed their position of authority.

- **9. (D) is correct.** The media tends to focus more heavily on candidates' personality than their policy platforms for the sake of achieving higher viewer ratings. However, this may distort the public's perception both of candidates and the party they represent.

- **10. (E) is correct.** Young people (18- to 25-year-olds) are the least likely group in the electorate to vote. This is partially because young people have not yet formed their political beliefs or determined their needs from government. As people age and bear more responsibilities, they tend to participate more actively in politics.

- **11. (A) is correct.** In the budgetary process, federal agencies and departments in the executive branch submit their budget proposals to the president and the OMB, which amend and combine them into a single proposal. Then the president sends this proposal to Congress, which, through its committees, ultimately decides how much money each department or agency gets to spend in the coming year.

- **12. (D) is correct.** In *Lemon* v. *Kurtzman* the Supreme Court ruled that aid to church-related schools (1) must have a secular purpose, (2) must have a primary effect that neither advances nor inhibits religion, and (3) must not foster excessive government entanglement with religion.

- **13. (D) is correct.** Some of Congress's enumerated powers are to appropriate money, confirm the appointment of justices, and regulate commerce. Congress also has the power to declare war, but it cannot send troops into war. It can make laws, but it cannot enforce them. These two responsibilities instead belong to the president, who is both commander in chief and head of the executive branch.

- **14. (B) is correct.** The Supreme Court's decision in *Craig* v. *Boren* (1976) codified the intermediate level of scrutiny for gender-based claims. It has been used in a variety of sex discrimination cases decided since *Craig*.

- **15. (E) is correct.** Incumbents have enormous advantages in congressional elections. They have better exposure, a political record with the constituency, and more campaign money with which to eliminate any chance of their challengers' success. As a result of these advantages, usually more than 50 percent of congressional incumbents are reelected.

- **16. (D) is correct.** Iron triangles, or subgovernments, often work like well-oiled machines to produce and implement policies in a specific policy area. Interest groups may suggest policies or lobby Congress to pass legislation, and then federal agencies and interest groups work together to implement the policy.

- **17. (D) is correct.** The only lobbying technique that involves the grassroots—members and constituents—is organizing an email or phone campaign. The other techniques use lobbyists and group leaders to approach government officials.

- **18. (C) is correct.** Political science research has consistently found party identification to be the strongest predictor of vote choice.

- **19. (D) is correct.** Many important and controversial Supreme Court cases in the 1960s addressed the rights of the accused. *Miranda* v. *Arizona* is one well-known case in which the Fifth Amendment right of protection from self-incrimination was enforced by the court. Other cases also extended the right of counsel to the poor and confirmed the exclusionary rule, preventing the use of evidence gained through unreasonable search and seizure from being used in trials.

- **20. (B) is correct.** The Supreme Court is the interpreter of the Constitution, but Congress is the keeper of it. If the Supreme Court finds a law unconstitutional, Congress has the authority to amend the Constitution to suit the law. Then the Supreme Court would have no choice but to interpret the law in light of the amendment to the Constitution.

- **21. (D) is correct.** General and runoff elections are elections use to select governing officials. Initiatives and referenda are elections in which voters play a role in deciding whether a specific policy proposal becomes law. There is no national primary election in the United States.

- **22. (C) is correct.** A bill may be amended or altered during debate in either the House or the Senate. It is often the case that the two houses pass different versions of the same bill. When this happens, the bill is sent to a conference committee composed of members of both houses. The committee works to develop a compromise between the bill's two versions. If the compromise is accepted by a majority of each house, the final piece of legislation is sent to the president for his signature.

- **23. (B) is correct.** The president has the power to negotiate executive agreements as well as treaties. Treaties are more formal and tend to address major issues; these require the approval of Congress. Executive agreements, however, deal with smaller matters, so it is often easier for the president to handle them independently.

- **24. (A) is correct.** Thousands of cases are appealed to the Supreme Court each year, but only a few are actually placed on the docket. The justices meet regularly to review appeals and, as a group, choose to hear only those cases they feel are most deserving of appeal or may have the greatest impact on the interpretation of the law. Answer *C* is true, but it does not answer the question.

- **25. (D) is correct.** The passing of the Fourteenth Amendment offered the Supreme Court the opportunity to assert federal supremacy over state laws. This amendment grants all people the right to due process of the law. The court has cited the Fourteenth Amendment in numerous civil liberties and civil rights cases. The gradual process of binding states to the provisions of the Bill of Rights is known as incorporation.

- **26. (C) is correct.** Although incumbents do often benefit from a record of good service to their constituencies or a clean political record, their *greatest* advantage in an election is name recognition. Incumbents receive a great deal of press coverage from local media outlets. As a consequence, their names are more easily recognized by voters. This leads to a tremendous advantage, because on Election Day most voters can do little more than recall a candidate's name.

- **27. (D) is correct.** Television has allowed the president to "go public" more easily, building public support for his policy proposals through the use of the bully pulpit. This can be a powerful policymaking tool, especially for presidents with high approval ratings.

- **28. (E) is correct.** Although other statements may be true, the only true statement that is evident from the information contained in the table is that 527 groups generally favor Democrats over Republicans. This makes them distinct from other campaign financing organizations, where Republicans traditionally have an advantage.

- **29. (A) is correct.** If no candidate receives an Electoral College majority, then the election moves to the House of Representatives, which must choose from among the top three electoral vote winners. Each state delegation has one vote, which means small and large states have equal voice in the process.

- **30. (E) is correct.** More and more states are allowing early voting, which is voting that takes place before the announced Election Day. Registered voters are allowed to either vote by mail or show up at specially designated polling places to cast their votes.

- **31. (B) is correct.** Presidents do have a significant amount of influence over the federal budget because they only compile the budget proposal for all of the departments in the executive branch. Congress plays an equal, if not greater, role in authorizing and appropriating funds.

- **32. (C) is correct.** The Civil Rights Act of 1964 officially prohibited discrimination in any public facilities and in employment. It also authorized the Justice Department to enforce the act by investigating and suing any company that violated civil rights as outlined by the law.

- **33. (A) is correct.** The Rules Committee is very influential on legislation because it determines the length of debate for each piece of legislation. It also has the authority to declare whether or not a bill may be amended during debate. The less flexibility it affords a piece of legislation, the greater the likelihood that the bill will not be passed easily.

- **34. (E) is correct.** Committees oversee agencies, both by holding hearings and by setting their budgets. These are two ways the legislative branch checks the power of the executive branch. However, both committees and agencies are lobbied regularly by interest groups that hope to influence either policymaking or policy implementation.

- **35. (B) is correct.** *Texas* v. *Johnson* brought the issue of flag burning to the Supreme Court. The court ruled that flag burning is protected under the First Amendment as a form of speech. The case therefore set a precedent that symbolic speech is considered free speech in the eyes of the law.

- **36. (D) is correct.** Party realignment often accompanies a critical election. Such elections are noteworthy because they initiate a new party era. Such major changes often are a result of new party affiliations among the electorate.

- **37. (D) is correct.** States were reluctant to give over power to the new national government. As a result, the government was simply too weak—it did not have enough centralized power to give it legitimacy and, ultimately, to allow it to function.

- **38. (C) is correct.** The Federal Reserve Board oversees monetary policy. It is an executive institution that regulates the economy by controlling the flow of currency. For example, it has the authority to determine how much money banks have at their disposal and how much credit is available to the public.

- **39. (E) is correct.** One basic difference that defines the two parties is their contrasting ideologies. Democrats tend to favor liberal policies, such as social spending, whereas Republicans usually endorse more conservative policies, such as those that limit the role of the federal government.

- **40. (B) is correct.** In most years, defense spending changes only slightly from the levels of the year before. This is the very definition of an incremental policy change. The other statements are untrue and/or not actually demonstrated in the graph.

- **41. (E) is correct.** In a unitary system all power resides in a central government. State and local governments have duties and powers that are delegated to them by the central government. Most governments in the world are unitary governments.

- **42. (B) is correct.** Social Security has replaced national defense as the government's biggest expenditure. To pay for Social Security, social insurance taxes have risen somewhat comparably.

- **43. (D) is correct.** Only Congress can appropriate funds to be spent by the federal government. The bureaucracy engages in all of the other activities listed.

- **44. (C) is correct.** Public approval can be a powerful tool for the president. If public opinion is high, Congress is more likely to endorse his proposals. To go against a president who is well liked by voters might hurt a representative's or senator's own chances for reelection.

- **45. (A) is correct.** Presidents are not legislators. They may propose policies indirectly or try to influence the policy process. This means that they must rely heavily on the support of other people to help them pursue their political agenda.

- **46. (E) is correct.** Interest groups play a role in democratizing government by serving as linkage institutions between politicians and the public. Interest groups represent the needs of different groups of people to lawmakers, so these groups help the constituency to be heard. Although not all groups may be heard equally, they at least have the opportunity to try to affect policymaking for the benefit of some citizens.

- **47. (C) is correct.** The new global economy and frequent military crises have increased the president's power and prominence as chief diplomat. The president has also become more powerful because he may act more independently than ever before. Television allows presidential candidates to reach the public directly without having to rely on political parties, and it also provides presidents with a means to address the public directly and to gain its support.

- **48. (C) is correct.** Federalism imposes a tiered structure on government. More than one level shares authority over the people. In the United States, people are subject to the laws of both state and federal governments, and they also may elect their leaders in both the state and federal governments.

- **49. (C) is correct.** Senators actually act more independently of their parties. This is partially due to the fact that they have longer terms than representatives do. Party affiliations and party leadership are also much stronger in the House, so representatives tend to vote along party lines.

- **50. (B) is correct.** Party identification plays a large role in the public's perception of the president. An American citizen is more likely to approve of a president who is of the same party. By virtue of being of the same party, it is assumed that the president is advancing political views with which the citizen agrees.

- **51. (A) is correct.** Once justices have been appointed to the bench, there is little that the government can do to directly influence their decisions. It may, however, through the solicitor general, submit briefs stating the official position of the federal government on the issue at hand. State governments, interest groups, and members of the public are also allowed to file *amicus curiae* briefs to endorse their views.

- **52. (E) is correct.** Congress, not the president, is responsible for conducting oversight of federal agencies. The president and agencies together make up the executive branch, and in this case, it is the legislative branch that maintains the system of checks and balances.

- **53. (C) is correct.** Some states allow citizens to participate directly in policymaking at the state level. A bill is listed on the ballot, and voters can either choose to approve or kill it. If they approve it by a simple majority, the bill bypasses the state legislature and becomes law—or in some states, it goes directly to the governor for his or her signature or veto.

- **54. (E) is correct.** The Voting Rights Act of 1965, a law designed to help end formal and informal barriers to African American suffrage, resulted in dramatic gains in African American voter registration, voting, and engagement in politics overall.

- **55. (D) is correct.** Generally, the winner of a state's popular election receives all of that state's electoral votes. This makes the more populous states powerful because they have more electoral votes to wield. In this case, the Republican would receive all six of the electoral votes.

- **56. (D) is correct.** One of the great ironies of Congress is that, as a representative institution, it does not do a very good job representing the demographics of the United States. Women, minorities, and those from lower-income brackets, are not well represented in either the House or the Senate.

- **57. (A) is correct.** The veto is one of the president's strongest legislative tools. Most of the time, it allows him the final say on every piece of legislation. The veto also encourages legislators to shape policy in such a way that the president will not choose to reject it, so it gives the president some say in policy formation.

- **58. (A) is correct.** According to the Constitution, each state has as many electoral votes as it has U.S. senators and representatives. Since the number of representatives each state has is based on the size of its population, more populous states have more Electoral College votes. California, New York, and Texas are the three most populous states in the U.S.

- **59. (D) is correct.** Blanket primaries list candidates from all parties, and voters are free to participate in the nomination of candidates from different parties. The general election usually features the nominees of the different parties. Open and closed primaries have candidates from only one party on the ballot. The difference is that only people registered with the party can vote in closed primaries, while in open primaries, a voters may "crossover" and vote in a party primary different from his or her registration.

- **60. (E) is correct.** The Constitution makes the vice president of the United States the president of the Senate. This is the vice president's only constitutionally defined job.

Free-Response Questions

This rubric provides examples of many, but not all, of the possible correct responses to the free-response questions.

1.

a. Identify changes from the original Constitution that increased the democratic nature of government.

- Seventeenth Amendment
- Nineteenth Amendment
- Twenty-Third Amendment

b. Explain how each of the two factors identified in part *a* has resulted in a more democratic nation.

Seventeenth Amendment: Under the original Constitution, state legislators selected U.S. senators. The Seventeenth Amendment, ratified in 1913, provides for the direct election of senators by the people.

Nineteenth Amendment: Women were disenfranchised in the original Constitution. The Nineteenth Amendment, ratified in 1920, gave women the right to vote.

Twenty-Third Amendment: The Twenty-Third Amendment, ratified in 1961, provided the District of Columbia with Electoral College votes in presidential elections. This gave the citizens of the District of Columbia a voice and influence in presidential politics.

2.
a. Identify possible sources of incumbency advantage

- Advertising
- Credit claiming
- Position taking
- Weak opponents
- Campaign spending

b. Describe how each of the items you identified in *a* works to incumbents' advantage.

Advertising: Incumbents gain visibility and name recognition from communicating with their constituents. Members of Congress have franking privileges that allow them to use congressional funds to send newsletters, memos, and emails to voters and potential voters in their districts. The name recognition that is gained from this gives incumbents an advantage on Election Day.

Credit claiming: Members of Congress engage in credit claiming, which involves enhancing their standing with constituents through service to individuals or the district. Casework and so-called pork barrel projects are two common ways representatives service their constituencies.

Position taking: Members of Congress often take policy stances that enhance their public images and might affect the outcome of an election. Because of the office they hold, they generally receive media coverage for such actions.

Weak opponents: Another advantage for incumbents is they are likely to face weak opponents.

Campaign spending: Incumbents tend to have a tremendous advantage in campaign fundraising. In House races, incumbents typically outspend challengers by a 15-to-1 ratio. Among other things, money buys name recognition.

c. Identify and explain why incumbents lose elections, notwithstanding the advantages they have.

Coattails: An unpopular president may lead to the defeat of members of his party in Congress.

Scandals: An incumbent tarnished by scandal or corruption is almost instantly vulnerable.

Redistricting: Incumbent House members may be redistricted out of their district as a result of the reapportionment and redistricting processes that take place after each census.

3. Identify and explain ways that shifting populations will have an impact on government and politics.

Changes in the demographics of the nation place new demands on the government. As the percentage of Latino/as in the population increases, for example, the prevalence of the Spanish language increases. This necessitates more English-as-a-second-language (ESL) programs and increases the cost to government to print materials in multiple languages. Other issues, such as immigration, may also become more salient in light of these changes.

The increasing percentage of minority groups in the population makes changing the representativeness of Congress increasingly important. Right now, minority groups are significantly underrepresented in our nation's legislatures.

Changes in the composition of society may change the partisan composition of the country. African Americans and most Hispanics (except Cubans) are more likely to identify as Democrats than Republicans. This has an effect on electoral politics in localities, states, and the nation at large.

4.

a. Identify items in the budget that cannot usually be amended during the budgetary process.

- Social Security
- Medicare

b. For each of the items in *a*, explain why spending is difficult to cut.

Social Security: Social Security pays benefits to senior citizens who have paid into the system during their careers because they no longer work to earn an income. The government must pay benefits to those entitled. Not only are Social Security recipients more likely to vote than other citizens, there are also a number of well-organized interest groups who oppose reductions in spending for Social Security. This makes it difficult for members of Congress to go on record supporting cuts in this program.

Medicare: Medicare is an entitlement program that helps pay for medical care for the elderly. The number of recipients has grown steadily. Congress, again, finds it difficult, if not impossible, to amend Medicare funding during the budgetary process. Senior citizens are very protective of their claim to health care benefits, which places members of Congress under significant pressure to not cut Medicare services.

NOTES

NOTES

NOTES

NOTES

NOTES

NOTES

NOTES

NOTES

NOTES

NOTES

NOTES

NOTES